Shades of Black

*Diversity in
African-American
Identity*

WILLIAM E. CROSS, Jr.

Shades of Black

Diversity in African-American Identity

TEMPLE UNIVERSITY PRESS
PHILADELPHIA

The author gratefully acknowledges permission to reproduce a
table from: Kenneth B. Clark and Mamie P. Clark, "Emotional
Factors in Racial Identification and Preference in Negro Children,"
Journal of Negro Education 19, no. 3 (1950), p. 346, table 9.

Temple University Press, Philadelphia 19122
Copyright © 1991 by Temple University. All rights reserved
Published 1991
Printed in the United States of America

The paper used in this publication meets the minimum
requirements of American National Standard for Information
Sciences—Permanence of Paper for Printed Library Materials,
ANSI Z39.48-1984 ∞

Library of Congress Cataloging-in-Publication Data
Cross, William E.
    Shades of black : diversity in African-American identity / William
E. Cross, Jr.
        p.   cm.
    Includes bibliographical references and index.
    ISBN 0-87722-759-4
    1. Afro-Americans—Race identity.   2. Afro-Americans—Psychology.
I. Title
E185.625.C76   1991
155.8'496073—dc20   90-36170
                                                                       CIP

To the memory of my mother,
Margaret L. Cross

CONTENTS

PREFACE

In setting the stage for the current work, the comments of two Black literary giants come to mind. Ralph Ellison (1964) once asked, "Why is it true when critics confront the American as Negro they suddenly drop their advanced critical armament and revert with an air of superiority to quite primitive modes of analysis?" Addressing a similar point, but in her distinctive style and voice, Zora Neale Hurston remarked during a 1944 interview with a reporter from the New York *Amsterdam News*: "There is an oversimplification of the Negro. He is either pictured by conservatives as happy, picking his banjo, or by the so-called liberals as low, miserable, and crying. The Negro's life is neither of these. Rather, it is in-between and above and below these pictures."

"Oversimplification" and "primitive modes of analysis" apply as well to the discourse on the psychology of the Black American. In this book, I attempt to demonstrate that diversity and texture have been and continue to be at the core of Black psychology. The social scientific literature on Negro identity written between 1936 and 1967 reported that self-hatred and group rejection were typical of Black psychological functioning. Justices of the U. S. Supreme Court employed such "scientific evidence" in reaching their historic 1954 school desegregation decision, *Brown* v. *Board of Education*. For years thereafter, the conventional wisdom stated that the average Black person suffered from low self-esteem and anti-Blackness. Similarly, the Black identity change that accompanied the Black 1960s was interpreted as a corrective for this negativity; the "new" Black identity was characterized by self-acceptance and a preference for things Black. Negativity in the past was replaced by positive corrections in the present. Simple enough . . . in fact, far too simple.

My good friend Urie Bronfenbrenner once remarked that the distinctive components and dynamics of a system, or Gestalt, are not always apparent when the system is intact and ongoing. In like manner, how scholars approach a topic such as Negro or Black identity is seldom transparent. The unraveling of a Gestalt may take many forms, but Bronfenbrenner has suggested that the best avenues toward deconstruction, analysis, and subsequent synthesis are (1) to conduct a laboratory experiment that tries to change a system, or (2) to make detailed observations when a system is undergoing change in its "real world" environment. It is through the latter, more than the former, that I first gained insight into the gaps and blind spots in the discourse on Black psychological functioning. The naturalistic event that was the focus of my observations and subsequent insight was the phenomenon of Black identity change, which Blacks experienced during the 1960s. Along with Bailey Jackson, Jake Milliones, and others, I attempted to capture the psychological stages associated with this identity change. Our resulting developmental models became known as models of nigrescence. *Nigrescence* is a French word that means "the process of becoming Black"; thus our models attempted to depict the psychology of the process of becoming Black.

Initially, observers of Black identity change, myself included, assumed that nigrescence involved comprehensive personality and identity changes. This expectation was explained, in part, by the romanticism associated with Black nationalism—with any nationalism, for that matter—in which elements of the traditional identity (the "Negro") are cast in pejorative terms, and things new (a Black identity) are seen in an overwhelmingly positive light. Even as the influence of romanticism waned, however, the concept of change from poor to effective mental health persisted. Perhaps the primary reason for utilizing a comprehensive-change perspective was that trends evident in the mainstream research on Black identity seemed to point in that direction. In depicting both the general personality and group identity in negative (if not pathogenic) terms, the empirical literature on Black psychological functioning appearing between 1939 and the beginning of the nigrescence period in 1968 made it seem that sweeping changes in the

Black psyche were in order. Consequently, observers of psychological nigrescence linked change to both the general personality dynamics of Black people and their group identity, since it stood to reason, in view of the earlier research, that both components of the Black self-concept had been documented as vulnerable.

Almost all the nigrescence models were based on clinical observations, case studies, and participant observations. This was true of my own model, the "Negro-to-Black Conversion Model," which was developed through self-analysis and participant observation studies. Observations were conducted during the Black Power phase of the Black Social Movement in my home town of Evanston, Illinois, and in neighboring Chicago. I attended rallies, joined various activist groups, and interacted with associates as they, and I, experienced nigrescence. Some of our friendships dated back to childhood; thus, in a few instances, I had vivid images of friends, depicting them before and after change. Although it was not a part of my vocabulary, and I do not mean to imply a level of sophistication that was beyond my grasp at the time, in a rather crude sense I was able to apply a life-span perspective to such images. That some of the information gained from these images helped me construct my nigrescence model goes without saying, but in the excitement of explicating the process of change, I overlooked another important dimension embedded in my notes: continuity. Eventually, circumstances made it possible for me to return to this overlooked issue.

In the fall of 1971, a small group of Black undergraduates at Princeton University met with the faculty of the Psychology Department to determine ways in which the department might offer more information on the Black experience. At the time, I was a graduate student within the department. There were a number of suggestions, including the development of an advanced undergraduate seminar on Black issues, and in the following spring, Princeton offered its first course on psychology and the Black experience, with me as the instructor.

Much to my good fortune, the students enrolled in the course, most of whom were Black, were dedicated psychology majors; a handful were destined to complete doctoral programs in psychology at major research institutions. The majority had begun to internalize their new Black identity; consequently, exchanges within the seminar tended to be substantive, if at times intense. If we expressed a bias, it was to be skeptical of overly pejorative or romantic interpretations of modal Black behavior, for either extreme insulted Black humanity by depicting it in simplistic terms. We reasoned, instead, that to be human is by definition to be complex, and thus an accurate analysis of Black psychological functioning would be multidimensional and would include positive as well as negative themes, functional and dysfunctional proclivities, and strengths in addition to weaknesses or vulnerabilities. We applied this perspective to a number of topics. My essay on nigrescence had recently been published, and as the students were engaged in Black Power activities on and off the campus, it was only natural that a major focus of the course became the study of nigrescence.

Some students observed that they had experienced or were still experiencing a change in their Black identity. They also noted that in many instances their parents, aunts, uncles, and grandparents might best be depicted by the traditional, or Negro, identity. (Of course, some students could identify relatives whose identity had changed or was changing.) Despite this difference in identity, the students could not truthfully characterize as pathological the mental health of their parents and relatives. On the contrary, some of the strengths the students identified in themselves, and that helped them account for their success at college, could be traced not to identity change but to their socialization by their (Negro) parents and extended families. The students' vision of their past was far from a tangle of pathology, though they could readily associate the traditional, or Negro, identity with many, if not most, of the significant others from that past. Moreover, although they testified to the exhilarating dimension of nigrescence, on balance they viewed themselves as no more or less subject to the trials and tribulations of being human after nigrescence than before. From this line of reasoning, they concluded that nigrescence was changing key elements of their self-concept but that the change was not comprehensive. Something about them had changed or was changing, but something about them remained the same.

At the end of the seminar, my thinking about nigrescence and the theory of Negro or Black identity had been altered significantly. Perhaps pathology was not typical of a "Negro identity," nor was mental health the province of "Blackness." Yet who could doubt that something about the person with a Negro identity was radically different from something about the person with the new Black identity. Given the possibility that the dimensions of the Negro identity were more often normal than pathological, perhaps not everything about the Negro identity *required* change.

In other words, nigrescence may not involve comprehensive change in the general personality and group identity of Blacks; perhaps, instead, we have a problem of change *and* continuity. To understand change and that which is new may not mean the negation of all that is old. In the final analysis, *any* identity change may involve (1) carrying over, in an intact state, certain traits or components linked to the "old" self; (2) the transformation of old elements into new elements; and (3) the incorporation of new dimensions of self that are not traceable to either old or transformed traits associated with the former self. The last two points pose no problems to traditional thinking about Negro psychodynamics. Given the proposition that negativity and psychopathology are inherent features of the Negro identity and personality, then a corrective should involve the transformation of pathological trends into positive proclivities, along with the incorporation of unique and new positive mental health tendencies that are not readily traceable to one's previous identity. But the efficacy of the traditional perspective is surely strained by the first point, especially when the focus is on the carryover of strengths, functional tendencies, and positive mental health patterns. While capable of predicting the transfer of weaknesses from the past to the present (because psychopathology is its point of departure), the transfer (let alone the existence) of strengths and proactive mental health features from the Negro identity to the Black identity is simply not accounted for by the traditional pejorative, or self-hatred, perspective. For this reason, describing and explaining the existence of positive mental health patterns in the modal attitudes and behavior of Blacks, covering the historical period before nigrescence, that is, 1939 to 1968, constitute a major challenge to revisionist theory and research on Black Americans.

The construction of such a revisionist perspective has been my passion for the last eighteen years. In addition, the current work reveals my attempt to bring nigrescence theory into line with the historical and contemporary implications of a revised perspective on Black identity. My goal is to purge Black psychology of both its overly pejorative and its romantic propensities, replacing them with a discourse centered on diversity and complexity in Black psychological functioning.

By way of a summary, my work shows that past racial identity studies frequently contained evidence of multiple images and that the self-hating Negro was hardly prototypical. I then try to identify the sociological and historical forces that tended to blind observers from the 1940s, 1950s, and early 1960s to the existence of such diversity. At various points in the text, I show how any number of scholars have been predisposed to search for evidence of self-hatred even when their empirical findings pointed to self-hatred as a minor theme.

Standing in the way of my reinterpretation of past studies (the focus of Part One) is the evidence of Black identity change documented to have taken place during the Black Power phase of the contemporary Black Social Movement (the focus of Part Two). My response is to show that the change was partial, not comprehensive. Blacks entered and left the period of Black identity change with essentially the same personalities and self-esteem characteristics, although the movement radically altered their world view, philosophical orientation, political stance, and value system.

The distinction between personal identity ("general personality") and group identity ("reference group orientation") is crucial to my analysis. Very briefly stated, research shows that until the onset of the so-called Black underclass, the material conditions of most working-class, middle-class, and even many poor Black families were such that parents were able to engender a great deal of psychological strength in their children and that this strength consistently manifested itself in psychological studies of Blacks as average scores on general personality measures. Nevertheless, Black families have held, and continue to hold, a multitude of ideas and ideologies about how one should interpret the significance of being Black (racial identity studies have typically been sensitive to these racial ideologies). The Black Social Movement of the 1960s achieved a high degree of ideological and cultural consensus among Black people, especially Black youth. But in changing their ideologies, the movement did not have to change the personalities of Black youth because most already *had* healthy personalities. Such mental health was a legacy of the personal psychological victories that their parents were able to achieve and to pass on to the next generation via family socialization, the church, and the community. Building on this legacy of personal strength, young people in the 1960s unfolded a social movement that pushed the community toward greater consensus on what it means to be Black. At the heart of this identity conversion was not so much the dynamics of personal self-hatred as the metamorphosis of a Eurocentric world view into an Afrocentric one.

This book is divided into two parts. Part One (Chapters 1–4) focuses on the more traditional literature; Part Two (Chapters 5 and 6) concentrates on the theory and research on nigrescence.

Chapter 1 explores the seminal investigations on Black identity conducted in the late 1930s and early 1940s by the husband-and-wife teams of Ruth and Eugene Horowitz and Mamie and Kenneth Clark. Since these pioneers established the paradigm that has dominated the study of racial identity, their studies are subjected to a close reading in order to map the assumptions and generic psychological theory they applied to the problem of identity development in Negroes.

Chapter 2 presents a comprehensive review of the general literature on Black identity written between 1939 and 1980. Although the discourse on Black psychological functioning has turned on the presumed relationship between group identity and self-esteem, the review uncovers the rather curious finding that until the early 1970s, most studies of Black identity focused exclusively on either the group-identity or the self-esteem component of the Black self-concept. Thus, the relationship between the two variables was often taken for granted, and researchers typically collected data on only one variable. These unitary results were then used as a platform to make inferences about the "missing" variable. Thus the results of studies of group identity were used as a basis for making inferences about the dynamics of Black self-esteem and, conversely, findings from studies of self-esteem became the vehicle for discussions of Black group identity.

Chapter 3 represents the first review of forty-five studies that directly explore the relationship between self-esteem and group identity in Black Americans.

Chapter 4 attempts to explicate what has been found wanting in traditional theory on Black identity, along with an outline of the contours of its replacement. The chapter makes reference to a cluster of "forgotten" studies. Had these studies been taken more seriously when they first appeared in the 1930s, 1940s, and 1950s, they may very well have obviated the need for the current text.

Chapter 5 deals with research on nigrescence, or Black identity development models, written in the early 1970s. Much of what was originally written was right on target. Yet the research also reveals that important aspects of our contemporary vision of how Black identity operates in the daily life of a Black American need to be revised to account for the diversity and variety one discovers in Blackness.

Consequently, Chapter 6 is a major revision of my own nigrescence model, which attempts to take into account the structure and dynamics of Black identity as it operates in the present and likely operated in the past. Self-hatred is placed in the broader context of Blackness as diversity, complexity, and three-dimensionality.

ACKNOWLEDGMENTS

I suspect that, especially in the humanities and the social sciences, every text is the product of a "committee." When an idea for a book captures the imagination of a scholar, it is first given various "validity" tests through discourse with numerous friends. Over time, such exchanges help the author develop a more vivid imagination and/or keener insight, and what finally is published as a singular effort is really the work of many contributors. Thus, let me begin by thanking a cluster of friends, students, and associates who over the past ten years have helped me achieve a clearer focus: William S. Hall, James Turner, Ted Short, Judith Little, A. Wade Boykin, Thomas Parham, Philip White, Moncrief Cochran, Rita Hardiman, Harriette McAdoo, Michael Thornton, Margaret Spencer, Hortence Spillars, Janet Helms, and Nicole Carrier. I am especially grateful to Badi Foster, Gerald Jackson, and Bailey Jackson for the extended time each has devoted to discussions with me on the nature of Black identity.

Gerald Jackson, Urie Bronfenbrenner, and Sander Gilman read one or more chapters and provided invaluable feedback. I must single out Professor Gilman's contributions, for he helped me work through several protracted episodes of writer's block. His work on Jewish self-hatred was in no small way a source of inspiration for my effort on Blackness.

There are several people who to this day are probably unaware that they have acted as role models for me. I was at Princeton University when Leon J. Kamin completed his text on the science and politics of IQ testing, and though it likely falls short of the mark, I have attempted to fashion the current work along the lines of his work. Professor Kamin and my undergraduate mentor of long ago, Bernard Spilka, always stressed that the works of psychologists should never be taken at face value, for every so-called objective investigation has its political and cultural context.

I thank Robert Harris, director of the Africana Studies and Research Center at Cornell University, for reducing my teaching load at a crucial point in the development of the manuscript. Bob is also the one who brought my manuscript to the attention of Temple University Press. Thanks are extended as well to the support staff of the Africana Center, which consists of Daisy Rowe, Carolyn Wells, and Sheila Towner. I am most grateful to Ms. Towner, for typing the entire manuscript through many revisions.

In what I hope is not the ultimate commentary on the worth of the current work, I was not able to attract research funds to conduct the comprehensive literature reviews that appear in Chapters 2, 3, 4, and 5. These reviews involved the close reading of countless unpublished dissertations, and as I did not have the funding to support the purchase of these works, I will be forever grateful to the reference staff of Olin Library at Cornell University. There are "hidden costs" in any interlibrary loan system, and in many ways, Olin Library helped "fund" the current effort, as their liberal interlibrary loan policy gave me access to materials that normally I might have been required to purchase. Along these lines, I want to thank Thomas Weissinger, director of the Library for the Africana Studies and Research Center of Cornell University, for acquiring, as part of the library's permanent collection, a cluster of the more important unpublished dissertations on Black identity.

I conducted most of the literature reviews; however, Valerie D. Whittlesey and Judith A. Little provided invaluable assistance. Dr. Little's contribution to the materials in Chapter 3 proved particularly important.

I received continuous support and encouragement from my family, including my father, William E. Cross, Sr., my brother, Charles F. Cross, and my sisters Dolores Adams, Shirley Tucker, Charlene Mardis, and Judith Hagan. My brothers-in-law, Herman Hagan, Thomas Walker, Samuel Adams, and Robert L. Tucker, and my sisters-in-law, Mary Pat Dailey-Cross, Brenda Cooper, and Joclyn Goss, have also been extremely supportive, as has my mother-in-law Joyce Jackson. My spirits were on occasion wonderfully revised through play with my nieces, Ashleigh and Leigh Cross, Nikka Cooper,

Lauren Goss, and my nephew, Marion Hagan. Most important has been the support provided by my wife, Dawn M. Jackson, and my marvelously unpredictable daughter, Tuere Binta Cross.

I am very appreciative of the efforts of Henry Louis Gates, Jr., who made it a personal mission that this work should find a receptive publisher. Irene Glynn's copyediting was both meticulous and caring, and I am most grateful for it. Finally, my thanks go out to Janet M. Francendese, senior acquisitions editor at Temple University Press, who on any number of occasions helped nurse this novice through the trials and tribulations of publishing his first book.

PART ONE

Rethinking Self-Hatred

CHAPTER 1

Landmark Studies
of Negro Identity

Whether from the vantage point of Black or white observers, concern for the psychological significance of Blackness in a white world has been a pivotal theme in the social history of Afro-Americans. No fewer than three of the fifteen articles published in the first volume of the *Psychoanalytic Review* in 1913 focused on the psychology of the Negro. Two of the articles were written by John E. Lind, a white psychiatrist stationed at the Government Hospital for the Insane in Washington, D.C., known today as Saint Elizabeth's Hospital. Lind and his colleague A. B. Evarts, the author of the third article and a psychiatrist also employed by Saint Elizabeth's, considered themselves students of the mind of the Negro. They shared the belief that in the primitive and inferior Negro, one could discover how the (white) mind probably operated at an earlier point in evolutionary history. Lind and Evarts were no less excited about the chance to study exchanges between the "divergent" races: "The existence side by side of the White and colored races in the United States offers a unique opportunity, not only to study the psychology of a race at a relatively low cultural level, but to study their mutual effects upon one another" (Evarts 1913, 388).

Apparently Lind understood German, and from the origin of psychoanalysis to at least 1914, he kept abreast of the debates taking place among Freud and his associates by reading their German manuscripts and periodicals. Thus, several years before its English translation appeared, Lind used the seminal article by Alfred Adler, "Ueber den Nervosen charakter," to frame the analysis of a complex peculiar to the Negro:

> This complex is based upon the social sub-ordination of the ne-
> gro in the United States, and as the most obvious racial distinc-
> tion serving to set him apart from the more favored race is his
> color, I shall refer to it hereafter for the sake of convenience as
> the "color complex." That the color complex is present even in
> Negroes presenting no evidence of psychosis might almost be
> accepted as a truism. I shall mention, however, a few evidences
> of this. In the somewhat primitive theological conception which
> obtains among the Negroes, the Deity is personified as a White
> man, the angels also are White. Apparent exceptions to this
> must be noted. I have seen works of art for sale in stores cater-
> ing to the Negro trade, representing scenes in Paradise, transla-
> tions, etc., where the celestial figures were Black, a startling,
> vivid Black. The motives prompting such production, as well as
> those which might actuate their purchase and their acceptance
> as a faithful representation of the future state are probably a
> note of defiance, a protest against the orthodox color scheme
> of salvation, and by inference a recognition that the latter does
> not exist. But these are exceptions and the rule which will be
> verified by anyone who has had considerable dealing with the
> Negroes is that the future blessed state according to their ideas
> is one in which they will display a spotless integument and the
> first ceremony in the ritual of their entrance to Heaven is the
> casting aside of the ebony husk. (Lind 1913–1914, 404)

On the following page of the article, Lind continues:

> Whether then we accept or deny the hypothesis of the ubiquity
> of the color complex in the mentally normal Negro, no exhaus-
> tive study of psychoses in Negroes is necessary to show that it
> exists in very many of these and often molds largely the topog-
> raphy of the delusionary field.
>   Adler in his monograph on the nervous character is in-
> clined to give a less important part in the etiology of mental
> disturbances to the sexual factor than Freud. He discusses at
> length, the conflict in the life of the individual with the "will to
> power," of Nietzsche, and holds that this, with a sense of inferi-
> ority, is at the bottom of a large proportion of disturbances in
> the individual psychic life. (p. 405)

Lind's remarks might seem to anticipate issues raised years later by Kenneth and Mamie Clark; actually, the conceptualizations are historically linked. Adler's thesis on the "sense of inferiority and will to power" evolved at a time when many were seeking an explanation for the existence of self-hatred among European Jews (Gilman 1986), and this concern, along with its psychoanalytic underpinnings, was transported to the United States by Kurt Lewin (1941) in his polemic on *Jewish* self-hatred. In turn, Lewin's essay became a major reference in discussions of *Negro* self-hatred in the writings of Kardiner and Ovesey (1951) and Kenneth Clark (1955). But this is jumping the gun a bit. Let us turn next to the mid 1930s.

The Work of Eugene and Ruth Horowitz

Eugene Horowitz and Ruth Horowitz were keenly interested in theory and research on social attitudes and personality, which they frequently explored in studies involving the racial attitudes and personality dynamics of Black and white children. Under the guidance of Gardner Murphy, Eugene Horowitz (1936) completed his dissertation on the racial attitudes of white children living in the South, North, and within a communist commune in New York City. (His sample also included a significant number of Black students, but his focus was on the white subjects.) Part of Horowitz's methodology required subjects to rank-order photographs of the faces of Black and white children; then, in the Show Me Test, the children selected preferred companions from the same set of photographs.

> For the Show Me Test, the children selected companions for a variety of imagined situations. On each occasion, no limit was placed on the selections; as many boys could be chosen as a child might want; and on successive occasions, the same or different boys might be selected. For this test the situations were:
>
> 1. Show me all those that you want to sit next to on a street car.
> 2. Show me all those that you want to be in your class at school.
> 3. Show me all those that you would play ball with.
> 4. Show me all those that you want to come to your party.
> 5. Show me all those that you want to be in your gang.
> 6. Show me all those that you want to go home with you for lunch.

7. Show me all those that you want to sit next to in the movies.

8. Show me all those that you would go swimming with.

9. Show me all those that you like to have for a cousin.

10. Show me all those that you want to be captain of the ball team.

11. Show me all those that you want to live next door to you.

12. Show me all those that you like. (E. Horowitz 1936, 9–10)

The Show Me Test was based on an earlier study by Deutsch (1923) that Horowitz had learned about from Gardner Murphy (see, esp., Murphy and Murphy 1931, 607). Before selecting his measures, Horowitz became aware of a broad range of options, including the possible use of matched Black and white dolls:

> These techniques were developed after preliminary experimenting with outline drawings, a set of matched dolls, and the later use of a questionnaire and free composition, using two "matched" photographs. The need here was for testing techniques applicable to children over a wider age range than any of these techniques provided except the outline drawings; and the latter were found to be less satisfactory than the photographs, though they do permit greater comparability of stimuli presented in the tests. The realism of the photographs proved especially valuable. (Horowitz 1936, 12)

Eventually, Eugene joined with his wife, Ruth, to expand this review on the use of puppets, dolls, and pictures to elicit children's social attitudes. The Horowitzes' effort resulted in an important paper cited by Gardner Murphy, Lois Murphy, and Theodore Newcomb (1937, 280n) in their landmark text on experimental social psychology. In his dissertation and subsequent work (see Horowitz's chapter, Klineberg 1944), Eugene Horowitz was drawn to such devices as part of his concern for developing *objective measures of attitudes* (Horowitz 1936, 33). Ruth Horowitz, a clinician by training, saw that the dolls, puppets, and drawings had considerable potential for understanding the deep structure of personality. Her views were shared by Lois Murphy, and together they wrote an article on projective methods in the psychological study of children; of course, dolls, puppets, photographs, and toys were prominently featured (Horowitz and Murphy 1938).

One purpose of the dissertation by Eugene Horowitz (1936) was to show that racial attitudes and racial conflict were not instinctually based. He hoped that the inclusion of white children raised in a variety of circumstances would demonstrate considerable variability in their racial attitudes. As it turned out, his inclusion of a modest Negro sample also helped his case, for in a somewhat surprising turn of events, the Negro children showed a slight but statistically significant preference for the white photographs on the Show Me Test of racial preference:

> Yet that the prejudices are derived from social sources rather than through biologically transmitted traits is rather clearly demonstrated by consideration of the results from the Communist sample. Most of the White children in the various comparable samples showed a very marked preference for White as compared with Negro boys. The Negro lads tested showed a slight preference for Whites, whereas the averages for the Communist children hovered about the chance line. The unfavorably prejudiced attitude is attributed to environmental forces, not to specific experiences with Negroes, but to such social forces as apply with about equal pressure to children North and South, to children with little contact with Negroes and to those with much contact, to children in prosperous urban Georgia and to children in impoverished rural Georgia—social forces which extend to the Negro community and develop even there a preference for White as compared with colored lads, social forces which do not, however, penetrate, or are negated by, the training given to the Communist-trained children. (E. Horowitz 1936, 30)

What is intriguing is that clearly Eugene Horowitz did *not* equate same-race preference with "mental health"; from his point of view, a person who makes judgments by character rather than physiognomy will produce a "chance" choice pattern. This position was argued, almost as an aside, forty years later by W. Curtis Banks (1976).

Her husband's finding of a preference for white photographs by Negro subjects piqued the interest of Ruth Horowitz; in contrast to Eugene, she thought that race consciousness transcended surface issues and touched on intrinsic dimensions of personality. As a follow-up to Eugene's work, Ruth conducted what is now recognized as the first modern empirical study of racial identity in Black and white children (R. Horowitz 1939):

The data reported here are part of a longer study designed to
get at children's ideas about themselves, at a phase of development when the children can communicate them, and when the
ideas might still be conceived to be in the process of formation:
roughly, the nursery school age. The following discussion is
limited to children's emergent awareness of themselves, with
reference to a specific social grouping. It deals with the beginnings of race-consciousness conceived as a function of ego-development. (p. 91)

Of the 24 nursery school children involved in her study, 17 were
white (11 boys and 6 girls), 7 were Negro (5 boys and 2 girls), and all fell
within the age range of two years, three months to five years, one month.
Two projective techniques were individually administered, both of which
represented variations on Eugene Horowitz's Show Me Test. For the choice
tests, the children self-identified ("Show me which one is you") in response
to three tasks or items: a pair of photographs showing a Negro and white
child, a pair of line drawings showing a Negro boy and a white boy, and a
set of line drawings showing a Negro boy, a white boy, a clown, and a
chicken. The girls self-identified on the first item; for the remaining, male-
oriented items, they were asked to identify their brothers or cousins. The
boys needed no special instructions other than to self-identify on all items.
In the second technique, known as the portrait series, ten portrait pictures
were shown one at a time and for each the child was asked, "Is this you? Is
this ———? [name of child]."

Starting with the choice tests, the results showed that the proportion
of Negro and white children making incorrect self-identifications was nearly
identical; this pattern held for photographic as well as line-drawing stimuli.
The Negro and white girls were rather consistent in their self-identification
patterns; consequently, Horowitz accorded greater emphasis to an analysis
of the male data, for which more contrasts were evident. On the choice
tests, the Negro boys outperformed the white boys:

On the whole the White boys present a more confused picture
than do the Negro boys. Two of them identified with Negro
boys consistently (that is, every time they had a choice to make,
they chose to identify with the Negro picture), and chose pictures of Negro girls as their sisters. One of them chose a White
girl for his sister first, hesitated, and changed his choice, retain-
ing the second even on a retest given on the same day. No Ne-

gro boy consistently identified himself with pictures of White boys. While 33 per cent of the Negro boys made consistently correct identifications only 20 per cent of the White boys were consistently correct. The Negro boys who made consistently correct choices were slightly older than the White boys that did, but many of the White boys making incorrect identifications were older than any of these. (R. Horowitz 1939, 94)

At this point in the analysis, Horowitz had failed to replicate the finding of her husband's earlier study, which showed a modest tendency for Negroes to prefer whites. But, of course, she did not gain historical significance by demonstrating confusion and self-hatred in *whites*. On the portrait series, only 25 percent of the selections made by white boys were incorrect self-identifications; the figure for the Negro boys was 42 percent. Looked at from a slightly different angle, 33 percent of the white boys but as many as 66 percent of the Negro boys made one or more incorrect self-identifications. These figures are impressive except for one fact: The size of the Negro sample on which her analysis was based must have been 3! Recall that there were only 5 Negro boys in the sample to begin with; consequently, their frequency choices could only have been any one of five possibilities: 20 percent, 40 percent, 60 percent, 80 percent, or 100 percent, none of which works out to a figure of 66 percent, the proportion reported by Horowitz. This could have been a misprint, but earlier in the paper she indicated that, in contrast to the choice tests, the portrait series "did not give as satisfactory results . . . [because with] this technique there was a tendency on the part of some children to say 'yes' or 'no' to all the pictures" (p. 92). In other words, some children had to be dropped from the analysis of the portrait series. More than likely, 2 children were dropped from the sample of 5 Negro boys. Such a figure would be consistent with the percentage of Negro boys reported as having incorrectly identified, since 2 out of a sample of 3 equals 66 to 67 percent. Regardless of the small ($N = 5$) or puny ($N = 3$) Negro sample, and aside from the reliability and validity problems she encountered with the portrait series, Horowitz worked on to her now-famous interpretation concerning "wishful thinking" in Negroes. She concluded that the superior performance of the Negro children on the choice tests showed that Negro children become aware of racial differences at an earlier age than do whites. Moreover, the forced-choice, paired-comparison format of the choice tests meant that greater "reality constraints" were being placed on the Negro children, which may have acted to suppress any wish-fulfillment tendencies. But she reasoned that with the portrait series, the *absence* of a comparative frame may have revealed, especially among the Negro children, a deeper level of psychological functioning:

> Concomitant with their perception of differences and sim-
> ilarities, however, some of the children tended to identify
> themselves by other criteria than skin color when the situation
> permitted. We remember from the data of the second test that
> when the restriction of the forced choice was removed, in the
> portrait series, the Negro children identified more freely with
> members of both groups than did the White boys. What this
> means we can only guess. It can, of course be interpreted as
> "wishful activity." (p. 97)

Continued careful reading of the Horowitz work uncovers all the truths, half-truths, and exaggerations that have become commonplace in Negro identity studies employing racial-preference measures: (1) The subjects in the study are preschool children, yet affirmations are made about the relationship between the study's finding and the probable psychodynamics of Negro adults; (2) although only social attitude is assessed systematically (i.e., racial attitude), the results are discussed "as if" both social attitude and personality had been measured; and (3) "proof" of depth psychology involvement is equated with anecdotal evidence gleaned from the children's behavior and speech during the collection of social-attitude data. More important, Ruth Horowitz's study set the stage for the theoretical and methodological orientation to be embraced by researchers of racial identity from 1939 to the present.

THEORETICAL ORIENTATION OF RUTH HOROWITZ

Ruth Horowitz was wrestling with two dimensions of self-development: social attitude and personality. She was very critical of previous but unnamed works (her study did not include a list of references) that approached social attitude as devoid of psychodynamic content:

> While interest in attitudes of various kinds seems widespread in
> the field of psychology, there is as yet very little in the litera-
> ture to shed light on the dynamics of attitude function and atti-
> tude formation. Even studies focused on relationships between
> attitudes and various environmental factors rarely concern
> themselves with the attitude under scrutiny as an aspect of the

personality which finds partial expression through it. Instead, it seems customary to speak of attitudes as if they were entities per se which became somehow attached to the persons of various individuals, in the nature of a decorative appendage. (R. Horowitz 1939, 91)

Her critique led, not to the invention of new personality constructs, but to a debate about the way in which two previously established subordinate dimensions of the self-concept interacted. For Horowitz, the ontology of the ego, person, or self could be traced through the formation of social attitudes, such as one's race consciousness, gender consciousness, or group identity, and the concomitant progressive unraveling and elaboration of personality:

These data seem to point to the concept of group consciousness and group identification as an intrinsic aspect of ego-development and basic to the understanding of the dynamics of attitude function in the adult personality. Before the ego has been completely formed, in the very process of becoming, we find it subtly appropriating a visible symbol that has been socially institutionalized to aid in its work of marking itself off from all the not-self of which, until such demarcation has been established, it partakes. This may mean, however, that the self is defined in terms that make successive demarcations necessary, since in the perception of a difference an assertion of identification is involved. The individual's attitude toward his group evidently is an integral part of himself, in terms of which he is fashioned, under some circumstances of life. (p. 99)

Eventually, researchers used the term *self-concept* (SC) instead of ego development or self-development; the term *group identity* (GI) takes hold and is applied in the Horowitz study and thereafter, while the term *personality* attracts a plethora of competing labels. For the remainder of this work, *personal identity* (PI) will refer to "personality." The three terms can be put together as a formula, $SC = GI + PI$, which is to say that Horowitz studied the dynamics of self-concept (SC) through an exploration of group identity (GI) and personal identity (PI), and she strove to demonstrate that although GI and PI were distinctive structural components of SC, each was psychodynamically interwoven. Metaphorically, her vision of GI and PI was more akin to a ball or sphere, rather than two overlapping circles, in which the unity of self is publicly displayed either as a social attitude or its parallel personality dynamic, depending on the angle at which the sphere is viewed, with the innermost dimension of self hidden away at the core of the sphere. Moreover, given her grounding in clinical psychology and psychoanalytic ego psychology, she believed that insights developed in the study of children allowed the results to be discussed "as if" adults had also been studied.

There is reason to believe that Ruth Horowitz's conceptualization of the relationship between PI and GI was mildly, perhaps even sharply, in contradistinction to that held by Eugene. In his dissertation (E. Horowitz 1936) and in an important review article on social attitudes included in the classic text by Otto Klineberg (E. Horowitz 1944), social attitudes are approached as values, belief systems, ideological frames, or what today we would call "cognitions," and issues of personality, while noted, are given less weight in his overall scheme. True, in the article he co-authored with his wife (Horowitz and Horowitz 1938) can be found the statement, "Social attitudes of the younger children are but aspects of the personality of children" (p. 327); but in the article on white racism authored by him alone (E. Horowitz 1944), social attitudes are equated with social norms toward which, by definition, a variety of personality types or traits might be drawn. Thus, from Eugene Horowitz's vantage point, a white person of comfortable circumstances may embrace negative attitudes toward Negroes out of a simple propensity toward social conformity, while wretched poverty might explain the frustration and aggression underlying the racism of many poor whites (E. Horowitz, 1944; see, esp., 244–247). He relied less on unconscious explanations and was critical of those, such as Lewin (1941), who analyzed race attitudes held by Negroes in a categorical fashion. Even when Horowitz approached the phenomenon of anti-Negro attitudes in Negroes, his analysis led to a textured and flexible perspective in which low self-evaluation as well as high self-evaluation may result, depending on the circumstances of the person and the way in which the individual Negro responds to anti-Negro sentiment (Horowitz 1944, 220–221, 246–247).

Ruth Horowitz, in contrast, believed that to explain the dynamics of social attitudes or group identity in terms of "social conformity" was to "speak of attitudes as if they were entities per se which became somehow attached to the persons of various individuals, in the nature of a decorative appendage" (R. Horowitz 1939, 91). Social attitude or group identity, to her, was a part of personality, and personality was explainable through deep-seated and unconscious motivations, symbols, and meanings (Horowitz and

Murphy 1938); consequently, by her logic, group identity had to be viewed "as an intrinsic aspect of ego-development" (Horowitz 1939, 99).

If Horowitz's racial-preference study (1939) was not completely concerned with extending the ideas of her husband, whose conceptual frame was she using? Since she did not provide a list of references, one can only speculate. Her generic ideas about ego development and personality development follow the traditional psychoanalytic framework in a predictable fashion and are not a point of puzzlement. But what of the origin of her ideas about group identity? Her theorizing greatly parallels, or can be considered a logical extension of the work of symbolic interactionists such as Mead (1934), but more so than sociologists, Horowitz's thinking shows a remarkable similarity to that of Alfred Adler and, especially, Kurt Lewin (1936, 1941). The Horowitzes were in correspondence with Lewin as early as 1936; shortly thereafter, Eugene worked with Lewin on a research project, which took them to Palestine for a joint lecture series. In the late 1930s, Lewin was corresponding and visiting with scholars from Columbia University and the City College of New York. It was an inner circle of which the Horowitzes would shortly become a part. In his 1935 piece on the "Psycho-Sociological Problems of a Minority Group," Lewin presented "group identity" as a quasi-personality variable, but in his extremely influential polemic (Lewin 1941) on self-hatred among Jews, Lewin affirmed that group identity and personality are linked directly. Since Ruth Horowitz had access to Lewin's ideas through social discourse, before Lewin published them in 1941, perhaps he is the point of origin for her 1939 formulations about self-development, group identity, and personality. In his 1941 essay, Lewin sees negative self-development, or self-hatred as a social attitude that "usually influences deeply the total personality" (Lewin 1941, 192). He cites as an example its occurrence in Negroes: "One of the better known and most extreme cases of self-hatred can be found among American Negroes. Negroes distinguish within their group four or five strata according to skin shade—the lighter the skin the higher the strata" (p. 189).

The solution to this dilemma, for Lewin, lay in the individual's coming to realize that "there is nothing so important as a clear and fully accepted belonging to a group whose fate has a positive meaning" (Lewin 1941, 198–199). Translated in the light of Ruth Horowitz's thinking, a *positive* SC depends on the person's having a *positive* group identity, which in turn will be reflected in a *positive* personality: $SC(+) = GI(+) + PI(+)$. It does not take much to interpret this perspective to mean that in a racial-preference experiment, Negro children with a positive self-concept will show a same-race preference pattern; a white preference in Negroes bespeaks a negative group identity and, by inference, a damaged personality. At the end of her experiment, Horowitz codifies "Negro preference for White" as "wishful activity" or wishful thinking; the Clarks do the same in 1950. But by 1960 the term that dominates the literature is Lewin's concept of Negro self-hatred. (We return to Lewin at a later point in our discussion.)

METHODOLOGICAL ORIENTATION OF RUTH HOROWITZ

While some may question my opinion on the difference in theoretical perspective between Ruth and Eugene Horowitz, such divergence is more apparent in how they conceive and interpret racial-preference tasks. Although they made use of the identical procedure (Show Me Test), and used almost identical materials (one uses drawings of children, the other photographs), Eugene Horowitz referred to the Show Me Test as an *objective measure* of social attitude, while Ruth Horowitz described (Horowitz and Murphy 1938) and applied it (Horowitz 1939) as a *projective device*. In each instance, the resulting protocols are identical and unidimensional, but somehow Horowitz felt justified in approaching her data "as if" it clustered along both a group identity dimension and a personal identity dimension. As it turns out, the "missing data" were actually there in the form of observational and anecdotal material. Ruth Horowitz presented observational and anecdotal material to support her contention that the social attitude (i.e., racial self-identification) offered reliable insight into the personality dynamics linked to the social attitude. Thus, for her, racial self-identification not only "measures" group identity, it "reveals" personality. Consequently, she felt no need to measure each construct independently, for the one measure produced confirmatory evidence about each dimension, both of which she viewed as intrinsically connected. Horowitz seemed to approach the administration of racial self-identification as one would a clinical diagnostic situation in which all the subject's (client's) behavior is viewed as "evidence." This distortion was carried over to the work of the Clarks, and it "pressed" them to rely on only one measure when they were really interested in making statements on what would seem to require two independent measures.

Vivian Gordon (1980) has suggested that, especially when people have employed racial-preference and self-identification devices in the study of Negro or Black identity, theorists have gravitated toward a single-trait theory of Negro self-concept while, over time, theory and research have become more multidimensional. As we have seen, however, Ruth Horowitz and those, such as the Clarks, who extend her work, do not operate with a single-trait theory of identity. To the contrary, Horowitz and the Clarks operate with a complex model of human functioning that is multidimensional and dynamic. Nevertheless, her conception of the theoretical relationship between personal identity (PI) and group identity (GI) led Horowitz to believe that the Show Me Test could produce information that confirmed the unity of the complex self. At the level of structure of the self-concept, Horowitz (and the Clarks) embraced a perspective almost identical to that advocated by modern multidimensional theorists (e.g., Judith Porter, Harriette McAdoo, and Morris Rosenberg). But Horowitz and the Clarks provided few alternatives for the way in which the different layers of the self may interact and function, psychodynamically, other than in a linear fashion. Horowitz and the Clarks operated with the same constructs that are the central focus of contemporary Black identity studies, but their orientation left little room for the possibility that, in some or many instances, group identity may not predict personality, or vice versa. The presumption that the various levels of identity are orchestrated by highly significant linear relationships gives the work of Ruth Horowitz and the Clarks the appearance of being a unidimensional theory; at best, however, they had their eyes on two highly complicated domains: that of general personality, or personal identity (PI), and that of group identity (GI).

Let us now shift the spotlight from the Horowitzes to the Clarks, but first, I must note an ironic point. To a great extent, the significance of the Horowitzes' contribution to the discourse on Negro/Black identity has been underestimated; the influence of the Clarks, exaggerated. The Clarks are frequently credited with a novel theoretical perspective and a unique methodology in the study of Negro identity, but this is clearly not so. Their theoretical orientation was a replay of Ruth Horowitz's position, and given that Eugene Horowitz considered using matched Black and white dolls in his 1936 study, access to knowledge about his work is the likely source for Mamie Clark's use of dolls in her racial-preference studies. Furthermore, the kinds of questions the Clarks employ in their doll studies are traceable to Eugene Horowitz's Show Me Test. In a sense, then, the theoretical and methodological pillars of what will eventually become the "Negro self-hatred" literature are easily linked to Ruth and Eugene Horowitz.

And what becomes of this couple? They seem to disappear from the scene, only to have their articles reprinted in texts edited by Newcomb and Hartley (1947) and Hartley and Hartley (1952). But the Hartleys and the

Horowitzes are one and the same, for the Horowitzes changed their name to Eugene and Ruth Hartley![1] In fact, the first publication of the Clarks' findings of their original doll study was in a text edited by Theodore Newcomb and Eugene L. Hartley. Another important figure in the discourse on the meaning of Negro identity also changed his name, as Eric Homburg became Erik H. Erikson. Alfred Adler, from whose works the terms "self-image" and "inferiority complex" are derived, was born a Jew, but as a young man he "had himself baptized" (Sperber 1974, 30). That key contributors to the discourse on Negro identity manipulated dimensions of their own ethnicity in order to "pass" in American or European society is an irony seldom mentioned. Since so much theorizing about identity and personality is implicitly or explicitly informed by autobiographical reflections, it is a mystery how the texture and complexity with which each of these people approached the relationship between personal identity and group identity in their own lives failed to produce some skepticism about the meaning of racial preference in Blacks.

The Studies of Kenneth and Mamie Clark

About the time that Ruth Horowitz was conducting her study, Francis Sumner, a famous Black psychologist at Howard University, contacted Gardner Murphy at Columbia University about a bright student hoping to earn a doctorate at Columbia. Eventually Kenneth Clark was admitted to Columbia; later, Mamie Clark was admitted as well. It is at Columbia that the Horowitzes passed their knowledge about social attitudes, racial identity, and projective techniques on to the Clarks. There, the Clarks also became familiar with the work of Eric Homberger, Kurt Lewin, Gardner and Lois Murphy, and Otto Klineberg. The racial studies with which the Clarks are associated reflect a focus that began with Mamie Clark's master's thesis at Howard University.

The Clarks co-authored five articles on Negro identity between 1939 and 1950, but these publications actually reflect *two* data sets, one collected in 1939 and the other between 1939 and 1941 or 1942. That is, one data set

---

1. In a telephone conversation with Ruth and Eugene Hartley on May 13, 1986, Eugene indicated that during World War II, he had twice applied for a commission as a psychologist with the U.S. armed forces and had twice been turned down. Word filtered back to him that his "last name" was blocking his appointment. He and Ruth then changed their name to Hartley, and he reapplied and was given his commission. Thus, Eugene, an American Jew, had to "disguise" his identity in order to participate in the Allied struggle against the Nazis.

produced three publications (1939a, 1939b, 1940); the second provided the findings reported in two additional articles. Thus the Clarks did not conduct five studies over eleven years, they conducted two studies within about three years. This issue is not raised to slight the Clarks, for they *never* misrepresented their data. But one must remember that the Clarks did not conduct a plethora of studies, each of which replicated the results of the other. Although they are famous for their doll *studies*, they actually conducted only one doll study that included a northern and southern sample. The significance of the Clarks rests, not in their theoretical and methodological formulations (on both counts, they simply continued the work of the Horowitzes), not on their development of a large corpus (they conducted and published few studies), but in their ability to synthesize their research with the research of others in support of a pejorative interpretation of Negro identity (Clark 1955) and the advocacy of certain social policies (Clark 1965, Clark and Hopkins 1969).

When Mamie Clark decided to complete a master's degree in psychology at Howard University[2] by conducting a study along the lines of one published by Ruth Horowitz (1939), two people put her in direct contact with Horowitz. Max Meenes, a friend of the Horowitzes, was teaching at Howard and helped Mamie Clark shape her research. Kenneth Clark, by then a doctoral candidate at Columbia, was able to act as a conduit for both Ruth Horowitz and Mamie Clark as he traveled between New York City and Washington, D.C. It is Ruth Horowitz's recollection that, at one point, Mamie Clark thought of co-authoring a publication with her, but, as things worked out, Mamie's first article set a pattern in being co-authored with her husband, Kenneth Clark.[3] They became one of the most famous husband-and-wife teams in the social history of the Black intellectual community.

Theory and Methodology, 1939–1955

Unless one reads their publications in the order in which they were *submitted* for publication (Clark and Clark 1939a, 1940, 1939b, 1947, 1950), the Clarks might well be accused of being atheoretical. For the most part, only in their first article (Clark and Clark 1939) and in Kenneth Clark's first

---

2. In Richard Kluger's *Simple Justice* (New York: Knopf, 1975), he incorrectly states that Mamie Clark completed her master's thesis at City College in New York. Actually, her postgraduate training included a master's from Howard and a doctorate from Columbia.
3. In her master's thesis (1939), Mamie Clark acknowledged the assistance and support of nine people, including Francis Sumner and Max Meenes of Howard University, Otto Klineberg, Eugene Horowitz, and Ruth Horowitz of Columbia University, and Kenneth B. Clark.

book (1955) was their frame of reference made explicit. The in-between articles presuppose that the reader is very familiar with the literature review and hypotheses explicated in their initial publication (Clark and Clark 1939a, 591–594).

Although they employed her methodology and shared much of her theoretical orientation, Ruth Horowitz was not invited to be a joint author in any of the three articles that record the outcome of their first data set (Clark and Clark 1939a, 1939b, 1940) because, as the publications evolved, the Clarks were essentially contesting important aspects of Ruth Horowitz's seminal work (1939). In this we see the influence of Francis Cecil Sumner. Sumner was a match for any academic research psychologist, and had he been allowed to teach at a university worthy of his intellect, competence, and sophistication, he could easily have attained the status of Gardner Murphy. More than likely, Sumner's critical eye cued the Clarks to the flaws in Ruth Horowitz's study. The Clarks' first article in 1939 set the stage for the conflict, which is explored openly in their 1940 work. The Clarks saw the self developing in stages similar to those advocated by Jean Piaget and James A. Baldwin, and believed that at an early age, children might confuse their fantasy world with themselves. Thus very young children might identify with a "cuddly" and "furry" rabbit or lion; as the children grow older, comparison would be determined by the physical properties of their bodies with the properties and features of beings around them. To explore this perspective, the Clarks tested 150 Negro preschoolers—50 three years olds, 50 four year olds, and 50 five year olds—with a modified version of the Show Me Test. At the end of their first article, the Clarks noted:

> In an effort to get some indication of the nature of development of consciousness of self in Negro preschool children, with special reference to emergent race consciousness, 150 Negro children in segregated schools were shown a series of line drawings of White and colored boys, a lion, a dog, a clown, and a hen and asked to identify themselves or others. The results were as follows:
> The total group made more choices of the colored boy than of the White boy.
> The ratio of choices of the colored boy to choices of the White boy increased with age in favor of the colored boy.
> Choices of the lion, dog, clown, and hen were dropped off at the end of the three-year level, indicating a level of devel-

opment in consciousness of self where identification of one's self is in terms of a distinct person rather than in terms of animals or other characters. (Clark and Clark 1939a, 598)

In their 1940 article, based on the same data set, the Clarks continued to trace the differentiation of the self, only now the children were classified by age and skin color (light, brown, and dark). In her study, Ruth Horowitz (1939) had reported that Negro children responded in a manner that suggested they knew they belonged to one group (Negro society), but "wished" they could be something they were not, that is, white. The Clarks were critical of this conclusion, especially as they discovered various mediating variables that might have accounted for Horowitz's findings. Ruth Horowitz's sample was small ($N = 24$), she did not control for age, and she did not differentiate subjects by skin color. Instead, she aggregated her data, something the Clarks believed was inappropriate for this experiment: "A mass presentation of the data completely disguises any factors which may be operative in the dynamics of self consciousness and racial identification" (Clark and Clark 1939a, 595).

Controlling for age and skin color, the Clarks showed that the children were *not* orienting themselves according to an awareness of belonging to a socially defined group; instead, the children made comparisons and achieved greater degrees of self-differentiation based on the properties of their bodies. Thus very-light-skinned Negro children were more apt to compare themselves to the light-colored figures on the Show Me Test, while dark-skinned children identified themselves with the dark figure. Aggregating the choices of the light-, brown-, and dark-skinned children distorted the distinctive pattern for each group. Not only was Ruth Horowitz's "wishful thinking" conclusion derived from an analysis of aggregate data, but most of her children (16) were between the ages of two and three; only 8 children were between the ages of four and five.[4] Besides questioning whether two-and three-year-old children even have a notion of "race" as a sociological construct, the Clarks clearly believed "that the operation of the mechanisms of 'wishful thinking' and fantasies in reference to self-identification is too sophisticated an operation for the three-year-old developmental level" (Clark and Clark 1940, 164).

---

4. Although it is never stated, the Clarks must have known or suspected that Ruth Horowitz's Negro sample included a significant number of light- and brown-skinned children.

The Clarks could find little evidence of "wishful activity" in the behavior of the children in their sample, and they concluded on the following note:

> The general tendency of the dark children to identify themselves with the drawings of the colored boy is not incompatible with the objective fact of their own skin color. This same thing holds true of the medium children with certain already stated modifications. There would be, however, a definite incompatibility if the majority of light children identified themselves with the drawings of the colored boy, hence the persistence of their identifications with the White boy. It is obvious that these children are not identifying on the basis of "race" because "race" is a social concept which they learn at a higher stage in their development. They are, however, definitely identifying on the basis of their own skin color which is to them a concrete reality. (Clark and Clark 1940, 168)

Surprising, isn't it? The couple whose work has generally been synonymous with the documentation of Negro self-hatred ("wishful thinking") actually rejected the notion in their first foray into the field, thus protecting Negro children from what the Clarks perceived as premature, if not flippant, theorizing about the psychology of the Negro.

This distinction between the work of Ruth Horowitz and that of the Clarks is significant, but we should not lose sight of the extent to which the Clarks were in agreement that self-concept (SC) had two components and was equal to the sum of one's personal and group identities ($SC = PI + GI$), and that they held a complex and textured perspective on human functioning. Their argument was simply that the ontogeny of the GI factor was much more complex than Ruth Horowitz had envisioned.

Although the first and second articles by the Clarks announced the appearance of two first-rate scholars, the third and final work based on their original data set reminds us that the two authors were still students and had limited knowledge of related studies. In this third work (Clark and Clark 1939b), they used a large subsample of the first data set and added two new samples for a three-way comparison of racial identification and segregation: racially segregated nursery group, semisegregated nursery group, and integrated nursery group. The procedures employed with the semisegregated and integrated groups were the same as those used in testing the segregated subjects that Mamie Clark ran as part of her master's work. Again, this third work is not so much a new study as a modest extension and manipulation of her original data set.

The semisegregated group was so labeled because, although all the children and most of the teachers were Negroes, the nursery school staff included one white teacher and one white cook. Not surprisingly, the children's performance on the Show Me Test was practically identical to that of the segregated students in the original study (Clark and Clark 1939a, 1940), as an increasing identification with Negro images was evident with age. In contrast, the children from the racially mixed preschool showed a "chance" or no-preference pattern across age. The Clarks were at a loss to interpret these results and they introduced a deficit orientation to explain the children's behavior. In so doing, they revealed their limited knowledge of related studies, for the reader will recall that this is the same kind of finding Eugene Horowitz encountered in his doctoral thesis: White children socialized in a progressive environment placed less emphasis on race, as evidenced by a "chance" preference pattern on the Show Me Test; segregated and ethnocentric white children produced a white-monoracial preference pattern (Horowitz 1936). The Clarks actually described the Negro children in the progressive, mixed racial group as retarded! "This retardation and seeming confusion of identifications of these subjects in the mixed nursery school suggest that other factors not present in the semi-segregated or segregated group situation are operative in modifying the expressions of this function" (Clark and Clark 1939b, 163).

Their article listed but three references, two of which refer to their own work (Clark and Clark 1939a, 1940) and one to Ruth Horowitz's (1939) study. This became a trademark of the Clarks' studies: They referenced only themselves and Ruth Horowitz. I was struck by this tendency because I assumed that just as the first data set reflected Mamie Clark's master's thesis, so the doll study would reflect her (or Kenneth Clark's) doctoral dissertation. As doctoral students, surely the Clarks gained a broader perspective. Yet a trip to the library of Columbia University made it evident that neither one made racial identity or anything vaguely related to the Negro experience the subject of a doctoral dissertation. The famous doll study was almost an aside, which may in part explain why their last two empirical studies on identity (Clark and Clark 1947, 1950) were not framed by a meaningful literature review, nor were the results anchored in theory.

We see that the notion of Negro self-hatred *cannot* be traced to the Clarks' three publications between 1939 and 1940. We must look to their second data set, the results of which were recorded in 1947 and 1950.

To continue their work on the ontogeny of identity in Negro children, the Clarks received a grant from the Julius Rosenwald Fund for 1940–1941. In the time between Mamie Clark's master's thesis and preparation for the new study, the Clarks made a crucial distinction that Ruth Horowitz (1939) discovered almost by accident and that the Clarks totally missed in their critique of her study. Horowitz (1939, esp. 97–98) tried to make a distinction between the tendency of Negro children to show a keen awareness of skin-color differences on racial-recognition and racial self-identification tasks ("Show me which is the Negro child," "Show me which is the White child," "Show me which one looks like you"), versus the color *preferences* of children. Horowitz's methodology, as the Clarks pointed out, was fraught with problems, but their critique addressed only the issue of racial self-identification; that is, controlling for age and skin color, they showed that Negro children performed quite appropriately on racial identification tasks. But the Clarks' early work did not address *racial preference*. Just as Horowitz prematurely or incorrectly interpreted some of the variability on what was essentially a self-identification task as evidence of conflictual racial preference ("definition of the self is not so much in terms of what one is as it is in terms of what one is not"), the Clarks countered by incorrectly making statements about the absence of "wishful thinking" (conflictual racial preference) on what was still only a test of racial self-identification. On further thought, the Clarks must have considered that it might be possible to show that Negro children (1) correctly self-identify on racial identification tasks, but (2) show a white orientation ("wishful thinking") on tests of racial preference. Such a dualistic methodology would demonstrate that Negro children, although aware that they are "colored," prefer or wish to be white. A finding of this nature would give credence to Horowitz's speculations. Scholars often find it difficult to apologize to each other in public, and I cannot help but wonder if the Clarks were sending a cryptic message to Ruth Horowitz when, at the end of their racial-preference experiment, in which they found the above to be *true*, they chose to word their findings in the following manner:

> The discrepancy between identifying one's own color and indi-
> cating one's color preference is too great to be ignored. The
> negation of the color, brown, exists in the same complexity of
> attitudes in which there also exists knowledge of the fact that
> the child himself must be identified with that which he rejects.
> This apparently introduces a fundamental conflict at the very

foundations of the ego structure. Many of these children attempt to resolve this profound conflict either through *wishful
thinking* or phantasy. (Clark and Clark 1950, 350; italics added)

In order to explore the distinction between racial self-identification
and racial preference, the Clarks amassed data on 253 Negro children, 134
(southern group) of whom were tested in segregated nursery and public
schools from three cities in Arkansas, and 119 (northern group) in racially
mixed nursery and public schools in Springfield, Massachusetts. The distribution of the sample allowed the Clarks to examine the effects of region of
the country (North or South), sex (male or female), skin color (light, me-
dium, or dark), and age (three years of age through seven). In one of their
earlier publications, (Clark and Clark 1939a, 597) they noted that the line-
drawing portion of the Horowitz Show Me Test was more sensitive and
revealing at some age points than at others. As a preliminary to their new
research, they pretested other projective tests of racial attitudes in the hope
of finding devices that were equally sensitive for children ages three
through seven. Eventually they came to favor a Coloring Test, but they also
devised a Doll Test and a questionnaire. In their new study, they applied
these two assessment techniques along with the line-drawing section of the
Show Me Test, although it is not clear whether the results of the portions of
the Show Me Test were ever published.

In some circles, the Clarks have been credited with developing the
Doll Test as a novel procedure for assessing racial attitudes; as documented
earlier, both Eugene Horowitz (1936) and Ruth Horowitz (Horowitz and
Murphy 1938) had considered using or had reported on the use of matched
dolls in testing and/or conducting therapy with children. The Clark Coloring
Test *was* unique. Two publications record their findings, the first (Clark and
Clark 1947) on the doll study and the second on the coloring task (Clark
and Clark 1950). The doll study appeared in a text whose history is worth
noting.

The Society for the Psychological Study of Social Issues (SPSSI) was
established in 1936 to promote teaching and research in social psychology.
In 1943, "the Society was convinced that the teaching of social psychology
. . . was being unnecessarily handicapped by the paucity of teaching materials" (Likert 1947). Soon afterward, the SPSSI established a committee to
investigate the problem and eventually recommended that a book of readings be sponsored for publication. The book was destined to become a
classic in the history of psychology in general and social psychology in par-

ticular. Production on the book was delayed by World War II, but in 1947, the Committee on the Teaching of Social Psychology of the SPSSI finally published *Readings in Social Psychology*. The contents page lists persons who helped found the society as well as the names of those who would dominate the field of social psychology through the 1960s. One of the last articles written by Kurt Lewin appears in the text (Lewin died shortly before the volume went to press). The names of all twenty-seven members of the committee appear on the title page, although the text is generally referenced by the names of the committee co-chairmen, Theodore M. Newcomb and Eugene L. Hartley. Besides editing the work, Newcomb and Hartley contributed articles; Hartley appears as Eugene L. Horowitz in an early article reprinted in the text and, as co-author of a later article written with his wife, as Eugene and Ruth Hartley.

In a section on the socialization of the child, sandwiched between articles by Piaget and George Herbert Mead, is the article co-authored by Kenneth and Mamie Clark in which they report the results of the one and only doll study they published (Clark and Clark 1947). The article opens with a three-sentence introduction that makes it clear that the Clarks were approaching the study from the $SC = GI + PI$ perspective: "The specific problem of this study is an analysis of the genesis and development of racial identification as a function of ego development and self-awareness in Negro children" (p. 169).

Moreover, there is no confusion about which dimension of self-concept (SC) their methodology was attempting to assess: "Because the problem of racial identification is so definitely related to the problem of the genesis of racial attitudes in children, it was thought practicable to attempt to determine the racial attitudes or preferences of these Negro children—and to define more precisely, as far as possible, the developmental pattern of this relationship" (p. 169).

From their vantage point, the Doll Test was assessing racial identity, or what Ruth Horowitz called group identity (GI). At the end of the article, they make a statement about the personality (PI) dimension of the self, but this is documented, not on the basis of the racial attitude (GI) data, but through an interpretation of the comments made and the behavior exhibited by the children as they took the Doll Test. Thus, conceptually speaking, the Clarks were not operating with a unidimensional model of SC (i.e., $SC = GI$ or $SC = PI$); instead, they thought their measurement technique produced both GI and PI information, the exact assumption made earlier by Ruth Horowitz.

The Clarks approached their second data set hoping to be able to differentiate racial knowledge and self-identification from racial preference. They attempted to accomplish this by having each child (the children were tested individually) hand the experimenter either a white or a Black doll, on display and easily within reach, in response to the following requests:

1. Give me the doll that you like to play with—(a) like best.
2. Give me the doll that is a nice doll.
3. Give me the doll that looks bad.
4. Give me the doll that is a nice color.
5. Give me the doll that looks like a White child.
6. Give me the doll that looks like a colored child.
7. Give me the doll that looks like a Negro child.
8. Give me the doll that looks like you.

According to the Clarks, "Requests 1 through 4 were designed to reveal preferences; requests 5 through 7 to indicate a knowledge of racial differences; and request 8 to show self-identification" (p. 169). At Columbia, the experimental psychologist R. S. Woodworth had chaired the committees of both Mamie and Kenneth Clark, which is to say they were familiar with the problem of "order effect." Nevertheless, after a discussion about controlling for order effect in the display of the Black and white dolls, they then reveal having *avoided* controlling for order effect in the presentation of the eight questions/requests to each child in order to maximize a desired outcome!

> It was found necessary to present the preference requests first in the experimental situation because in a preliminary investigation it was clear that the children who had already identified themselves with the colored doll had a marked tendency to indicate a preference for this doll and this was not necessarily a genuine expression of actual preference, but a reflection of ego involvement. (p. 169–170)

Since later (Clark 1955) they argue that this and other preference tests reflect stable, persistent, and profoundly important dimensions of the Negro personality, their methodology seems paradoxical.

In any case, the Clarks report that the children clearly had knowledge of racial differences and that they apppropriately self-identified (they knew about race or color and they knew they were Negroes), yet even when age and skin color were controlled, the children had a preference for white skin and a negative attitude toward their own skin color. They also report that, by age seven, the trend was reversing; older children preferred the brown doll. The preference for white was more evident in the northern than the southern group. The article does not include a summary or discussion section and ends abruptly after the presentation of anecdotal material.

Three years later, the second and final article (Clark and Clark 1950) based on the same study was published in the *Journal of Negro Education*. Here the Clarks report the result of the Coloring Test. This test consisted of a box of crayons and a sheet of paper on which appeared the outlines of various objects (leaf, apple, orange, etc.) and a boy and a girl. Each child was first asked to color each object as a way of determining the child's understanding of the relationship between object and color. For those who passed this portion of the experiment, the child's racial self-identification was measured by asking him or her to color the outline of the human figure that matched their sex with a color that matched their color. Finally, the child's racial preference was determined by asking each child to color the opposite-sex human figure in a color "you would like little boys (or girls) to be." Of the 253 children who completed the Doll Test, the drawings of only 126 were used in the analysis of the Coloring Test.

An important error appears in the Clarks' introduction to this study. In their prefatory remarks, the Clarks review the results of previous studies, all five of which appear in a footnote. They also state: "Previous *studies* [emphasis added] have shown the majority of these subjects prefer a White skin color and reject a brown skin color" (p. 341). This statement makes it appear that several, if not all, of the studies referenced found the above to be true; yet an examination of the list shows that four were racial identification studies (Ruth Horowitz's 1939 study and the Clarks' three publications based on Mamie Clark's master's thesis at Howard) and that only one, the Clarks' 1947 Newcomb and Hartley piece, was a racial-preference study. Thus, at the time of the publication of the Coloring Test results, only *one* preference study had been conducted, and the Coloring Test publication constituted a second report on the Clarks' one and only racial-preference data set.

Although the children who took the Doll Test were the same children who completed the Coloring Test, in their findings the Clarks did not explore the relationship of a child's performance on one test to the other. Since they were working with categorical rather than continuous data, the computation of a correlation coefficient was not possible, but the relationship could have been studied through chi-square. Apparently, for reasons they do not state, this was not done; consequently, comparisons were done in terms of "trends" and "tendencies."

The Clarks comment that, compared to the Doll Test, the Coloring Test is a "more sensitive method for bring(ing) out some of the subtleties, complexities and conflicts involved in the pattern of the children's attitudes toward skin color (p. 345)." One can probably take this to mean that the Coloring Test presented a more meaningful and *accurate* analysis of the phenomenon under study. But if this were so, the quantitative results of the Coloring Test stand in rather stark contrast to the quantitative findings of the Doll Test. With the Doll Test, the Clarks were able to control for age, skin color, and region; when analyzing the Coloring Test, racial preference, more so than color knowledge or self-identification, was confounded by skin color. Recall that it was the Clarks who had previously admonished Ruth Horowitz for her failure to control for skin color; thus it is somewhat surprising that so much of the analysis of the Coloring Test was completed on aggregate data, in which 25 of the 29 light-skinned children were part of the northern sample, and only 4 were from the South. In any analysis involving the northern and southern children, the light-skinned children should have been dropped, and the Clarks, much to their credit, did drop them at one point (see Table 1), even though they end by interpreting their results primarily in terms of the aggregate data, *including the light-skinned subsample*. Looking at Table 1, which shows the color preferences for the medium- to dark-skinned children, we discover that the major finding was not the children's display of a white preference but a strong, in the case of the northern sample, and an unequivocal, in the case of the southern children,

Table 1

Racial Preference of Northern and Southern Medium- to Dark-Skinned Children

| Racial Preference | Six Year Olds | | | | Seven Year Olds | | | |
| | North | | South | | North | | South | |
	N	%	N	%	N	%	N	%
Brown	4	15	18	67	13	60	23	80
White	20	77	8	30	4	18	5	17
Irrelevant	2	8	1	3	5	22	1	3

Source: Reported in Clark and Clark 1950, 346, Table 9.

preference for *brown* at age seven. Of the southern sample, 67 percent showed a preference for brown at age six, and an astounding 80 percent did so at age seven! This was the highest choice frequency of any cell in the Clarks' analysis of preference for either the Doll Test or the Coloring Test. No less dramatic was the *change* in preference demonstrated by the northern group. At age six, 77 percent prefer white and only 15 percent prefer brown; at age seven, the trend has completely reversed, with 60 percent of the northern sample preferring brown. Compared to the northern six year olds, this represented a 37 percent decrease in the preference for white, and a 45 percent increase in the preference for brown. The Clarks totally avoided the implications of the trend for the southern sample, and primarily construed the pattern of the northern children as reflective of emotional conflict.

If the conclusions the Clarks reached were somewhat remote from their quantitative analysis, what explains the origin of their pejorative pespective? The answer seems to lie in the anecdotal data the Clarks collected from children in their study and "clinical" observations they made of other children in *psychiatric treatment*. For children in the study, 17 percent (20 out of 119) of the northern and 40 percent (54 out of 134) of the southern sample made comments while taking the Doll Test; the Clarks evaluated these comments at the end of their presentation of the results of the Coloring Test. Even here, one is impressed by the extent to which the Clarks pursued a unidimensional and pejorative frame in the face of flimsy qualitative evidence. Of the total number of children who made remarks during the Doll Test ($N = 74$), only 11, or 9 percent, of the children from the North ($11/119 = 9$ percent) and 25, or 18.6 percent, from the South ($25/134$) made anti-Black statements. For the entire sample, only 14 percent ($11 + 25 = 36$, or 14 percent of 253) made anti-Black comments, 7.5 percent said the brown doll was ugly, fewer than 1 percent said the brown doll was dirty, and none of the children from the North and only two from the South used the word *nigger* in discussing their preferences. Putting it another way, if 14 percent made anti-Black statements, 86 percent did not, including a group of northern and southern seven year olds who evidenced a clear-cut brown preference on the Coloring Test. Reading these figures, one becomes interested not only in the self-denigration themes suggested by the 14 percent, but the other alternatives implied in the attitudes of the remaining 86 percent. Instead, from the Clarks, who in 1939 and 1940 were quick to point out the numerous ways one might approach the analysis of self-identification data other than from a unitary and negative frame, comes a single-mindedness in the analysis of their racial-preference data, data that seem no less in need of a textured perspective.

What convinced the Clarks to pursue their story line was not the trend of the quantitative or qualitative data but the impact made on them when some of the children did articulate group rejection or anti-Black sentiments. Note Kenneth Clark's comments to Richard Kluger, published in *Simple Justice*:

> "We were really disturbed by our findings," Kenneth Clark recalls, "and we sat on them for a number of years. What was surprising was the degree to which the children suffered from self-rejection, with its truncating effect on their personalities, and the earliness of the corrosive awareness of color. I don't think we had quite realized the extent of the cruelty of racism and how hard it hit." The interviewing and testing proved a moving and shaping experience for Clark. "Some of these children, particularly in the North, were reduced to crying when presented with the dolls and asked to identify with them. They looked at me as if I were the devil for putting them in this predicament. Let me tell you, it was a traumatic experience for me as well." (Kluger 1975, 400)

The Clarks then assume that the negative remarks made by a handful of children in their study or clinical practice represent *pervasive* themes in the psychodynamics, not only of Negro children in general, but of the average Negro teenager and adult (Clark 1955). It is a perspective in which the actuality of race as a debilitating factor in the lives of a fraction, albeit a significant fraction, was confused with the *potentiality* of race damaging the lives of the majority. Race as a "hassle," "imposition," "stigma," and "mark of oppression" is at the core of their analysis. To the extent that Negro identity was a two-sided story, one about oppression and its consequences and the other about culture and the way people survive and, on occasion, transcend their oppression, the Clarks become experts not on Negro identity as a cultural phenomenon, but as a clinical case study in imposition.

That the Clarks' vision of the average Negro was informed by the troubled personalities they saw in their clinical practice goes without saying, but the absence of a cultural frame also reflected a school of thought about Negro culture that captured their imagination in the 1940s. With the publication of his text on the Negro family in 1939, E. Franklin Frazier conducted a Sherman-like march though *any* counterthesis and concluded that African culture was totally destroyed by slavery and that the everyday life of the average working-class Negro was, no more or no less, a poor imitation of white American culture, doomed to failure by racism and discrimination. His perspective on the Negro middle class proved no less bitter. As individuals, Frazier saw Negroes, regardless of their status, as an extraordinarily vulnerable and crippled people. When Gunnar Myrdal sifted through the position papers on Negro life and "culture" in preparation for writing *An American Dilemma*, he eventually sided with the Frazierian perspective of "zero culture" or "pathetic culture," and excluded such works as those of M. J. Herskovits and Zora Neale Hurston (Stanfield 1985). Kenneth Clark was engaged by the Myrdal enterprise and, like Frazier, he survived the "final cut," probably because his vision of Negro culture and life was shaped, in part, by Frazier's thesis. Later, around the time that the Clarks were publishing the Doll Test and Coloring Test results, Frazier and Kenneth Clark assisted in the production of evidence that offered a psychological complement to Frazier's sociological profile of the Negro. Abram Kardiner and Lionel Ovesey contacted both men about their desire to conduct a psychosocial study of the American Negro, employing what was thought at that moment to be psychiatry's most potent and revealing diagnostic devices: the clinical interview and the Rorschach Test (a projective test of personality). In 1951, they published their findings in a text destined to become a classic in the pejorative perspective on Negro life and culture, *The Mark of Oppression*. In the preface to the first edition, Kardiner and Ovesey (1951) indicate that they were "greatly indebted to Dr. E. Franklin Frazier for advice concerning the book as a whole." Then they acknowledge persons and clinics who cooperated in the procurement of subjects; first to be listed are "Drs. Mamie and Kenneth Clark of the Northside Center for Child Development."

At an early point in their work, Kardiner and Ovesey embrace the Frazier and Myrdal frame of reference about Negro culture:

> The most conspicuous feature of the Negro in America is that his aboriginal culture was smashed, be it by design or accident. The importance of this basic fact for the Negro in America cannot be overestimated. It means, in effect, that the old types of social organization and all their derivatives could not continue, but a new type of emergent adjustment derived from the new conditions would have to be established. (p. 39)

For the remainder of the text, they explore the self-concept (SC) of Negroes and purport to find a group identity (GI) anchored in the idealization of white people and white culture and the concomitant rejection of Negro life and culture. They then try to show that the consequence of this negative group identity is "low self-esteem" (damage to PI). Besides popularizing low self-esteem, Kardiner and Ovesey introduce another term into the discourse on Negro identity: *self-hatred.*

The use of self-hatred in the social sciences and psychiatry dates back to the turn of the century when European Jews were attempting to explicate the essence of a "bad" and a "good" Jewish identity. In a masterful work, Sander Gilman (1986) traces the history of Jewish self-hatred. The nature and texture of Jewish self-hatred followed the course of European anti-Semitism, and in the mid nineteenth century, anti-Semitism was transforming itself into the "science of race." Jewish "differentness" was marked by statistical studies purporting to show that Jews suffered a higher incidence of psychopathology than other people. A Jewish propensity for hysteria and neurathenia was linked, in the minds of anti-Semites, to the legacy of Eastern Jewry, with its enthusiasm, mysticism, and alleged pattern of incest. Through exclusivity and inbreeding to the extreme, so the argument went, the central nervous system of the Jewish race had degenerated (i.e., psychosis Judaica).

Jews themselves were repulsed by the charge of incest, but they tended not to dispute the psychopathology statistics; instead, they sought to provide other explanations for Jewish mental illness. For example, an early supporter of Theodor Herzl and the Zionist movement, Martin Englander in 1902 wrote "The Evident Most Frequent Appearances of Illness in the Jewish Race," in which the Jews of the Diaspora were defined as mentally and spiritually exhausted by their search for freedom and happiness outside of Zion; the cure, of course, was "land air and light, i.e., the creation of a homeland." Gilman also noted the case of Cesare Lombroso, known for his studies of degeneracy in prostitutes and criminals, who when confronted with the charge that Jews themselves were a degenerate group, responded in 1893 with a work titled *Anti-Semitism and the Jews in Light of Modern Science.* Accepting as "fact" that the Jews suffered from a high incidence of mental illness, Lombroso saw this not as evidence of a racial or biogenetic trait but as the negative consequence of persecution.

Max Nordau saw Jews as being weak in "mind and body" from having been confined to the ghetto for too long. According to Gilman, Nordau in 1900 called for a "new muscle Jew" who would help create a new Jewish homeland along the lines of German nationalism.

On the eve of the twentieth century, Gilman saw the science of race

give way to the psychology of race, and Jewish observers began to explain
the high level of Jewish mental illness in psychoanalytic terms: Psychosis
Judaica gave way to "the Jewish complex." With the press of Zionists, who
were often at odds with assimilated German Jews, the good Jew, or the
healthy Jew, became the unassimilated, mystical, "pure," Eastern European
Jew; the unstable Jew was the assimilated or baptized Jew. Gilman noted that
in 1919, a young Jewish doctor named Rafael Becker compared Jewish and
non-Jewish psychiatric patients and reported his findings before a Zionist
organization meeting in Zurich. In his opening remarks, Becker paid hom-
age to the startling "statistical facts" about Jewish mental illness, but then,
according to Gilman:

> Becker denies any specific increase in mental illness because of
> a special proclivity of the Jews but sees in the increase in the
> rate of other forms of psychopathology the direct result of the
> acculturation of Western Jews. Even though Jews in earlier
> times suffered more greatly from oppression, their strong faith
> preserved their sanity. Only with the decline in Jewish identity
> in the nineteenth century has there been an increase in mental
> illness. Becker picks up a thread in late-nineteenth-century anti-
> assimilationist Jewish thought that places the roots for the
> moral decline of the Jew at the doorstep of Jewish emancipa-
> tion and acculturation. He introduces Alfred Adler's newly
> coined concept of "inferiority" to give a dynamic dimension to
> his assumption that Jews are more frequently driven into mad-
> ness than their non-Jewish persecutors (49). It is the "assimi-
> lated Jew" who is diseased, self-hating, and thus self-destructive.
> (Gilman 1986, 295)

For every observer who laid the blame of Jewish self-hatred on the German
Jew and romanticized the Eastern Jew, Gilman found an equal number of
Jewish spokespersons who reversed the polarity. Theodor Lessing published
Jewish Self-Hatred in 1930; in it, the "bad Jew" is the Jew of the East and the
"good Jew" is the German Jew who has become a separatist. The self-hating
Jew, according to Lessing, is the assimilated Jew who has not been awak-
ened to his nationalistic yearnings. Once awakened or converted, "good
Jews" are "intelligent, hard-working, and rational while their antithesis re-
mains limited, scholastic, parasitical and irrational" (Gilman 1986, 301).

As the polite science of race of the nineteenth century reappeared in
the draconian anti-Semitism of the Nazis, Jews stressed ever more the di-

chotomy between the hopeless, self-hating, acculturated German Jew and the healthy German Jew of separatist persuasion. As a case in point, Gilman reviewed an editorial in the *Jewish Panorama* of May 5, 1933, by Robert Weltsch.

> Weltsch's observations rely on a dichotomy between healthy self-criticism and diseased self-hatred. Healthy are those who reject their acculturated identities and see themselves primarily as Jews; diseased are those who remain mired within the corruption of a primarily German identity. Again it is the label of the Other, here the acculturated German, as self-hating and thus diseased that creates categories of the acceptable and the unacceptable Jews. Weltsch's Zionist orientation sees the "new Jew" as consciously rejecting the model of identity that predominated among German Jews during the late nineteenth and early twentieth centuries. His glorification of a separatist Jewish identity is parallel to the stress on national identities present throughout Europe. Just as the Nazis claimed that being consciously German was "healthy" and being Jewish was "diseased" (a metaphor that dominates Hitler's *Mein Kampf*), so, too, it was necessary for Jewish political ideologists to distinguish between "healthy" and "corrupt" Jewish identities. What is evident is that their own sense of self provided the model for the "healthy" Jew; that which they rejected, the model for the "ill" Jew. (Gilman 1986, 303)

The German model for the "healthy" Jewish identity eventually made its way to the United States, primarily through the writings of Kurt Lewin (1941) and Bruno Bettelheim (1947, 1960). Even here, the confusion over what is or is not a healthy identity becomes evident, with Bettelheim attacking the "pathology" of the assimilated Jew and Lewin, although genuinely more eclectic, having a somewhat skeptical view of the value of East European Jewish identity.

It was Lewin, not Bettelheim, who influenced the study of minority identity in the United States. Lewin's polemic on Jewish self-hatred appeared in the 1940s in time to be incorporated in the thinking of Kardiner and Ovesey and Kenneth Clark. By the time Bettelheim's more elaborate model appeared, the concept of self-hatred had already been established as "fact." Furthermore, Bettelheim's thesis argued against assimilation and stressed group solidarity. The primary architect of Negro identity, Kenneth Clark, held an opposite view and was thus less receptive to Bettelheim's implied separatism. Even the pragmatic group solidarity suggested by Lewin was seldom stressed by Clark. The irony is that although the Jewish debate on self-hatred was clearly anchored in issues of culture and group solidarity, culture and solidarity were seldom points of reference in discussions of Negro identity, primarily because American observers of Negro identity believed there was little Negro culture to speak of:

> In the light of these criteria, we can compare the Negro under slavery with the Ghetto Jew. The latter did not have his culture destroyed, but rather the whole culture was transplanted to a new environment—the Ghetto. Full participation in his own culture inside the Ghetto was permitted the Jew, but only limited participation in the master culture outside of it. Family organization, religion, tradition could continue unchanged. The ideals of the group were drawn from traditional sources, and the ideals of accomplishment were drawn from the intrinsic culture. The master culture in which the Ghetto was located was treated with disdain, and its ideals were rejected. The subservient position the group had in the master culture was, to a good measure, canceled out by the exaggerated value of the intrinsic culture. The extrinsic culture was "foreign." It was this contrast that kept the culture of the Jews alive for two thousand years.
>
> The case of the Negro was completely different from that of the Jew. There was not only limited participation in the extrinsic culture, but this could only take place by identification with the master's status. In other words, participation was vicarious—through the agency of another person. Moreover, slavery destroyed the intrinsic culture by depriving the old institutions of functional relevance and by destroying the functional interaction of various statuses. All of the latter were leveled to the one status, that of a vested interest belonging to someone else. Minimal instinctual gratification had to be permitted to preserve the utility of the slave, but much of his comfort and effectiveness were destroyed. Reciprocal action between members of the intrinsic group (slave) was extremely limited, and with the extrinsic group (master) was completely absent. (Kardiner and Ovesey 1951, 41)

Kurt Lewin used the term self-hatred in an essay on Jews in 1941, but the article appeared in the *Contemporary Jewish Record*, an "ethnic" periodical, and was seldom cited. The essay was reprinted in Lewin's collected works (Lewin 1948), and this source is usually cited. Lewin clearly articulated the $SC = PI + GI$ model and stated that, for people in general and minority-group members in particular, negative group identity (GI) was likely to result in self-hatred at the level of personality (PI). The dynamics of Lewin's essay are ever present in *Mark of Oppression*; not surprisingly, self-hatred and some variant of low or damaged self-esteem were the principal ways Kardiner and Ovesey codified their findings about the Negro personality. *Mark of Oppression* became *the* work researchers of racial preference used to "prove" that the doll studies explored the early evolution of Negro (self-hatred) personality development in children.

With this information as background, it is easy to see how the Clarks could argue against the "wishful thinking" hypothesis in 1939 and 1940 but become the principal advocates of Negro self-hatred by 1955. E. Franklin Frazier and Gunnar Myrdal set the stage for the Negro identity research, and it would be almost thirty years before their tangle-of-pathology thesis was seriously questioned. Between 1940 and 1965, researchers who tried to depict *any* portion of Negro life as a reflection of strength and a unique culture were simply labeled "romantics." This is not to say that the Clarks and others were intimidated by the pejorative camp. To the contrary, one has to imagine the excitement of researchers as they produced evidence that seemed to support certain propositions of their friends. Frazier must have been delighted when Kardiner and Ovesey embarked on a psychiatric study that might confirm hypotheses about pathology in Negro personality that logically flowed from his theory. The Clarks must have experienced a real sense of relief when they saw the Kardiner and Ovesey study bringing acceptance to their own work. Everything "fit"—Frazier's social history of Negro life, the self-hatred syndrome in Negro adults, and the ontogeny of this self-hatred traced to racial preference in Negro children. There really was no need for the Clarks to explore other implications of their racial-preference study (e.g., the tendency for most of the six and seven year olds to prefer brown) because Kardiner and Ovesey's discovery of rampant self-hatred in all walks of Negro adult life relegated such findings to noise in the data, rather than evidence of a cultural buffer. Finally, any chance that the Clarks might return to their racial-preference data set and discover overlooked trends was dashed when Kenneth Clark was asked to be an expert witness in behalf of those attempting to overthrow segregation laws.

Kenneth Clark was predisposed to see Negro life from a pathogenic perspective, and the opportunity to assist in the struggle to destroy legal

racism through a careful delineation of the negative effects of racism rein-
forced his views. A lesser person might even have contrived evidence, but
Clark was too ethical. Besides, the request by Thurgood Marshall's legal
team complemented the frame of reference spelled out by Kenneth Clark in
"The Effects of Prejudice and Discrimination on Personality Development in
Children," a paper he presented in 1950 at the Mid-Century White House
Conference on Children and Youth. A few months later, a key member of
the National Association for the Advancement of Colored People (NAACP)
Legal Defense Fund asked Clark for help in developing the Defense Fund's
case against segregation. Clark's monograph was eventually included as part
of the Defense Fund's brief to the U.S. Supreme Court, and in its May 1954
decision (*Brown* v. *Board of Education*) striking down segregation, the
Court cited Clark's report. In 1955, Clark's monograph became the basis of
his first book, *Prejudice and Your Child*. With the fame that followed, and
the apparent "correctness" of the views, it is doubtful whether Kenneth or
Mamie Clark would have reexamined the earlier findings.

Even if Kenneth Clark had not been linked to activities surrounding
the desegregation case, it is unlikely that he or Mamie Clark would ever
have found a cultural angle from which to reexamine their data, for the
Clarks were not trained theoreticians of Negro culture and Negro identity,
although their training and world view lent themselves to the development
of considerable expertise on the psychology of oppression among Americans who happened to be Negroes. Others may eventually perceive the
Clarks as experts on oppression and Negro (cultural) identity, but the Clarks
seldom suffer from such confusion. It is simply no accident that Kenneth
Clark's first book is titled *Prejudice and Your Child* rather than, say, "Negro
Identity: Issues of Culture and Oppression." In *Prejudice and Your Child*,
Clark summarizes the research on racial preference in Negro and white
children conducted between 1939 and 1955 and interprets the findings in
the light of works by Frazier, Kardiner and Ovesey, Lewin, Myrdal, and
others. Negro self-hatred is the central theme. Following a section on prejudice and its consequences, Clark outlines a "program for action" (pp. 85–
135), which includes these subsections: "What can schools do?" "What can
social agencies do?" "What can churches do?" "What can parents do?" Clark
gives no indication that he sees existing Negro culture as incorporating positive and effective mechanisms for transcending racism. Thus, in "What can
parents do?" the teaching of Negro history and culture in Negro homes is
not even mentioned; and except for one brief paragraph, the same is true of
his advice to schools.

But if the Clarks and others did not use the term Negro in any cultural context, what did they expect of children who identified as Negro? The Clarks saw "Negroness" as a *stigma*. In a color-blind world, Negro children would identify as "brown," not out of any cultural imperative, but as fact. According to the Clarks' way of thinking, the absence of racism would create a climate in which brown-skinned people would accept this fact just as they might accept having brown hair. Thus, choosing brown or rejecting brown was not a cultural matter but a factual matter that might be distorted or made clear in the presence or absence of racism. The logical extension of the Clarks' perspective on group identity was not cultural solidarity and certainly not cultural nationalism. Consequently, the Clarks were very unhappy about the Black identity movement in the 1960s and 1970s; they saw it as a sign of reactionary separatism.

The Clarks, though associated with the construct "group identity," never really advocated collective Negro enterprise or group (cultural) solidarity as a countermeasure and proactive strategy for Negroes living in America because, ultimately, they saw no possibilities in Negro culture. Instead, they produced an image of the Negro dominated by feelings of inferiority. In a sense, they provided extraordinary insight into what happens when racism cripples the mind and spirit, but they offered no explanation for, and even came close to denying, the existence of Negro identities that effected reasonable-to-average levels of self-esteem in the face of everyday negotiations with poverty and racism. One can find Stanley Elkins's *Sambo* or Richard Wright's *Bigger Thomas* in the psychological portraits provided by the Clarks, but what of the anti-Sambo slave prototypes found in John Blassingame's *The Slave Community* or the rich and varied figures who appear in the works of Zora Neale Hurston or the poetry of Langston Hughes and Mari Evans? To study the psychology of the Negro is to encounter a spectrum of identities, a spectrum represented in the *data* of the Clarks' five racial identity studies, though missing in the monadic image they forged from those data. Yet this singular, pejorative image provided a sharp tool with which the Warren Court could cut a path toward desegregation:

> "I told the staff that we had to try this case just like any other
> one in which you would try to prove damages to your client,"
> recounts Thurgood Marshall. "If your car ran over my client,
> you'd have to pay up, and my function as an attorney would be
> to put experts on the stand to testify to how much damage was
> done. We needed exactly that kind of evidence in the school

cases. When Bob Carter came to me with Ken Clark's doll test, I though it was a promising way of showing injury to these segregated youngsters. I wanted this kind of evidence on the record." (Kluger 1975, 397)

As "evidence of damage," the image served its purpose well. Beyond the courtroom, however, and especially in scholarly works that have appeared since the Court's 1954 decision, the image helped distort Black history and the social scientific analysis of Black life. By continuing to interpret the racial-preference studies with singular rather than contrasting images, the isolated and stark presence of the self-hating Negro became what the Clarks and others never intended: a stereotype.

▍▍▋▋▍▍
CHAPTER 2

Empirical Research
on Group Identity
and Personal Identity

Black identity research continues to be framed by the same two-factor model formulated by the Horowitzes in which self-concept is thought to consist of a general personal identity (PI) domain, and a racial or group identity (GI) domain. Restated as a formula, a complete picture of the self-concept is equal to the sum of information about a person's *personal identity* (PI) and *group identity* (GI), or $SC = PI + GI$. In this chapter, the empirical research on Negro and Black identity conducted between 1939 and 1980, including the studies by the Horowitzes and the Clarks, is analyzed in accordance with this formula. The chapter shifts from the close reading, or microanalysis, of a select group of Negro and Black identity studies in Chapter 1 to a macroperspective in which we search for trends or generalizations, as revealed by an analysis of a fairly inclusive sample of studies. Before we proceed, however, we must relabel one variable in the equation.

A less expansive version of this chapter appeared as "Black identity: Rediscovering the distinction between personal identity and reference group orientation," in M. B. Spencer, G. K. Brookins, and W. R. Allen, eds., *Beginnings: The social and affective development of Black children*. Hillsdale: L. Erlbaum, 1985, 155–171.

Racial identity, religious identity, occupational identity, and class or socioeconomic identity can be described as different kinds of "group identity." In the sociopsychological and sociological literature, however, one is more likely to see them cited as instances of "reference group orientation." Since one of this book's goals is to show the connection between Negro or Black identity and reference group theory (Hyman and Singer 1968; Teeland 1971; Urry 1973), a connection explored in Chapters 3 and 4, from this point on the formula will read $SC = PI + RGO$, where RGO stands for "reference group orientation."

Hundreds of investigations have been conducted on Black (and white) identity development in children and adults. When attempting to review this literature, a primary task is the articulation of a meaningful classification or data-reduction system. Such a system reveals the methodological issues and/ or hypothetical constructs that the reviewer plans to stress in describing, classifying, and analyzing each study. In previous reviews, Proshansky and Newton (1968) emphasized racial conception (how the child learns to make racial distinctions at a conceptual level) and racial evaluation (how the child evaluates personal group membership); Banks (1976) differentiated racial preference from racial self-identification studies; Williams and Morland (1976) focused on studies of racial attitudes, racial acceptance, and racial preference; and the five methods used to operationalize the construct "self-concept" (doll studies/participant observations/unscaled interviews/projective tasks/personality, or self-esteem, inventories) in studies of Black identity provided the point of departure for Gordon (1976, 1980) and Baldwin (1979). Looking at the equation $SC = PI + RGO$, we see that a common shortcoming of these reviews is that only one side of the equation is explored. Focusing on racial awareness or racial preference limits one to the RGO component of SC, while reviews such as the one by Taylor (1976) delineate only the PI variable. Furthermore, such reviews have seldom covered studies on the relationship (the correlation) between PI and RGO that is so crucial in answering questions about Negro and Black identity. The review by Porter and Washington (1979) was a step in the right direction, but it suffered from a number of limitations (see Chapter 3).

Framework for A New Review

This chapter covers empirical studies conducted on Negro or Black identity from 1939 to the present, with particular emphasis on the years 1939–1960, the period during which the pejorative view about Negro identity was established, and 1968–1980, the years in which Black identity change was recorded.

NEGRO SELF-HATRED, 1939–1960

Mark of Oppression by Abram Kardiner and Lionel Ovesey (1951) purported to demonstrate that self-hatred was a pervasive theme in the personality dynamics of the vast majority of Negro Americans. The book's publication marked the point at which many in the scientific community began to accept Negro self-hatred as an established "fact." With the U.S. Supreme Court's *Brown* v. *Board of Education* decision in 1954, and the publication in 1955 of Kenneth Clark's *Prejudice and Your Child*, Negro self-hatred gained a consensus in both the scientific and popular press. It is safe to say that by 1960, many assumed that Negro self-hatred was a thoroughly documented finding. This review focuses on empirical studies conducted between 1939 and 1960 that helped create the Negro self-hatred thesis.

NIGRESCENCE, 1968–1980

The Supreme Court school desegregation decision in 1954 began the contemporary Black Social Movement. The movement as a whole can be broken down into two phases: a *civil rights phase*, which lasted from about 1954 until the death of Dr. Martin Luther King, Jr., in 1968; and a *Black Power phase*, which took on the characteristics of a mass movement in the aftermath of King's murder in 1968 and continued to show mass movement activity through the mid 1970s. It was during the Black Power phase that the concept *Black identity* had its origin. Blacks were said to experience a Negro-to-Black identity transformation, captured in the phrase the *psychology of nigrescence*, or the psychology of becoming Black. Personality and self-concept studies conducted with Blacks between 1968 and the late 1970s were often designed to capture the nature and extent of Black identity change. The current review examines the empirical literature from the *nigrescence period* to determine what changes and/or continuities can be discerned.

Two-Factor Theory of Black Identity

The schematic in Figure 1 indicates that researchers of Negro and Black identity have generally operationalized their notion of self-concept (SC) through either personal identity (PI) or reference group orientation (RGO). In this review we try to determine the extent to which PI and RGO studies

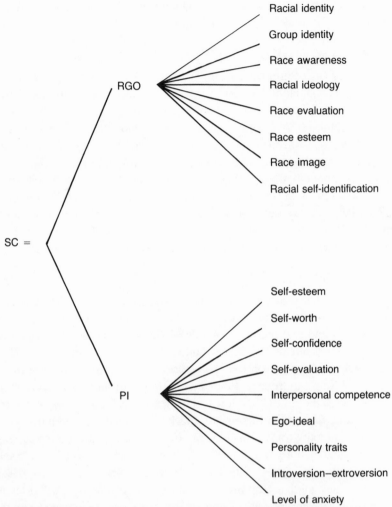

Figure 1. Schematic of two-factor theory of Black identity. Note that self-concept (*SC*) = personal identity (*PI*) + reference group orientation (*RGO*).

were used to argue either the self-hatred thesis or the Black identity concept. Since both concepts imply that there is a very strong relationship between the PI and RGO domains of the self-concept, we seek to determine how many PI × RGO *correlational* studies were conducted during each time period.

For the self-hatred period, we should expect to find a significant number of PI studies showing personality or personal identity damage in Negroes and another cluster of RGO studies showing that Negroes have a negative group identity. As a check on the fact that these two domains are, in fact, predictive of one another, we should also expect to find empirical evidence from the self-hatred period demonstrating that there is a very strong correlation between Negro personality damage and negative group identity attitudes; such evidence could come only from empirical studies in which independent measures of PI and RGO were administered to the same sample of subjects. Given that in Chapter 1 our close reading of a few of the self-hatred studies tended to call this thesis into question, we look for PI and RGO evidence from the self-hatred period that does not confirm self-hatred.

As to the period of nigrescence, we want to determine whether substantive change in the identity structure of Blacks has been demonstrated by both PI and RGO studies, and we try to isolate those PI × RGO correlational studies that show Black personality or personal identity dynamics can be predicted by the nature of the group identity or reference group orientation held by Blacks. Keep in mind that just as the self-hatred thesis may have been an oversimplification of Negro psychological functioning in the past, so also the "new" Blackness perspective may distort our understanding of contemporary Black psychology. Consequently, we look for evidence that suggests the new Blackness phenomenon is much more complicated than previously considered.

Before producing the results of the current literature review, we need to specify in greater detail what differentiates personal identity (PI) research from research on reference group orientation (RGO).

PERSONAL IDENTITY (PI)

In research on Negro/Black identity, PI studies have focused on variables, traits, or dynamics that appear to be in evidence in all human beings, regardless of social class, gender, race, or culture; in this sense, PI studies examine the so-called universal components of behavior. Everyone is thought to fit on a continuum of high or low anxiety, self-esteem, introversion–extroversion, depression–happiness, concern for others, and so on. The degree to which a trait may be prominent may differ by culture, class, or gender, but the traits or dynamics in question are felt to be present in every human being, some on a fragmentary level, others at a pronounced level. PI variables are thought to be the building blocks of personality, with culture, class, race, ethnicity, and gender mediating "how much is present" across cultures or different groups of people.

Another key point to keep in mind is that PI research tries to establish whether or not a person or group is characterized by adequate psychological well-being. Psychological functioning, interpersonal competence, ego strength, and pathology determine the dialects of PI research. Thus PI research is concerned with the direct measurement of psychological functioning, in the most general sense of that concept, and the indirect measurement of cultural or gender identity. In other words, given that one is told that subject A and subject B have high self-esteem and highly effective interpersonal skills, one could not predict whether the subjects were Black or white, men or women. What one could say is that whatever the sex or racial differences between subject A and subject B, both seem, within the context of American culture, to have elements suggestive of adequate mental health. The power of PI research is its presumed ability to delineate the mental health profile of a person or group.

Since the researcher believes that PI variables are present in all humans, the same assessment techniques or tests are used with different groups. PI-related research does not require the design of special tests for application with different groups of people, with the exception of language translations. For example, in studying self-esteem in men or women, Blacks or whites, Asians or Chicanos, researchers have typically used the same questionnaires or tests (e.g., Tennessee Self-Concept Scale and Rosenberg Self-Esteem Scale). The tests are not modified for each group because self-esteem is thought to be a trait in evidence in all groups. Consequently there is no such thing as a "Black version" of the Thomas Self-Concept and Values Inventory nor are there versions designed for use with women or men. In this sense, there is no such thing as "Black self-esteem" or "female self-esteem"; instead, more technically, research has studied the level of self-esteem in Blacks, whites, men, women. The same is true for PI-related phenomena such as introversion–extroversion, depression–happiness, concern for others, ego defense, anxiety, IQ, and field–ground dependence (see Figure 1).

How, then, does race enter into the equation of PI research on Black people? The answer is that in PI studies, race is always treated as an independent variable or subject variable. The researcher (1) locates some personality scale, inventory, or questionnaire (e.g., Minnesota Multiphasic Personality Inventory [MMPI], self-concept scale, Rorschach Test, locus-of-control scale, anxiety scale) that purports to tap "universal elements" of personality and that contains no reference to race, nationality, gender or religion; (2) the device is administered to Black and white subjects (in scales standardized on whites, the white "control" group may not be incorporated in PI studies, and comparisons are made on the basis of normative data); and (3) the researcher then determines whether or not race, as an independent variable, is statistically significant. That is to say, does the scale configuration (MMPI), level of self-esteem (Tennessee Self-Concept Scale or Coopersmith Self-Esteem Inventory), personality pattern (Thematic Apperception Test [TAT] or Rorschach), locus of control (I-E scales), or level of anxiety differ according to the race of the subject when race is treated as a classification factor?

REFERENCE GROUP ORIENTATION (RGO)

Although PI studies can reveal psychological functioning and the universals of one's self-concept, there remains the examination of those aspects of "self" that are culture, class, and gender specific. Since it could be said that PI research seeks to control for and thus "cut through" social class, ethnicity, and gender in its search for the common core of human behavior, RGO research takes just the opposite tack. It seeks to discover differences in values, perspectives, group identities, lifestyles, and world views. In a sense, RGO represents the ethnographic dimension of the self-concept. Although anxiety, fear, self-esteem, and happiness may reflect behavior found, to one degree or another, in all human beings, RGO research tries to discover what events or symbols within each culture or subgroup stimulates anxiety, fear, and so on. PI research is akin to the dynamics and structure of the self; RGO studies establish the content, context, symbols, values, and reference groups for the self. Though it is true that everyone eats food (a universal behavior pattern), what a person eats, how it is prepared, and the utensils involved are not the same across cultures but are very culture specific. Similarly, every human being relies on people or groups as a point of reference (i.e., a PI statement applicable to all humans), but which persons or groups one relies on reveals the specific nature of one's group identity or reference group orientation. For example, to say, "I like people," is a universal human propensity that offers little information about one's particular cultural frame, but to say, "I like and prefer to socialize with fellow Jews," leaves little doubt about the core of one's RGO.

This concern for reference group specificity has led researchers to develop RGO assessment devices (tests, questionnaires, doll-preference situations) that are very *particularistic*. Since the RGO researcher is not concerned with how a person feels in general, but how one orients oneself or how one feels regarding specific values, preferences, or symbols, not surprisingly these values, preference options, and symbols are generally made an explicit dimension of the dependent variable. Much has been made of the Clarks' use of dolls in their operationalization of the construct group identity (RGO), and Gordon (1976) has argued that this method is distinctive in requiring "forced choice" behavior; however, neither issue speaks to the central feature of RGO studies. The Clarks were not studying children's reactions to dolls per se; they were concerned with the most effective way of presenting *explicit symbols* of "race and color" to subjects who happened to be children. Had they been working with adults, race or color would have remained a central property of the stimulus condition; however, the nature of the choices offered adult subjects would have reflected objects more typical of adult life.

In the assessment of RGO, race or color is usually an explicit property of the stimulus condition, and it is *always* a factor in the scoring technique. In some projective devices or open-ended interviews, the researcher may not present race or color as a stimulus, but will search the protocols for race-explicit attitudes, feelings, and the like, that are spontaneously elicited by the nondirective stimulus. Generally speaking, however, not only is explicit race or color information a part of the dependent measure in RGO studies, it is also a salient component of the stimulus situation or items. The subject, in turn, must make a particular kind of preference or relate particular attitudes toward his or her socially ascribed group in order to achieve a "high in-group score," the obverse resulting in an "out-group," or self-hatred, score. Note, however, that "self-hatred" is clearly inappropriate, for it refers to a PI variable; nevertheless, in studies that have produced only RGO data, it is not uncommon for results to be discussed "as if" both PI and RGO information had been generated. We note that race or color-explicit stimulus scoring techniques are direct measures of one's "group identity" (Lewin 1948; Porter 1971), "racial attitudes" (McAdoo 1977), "racial orientation" (Goodman 1952), or "reference group orientation" (Cross 1978b, 1981). The last term is preferred, for in addition to binding these studies to the sociological literature on reference group theory (Hyman and Singer 1968), students and scholars of this technique have in fact been concerned with the creation of valid measures that reliably demonstrate how a child or adult orients himself or herself toward his or her socially ascribed group. In this light, and as shown in Figure 1, studies of racial attitudes, racial identity,

racial self-esteem, racial evaluation, racial preference, or racial self-identification are subcategories of the domain reference group orientation
(RGO).

Consequently, objective criteria can be used to discern PI from RGO
studies. PI studies treat race as a subject variable/independent variable; race
or color is excluded from the stimulus conditions and the dependent measures. In PI studies, the dependent measure operationalizes some "universal" personality element; therefore, with the exception of projective techniques and open-ended interviews, devices associated with PI studies
preclude the possibility of race or color being even unintentionally injected
into the scoring procedure. In most RGO studies, in contrast, the graphic
presentation of color or some other explicit race-related symbol constitutes
a salient dimension of the stimulus (e.g., the color of the dolls or, with
questionnaires, items that measure racial attitudes, opinions, feelings or racial ideologies). In *all* RGO studies, race-related information is an important, if not the most important, element of the dependent measure (e.g.,
frequency of Black vs. white doll selection; total score on pro-Black vs. anti-
Black ideology items; production of Black features on the Draw-a-Person
Test, positive vs. negative race-related themes on the TAT or Rorschach).

Given the above definitions, and referring again to Figure 1, we see
that the hypothetical construct SC has two superordinate domains, PI and
RGO, each of which is further reducible to a plethora of subordinate constructs, and, in some instances, the subordinate variables may also incorporate sublevels. As can readily be imagined, one could easily develop complex predictive models *within* each of the two domains, to say nothing of
the kind of models that would result from attempting to combine variables
across the PI and RGO domains. But while all that might prove very interesting, the great debate about Negro or Black identity has centered on the
general relationship between PI and RGO, not the dynamics and interface of
lower-level constructs. For Negro and Black subjects, evidence of adequate
mental health or the absence of psychopathology, as measured by various PI
devices (e.g., self-esteem scales, MMPI, adjective checklist), has been presumed to be linked to an in-group orientation, as measured by various RGO
measures (e.g., black doll preferences with young subjects, a high score on
a Black consciousness scale with older subjects). Conversely, opposite PI
trends were presumed to be traceable to an out-group orientation, and an
out-group orientation traceable to low PI scores.

Classification of Empirical Studies on Black Identity by PI and RGO

In preparing the current review, 181 studies were identified for classification, and it was determined that the list incorporated empirical studies referenced in previous critical and comprehensive reviews. The current review systematically excluded "field studies which relied on case study and participant observation techniques . . . and studies which used an unscaled or informal questionnaire or interview for gathering data" (Gordon 1980, 60–61). Such studies have played a minor role in documenting the alleged negative Negro identity from 1939 to 1967 and in documenting the alleged change in Black identity from 1968 to the present.

The studies were relatively easy to classify, which attests to the fact that researchers have generally been operating with either a PI- or RGO-related construct when designing their experiments. With the exception of the Draw-a-Person projective technique—clearly an RGO device, since when applied in racial studies, the dependent measure has typically been whether or not a subject's drawing was that of a Black or white figure—studies using projective devices were frequently problematic. Projective techniques allow subjects the freedom to organize their impression of, say, TAT or Rorschach cards, with a story of either PI or RGO import. Unless the researcher differentiates between the two protocols, it becomes nearly impossible for a reviewer to determine the basis on which some subjects were depicted as self-hating and others as healthy.

In other instances, the appropriate PI and RGO scoring categories may be in place, but the degree to which the projective stimuli are effectively "race neutral" may be at issue. To this day, the TAT is used with Black subjects to elicit "deep structure" personality dynamics, including "race neutral" elements. Nevertheless, Robert L. Williams and his students have repeatedly shown that the original TAT cards, which have figures that appear to be white, elicit stories with more negative content than do the same cards with Black-looking images (Williams 1981; see also the *Journal of Non-White Concerns* 10, no. 1 [1981] and 10, no. 2 [1982]).

Table 2 shows the results of classifying the 181 studies. The table also includes information on studies that have simultaneously applied independent measures of PI and RGO on the same sample, typically in a correlational design and henceforth to be called PI × RGO correlation studies. You will note that the information pertaining to this third category of study, PI × RGO, is added to Table 2 by broken lines. As I explain in greater detail

Superordinate and Subordinate Constructs Associated with Studies of Black Identity and Frequency of Studies: 1939–1960 and 1968–1980

Superordinate Constructs	Subordinate Constructs	Documentation of Negative Negro Identity, 1939–1960	Documentation of Black Identity Change, 1968–1980	Studies Reviewed (N)
Reference group orientation (RGO)	Racial attitudes, group identity, race awareness, racial ideology, race preference, race evaluation, race esteem, racial self-identification, race image, esteem for group, in- or out-group orientation, etc.	17 RGO studies. All showed negative Negro identity.	29 RGO studies. 18 (62%) showed a positive, 8 (28%) a negative, and 3 (10%) a varied Black identity pattern.	46
Personal identity (PI)	Self-esteem, self-worth, self-confidence, personal self, self-concept, general personality, interpersonal competence, primary-self, personality traits, anxiety level, unconscience-self, hidden personality dimensions, etc.	1 PI study.	89 PI studies. 66 (74%) showed positive, 13 (15%) negative, and 10 (11%) varied results for self-esteem.	90
PI × RGO	Generally an implicit factor in Black identity research in which PI and RGO constructs are discussed "as if" empirical studies demonstrated that PI × RGO measures follow a positive linear correlation of considerable magnitude.	None.	45 PI/RGO studies (see analysis in Chapter 4).	45

shortly, this was done to indicate that PI × RGO correlation studies have played an insignificant role throughout the history of the study of Negro and Black identity. This may strike many as an odd discovery, for the nature of the relationship between PI and RGO would seem to be at the core of this literature. Indeed, it has been, but only as a presumption or presupposition, not an empirically established fact. From 1939 to the present, most researchers have taken the PI × RGO relationship as a given; consequently, the vast majority of Negro and Black identity studies have been *univariate studies* in which either a PI or RGO device has been applied exclusively.

The last column of the table shows that of the 181 studies reviewed, 46 (25 percent) were classified as RGO, 90 (50 percent) were classified as PI, and 45 (25 percent) were PI × RGO correlation studies. More important, the two columns to the left show which studies contributed to the empirical documentation of a negative Negro identity and which played a role in empirically documenting change toward a positive Black identity.

From the pejorative perspective and for the time period 1939 to 1968, Negroes were *expected* to show core damage to their PI and RGO; consequently, it did not matter what PI or RGO measure was applied, or what was the age, gender, or social class of the (Negro) subjects. Pathological results were anticipated, and with history, the results allegedly demonstrated them. Nigrescence followed the same course, pointing to anticipated evidence of identity change across *almost any* personality or group identity measure, including samples drawn from various age groups and all walks of Black life. Thus, to test the validity of one perspective or the other, it is the overall trend of the literature that is important, not the trend associated with a particular subdomain or dependent measure. We should keep in mind, however, that in each time period, psychologists have been more enamoured with certain PI or RGO measurement devices than with others; for example, from 1968 to the present, PI has frequently been operationalized as self-esteem (Tennessee Self-Concept Scale, Coopersmith Self-Esteem Inventory, Rosenberg Self-Esteem Scale, etc.)

Negative Identity: 1939–1960

Self-hatred among Negroes was a well-documented trend of empirical studies on Black identity by 1954 and an accepted "fact" by 1960. In *Prejudice and Your Child*, Kenneth Clark applied any number of PI constructs (insecurity, low self-esteem and self-worth, anxiety, damaged personality) and RGO constructs to his summary of empirical studies on Negro identity conducted between 1939 and about 1954, creating the impression that this body of research incorporated a cluster of PI as well as RGO investigations. Clark was not alone; the same can be said of other key observers during this period (Pettigrew 1964; Proshansky and Newton 1968). Turning to Table 2, we note that eighteen empirical studies of Negro identity were reported between 1939 and 1960, and all but one was an RGO study. Each of these RGO studies recorded a Negro out-group orientation. In other words, the self-hatred argument, which would appear to be a PI-related hypothesis, was developed in the accumulation of evidence from RGO studies conducted with children, many of whom were of preschool age. In fact, aside from *Mark of Oppression*, the study by Kardiner and Ovesey (1951) of 25 Negro adults, most of whom were involved in psychotherapy (nonpsychiatric controls were not included in the study), empirical investigations of personal identity played a *minor* role in the discourse on Black identity that took place between 1939 and 1960. For example, in the now-classic work by Proshansky and Newton (1968), "Nature and Meaning of Negro Self-Identity," the authors do not cite one personal identity study in the section of their article that presents empirical evidence on the "development of self-identity in the Negro" (pp. 182–192). All the evidence cited comes from studies of reference group orientation, that is, racial-preference studies. Similarly, Pettigrew's (1964) important overview of Black American life contains a section on Black self-esteem and Black identity based primarily on reference group/racial-preference studies (he cited only one personal identity study). The irony lies in the fact that when each of the RGO studies for this period is reviewed, the experimenter clearly specifies in the methods section that an unambiguously RGO-related construct was assessed. On reaching the discussion section, however, the distinction between PI and RGO information is blurred, and the construct self-hatred is injected "as if" PI and RGO data had been collected or that it was an established fact that PI and RGO are highly correlated. The fact is that, between 1939 and 1960, one is pressed to find *one* PI × RGO correlational study.

Before moving on to the period of identity change, a summary would state that for the studies of Black identity conducted between 1939 and 1960, evidence was accumulated, primarily from RGO research, that Black children (compared to whites) tended to be out-group oriented and were considerably attracted to symbols representative of the white perspective. Although seldom mentioned by investigators or stressed in secondary reports on these studies, a considerable amount of variance attributable to Black in-group preference usually accompanied the tendency of Blacks to select white symbols more frequently. In fact, with age, there was a trend toward a Black preference among Blacks (recall the Doll Test and Coloring Test data in Chapter 1). Nevertheless, the lasting impression of this research has been the theme of a Black preference for white. Aside from biased "clinical" studies, no significant number of PI studies were conducted during this period; consequently, conclusions about the negative or positive nature of the personal identity of Blacks from 1939 to 1960 is purely speculative. Moreover, reference to the investigations of this period as "indirect" evidence of self-hatred, a PI variable, was misleading because empirical support *linking* PI with RGO was not forthcoming between 1939 and 1960. The tendency of researchers of this period to use reference group terms in labeling their dependent variables and psychoanalytic/self-concept construction in explicating their results remains a puzzle to most students of Black identity. Of course, the "empirical" link between PI and RGO consisted of anecdotal data produced by a small percentage of the children as they completed RGO tasks.

Identity Change: 1968 to the Present

To review a point made earlier, the Black Social Movement had a civil rights phase and a Black Power phase, and Black identity change was linked with the second, not the first, phase; consequently, studies assumed to reflect this change were thought to have been conducted between 1968 and the late 1970s (Butler 1976; Cross 1978a, 1985). Turning again to Table 2, we note that of the 181 studies reviewed, 163, or 90 percent, were conducted during the period from 1968 to 1980. Of these, 29 (18 percent) were RGO oriented, 89 (54 percent) were PI related, and 45 (28 percent) were PI × RGO correlational studies. The PI × RGO correlation studies, which played no role in the discourse on Black identity change, will be the object of discussion in the next chapter. For the time being, let us trace the trend for the RGO and PI studies.

TREND OF STUDIES, 1968–1980

Trend of RGO Studies.   During this period, 29 RGO studies were recorded, most of them representing replications, in one fashion or another, of the racial-preference studies conducted before nigrescence. Eighteen studies, or 62 percent, showed Blacks with an in-group orientation; 8 studies, or 28 percent, showed a negative identity; and 3 studies, or 10 percent, produced varied results. Thus, while 100 percent of the RGO studies conducted between 1939 and 1960 showed an out-group, or negative, identity, the same kinds of studies repeated *after* nigrescence showed a strong preference for Black in 62 percent of the RGO studies. Just as the earlier studies tended to show Blacks exhibiting a split pattern favoring white (subject selected white on average 60 percent of time and Black 40 percent), the new preference for Black was also accompanied by a split pattern (60 percent Black vs. 40 percent white). As in the past, researchers made little of this split pattern and emphasized the directionality of the preference rather than its inherent duality. Many have pointed to these studies as evidence of the new Black identity.

Trend of PI Studies. By the mid 1960s, psychologists and sociologists were applying newly devised self-esteem scales to the measurement of self-concept, and the intellectual excitement associated with these tests, to say nothing of their relative ease of administration, caused a literal explosion in their usage. The field of Negro and Black identity was no less affected. Of the 89 PI studies reviewed here for the 1968–1980 period, most employed some version of the new self-esteem tests, although other PI devices were also represented. More so than in RGO studies, there is a white presence, either in the form of normative data or in the use of whites as a control group. Table 2 shows the trend of the 89 PI studies conducted between 1968 and 1980, and Table 3 categorizes these studies across four comparisons. Of the 89 studies, 48, or 54 percent, recorded no difference in self-esteem/personality between Blacks and whites (B = W category); 18, or 20 percent, showed Blacks with higher self-esteem than that found in whites (B > W category); 13, or 15 percent, reported whites having higher self-esteem or more normal personality than Blacks (W > B category); and 10, or 11 percent produced mixed results (varied category). Combining the first two categories, 66, or 74 percent, of the studies reviewed showed Blacks with a PI level that matched or surpassed the level recorded for whites. Many suggested that these findings clearly showed a change in Black identity consistent with the degree to which the Black Social Movement of the 1960s had engaged Blacks at all ages and all socioeconomic brackets.

At first glance, it seems that a significant number of RGO and PI studies conducted during and after nigrescence showed Black identity changing toward an increasing in-group orientation (RGO trend) and higher levels of self-esteem and stronger personality characteristics (PI trend). Such an interpretation would lend considerable credence to the pejorative per-

Table 3

Classification of 89 Personal Identity (PI) Studies by Four Categories

---

B = W(*N* = 48, or 53.93%)

J. G. Allen 1972	James 1970
Atolagbe 1975	H. Johnson 1970
Barbarin 1977	C. Jones 1973
Beglis and Sheikh 1974	Kelley 1976
Bennett and Lundgren 1976	Klein 1974
Bridgeman and Shipman 1975	Knight 1969
P. Brown 1973	Kuhlman and Bieliauskas 1976
Cameron 1971	Lanza 1969
Carpenter and Busse 1969	Little 1971
Chang 1975	J. McAdoo 1970
E. Clark 1971	McElroy 1971
Cuniff 1971	Moses, Zirkel, and Greene 1973
Dale and Keller 1972	Pleasants 1973
Davids 1973	Powers et al. 1971
C. Davis 1974	Samuels 1973
Douglas 1969	Sisenwein 1970
Getsinger et al. 1972	Spivey 1976
Gross 1976	Thorsell 1976
Harms 1977	Tucker 1977
Hartnagel 1970	Watson 1974
Healy and DeBlassie 1974	Wax 1972
Hedgebeth 1970	D. White 1975
Hughbanks 1977	M. White 1973
	Yancey et al. 1972
	Yeatts 1968

B > W (*N* = 18, or 20.22%)	**W > B (*N* = 13, or 14.61%)**
Bachman 1970	Bridgette 1970
Burke 1975	Crain and Weisman 1972
Cicirelli 1977	C. Gordon 1972
Gregory 1977	Hauser 1972
Hunt 1973	Lefebvre 1973
Hunt and Hardt 1969	Long and Henderson 1968, 1970
Jamerson 1973	Miller 1975
J. Johnson 1970	Munro and Oles 1975
Olsen 1972	Peterson and Ramirez 1971
Powel and Fuller 1970	Posner 1969
Prendergast et al. 1974	Rodriguez 1972
Reeder 1978	Williams and Byars 1970
Rosenberg and Simmons 1971	
Soares and Soares 1969	
Strang 1972	
Trowbridge et al. 1972	
Wendland 1968	
M. White 1968	

Varied (N = 10, or 11.24%)

E. G. Allen 1969   Hughes and Works 1974
Burbach and Bridgeman 1976   R. King 1974
Durley 1973   Kohn 1969
French 1972   Laryea 1972
Hawkin 1971   Rubin 1974

Key: B = W, studies that reported no difference in self-esteem/personality
       factor between Blacks and whites.
 B > W, self-esteem/personality factor significantly higher for Blacks.
 W > B, self-esteem/personality factor significantly higher for whites
       compared to blacks.
 Varied, mixed results that distracted from ability to classify one way or the
       other.

---

spective of the past that saw Blacks suffering from a damaged PI and RGO. A
large number of the PI studies were conducted with adults; in replicating
the RGO studies of the previous era, children were frequently the subjects
in racial-preference (doll) studies. Since the Black Social Movement was first
and foremost an adult phenomenon, the PI studies have been used to argue
change in adult mental health, and RGO studies as evidence of the spread of
Black identity to young children.

As the dust has settled, certain challenges have been leveled at both
change trends, and while the RGO trend would appear to have weathered
the attack, the same cannot be said of the PI trend.

BANKS'S CHALLENGE TO THE RGO TREND

We noted that every single RGO study conducted in the earlier period
showed Negro children preferring white. From 1968 to 1980, 18 out of 29
(62 percent) experiments found evidence of Blacks preferring Black. In a
reexamination of this literature, Banks (1976) pointed out that in some of
these experiments, both Black and white children were used as subjects.
Black subjects were more likely to produce a nonmonotonic trend that
tended to be white oriented in the past and Black oriented in the present (a
monotonic pattern is the selection of one color 75 to 95 percent of the time,
and a second color 25 to 5 percent of the time; in a nonmonotonic trend,
one color is selected 55 to 65 percent of the time, while the second is
favored 45 to 35 percent of the time). As he looked more closely, Banks
thought he noticed a startling possibility: could observers have confused the
failure of Black children to favor Black in as monotonic a fashion as white

children prefer white with statistical evidence showing Blacks preferring either color beyond chance? That is, rather than focus on comparison data in which white behavior is used as a *standard*, Banks reexamined 21 racial-preference and racial self-identification studies and looked at the Black choice data to determine in which experiments Blacks showed a nonchance color preference. Applying the chi-square statistic, Banks found that each study fell into any one of three categories in which Blacks exhibited the following: category 1, a preference for white that could not be accounted for by chance; category 2, a mixed preference, or "chance," pattern; and category 3, a nonchance Black preference. Banks found 2 studies where the Negro children showed a nonchance preference for white, 4 experiments where they preferred Black, and 15 studies in which the Negro children showed no preference. Based on these results, and highly pertinent to our discussion here, Banks (1976) commented:

> Although it has been advanced that Black preferences have changed with the advent of racial pride movements in the 1960's, little actual evidence supports either contention that Blacks rejected their own race prior to that period or have consistently preferred their own race since then. (p. 1185)

From Banks's perspective, no change trend can be gleaned from the RGO studies, that is, unless one introduces the monadic preference exhibited by white children as the pattern Blacks "ought" to imitate. According to Banks (1976), Black children have been more likely to exhibit no preference instead of self-rejection or ethnocentrism:

> Reliance upon white comparative frames has largely perpetrated the notion of Black self-rejection in the absence of definitive evidence of preference behavior in Blacks. Even in those investigations which employed only Black samples, implicit a priori standards tended to reflect presumptions about the desirability of such high ethnocentric response sets as are common only in White samples. The fact that Blacks failed always to prefer Black stimuli evaluatively, or as objects of self-identification, has generally been interpreted as a failure to adopt positive racial self-regard. (p. 1185)

Of course, a number of scholars have countered that social comparisons are at the heart of any reference group analysis and that it is perfectly valid to point out differences in the racial frame of reference held by different groups (Milner 1983; Williams and Morland 1976). But rather than pursue this line of reasoning, let us apply a time perspective to Banks's results to demonstrate that even his data confirm a change in RGO.

Look at Table 4, which shows the 21 evaluative preference (RGO) studies Banks classified as evidencing white, Black, or chance preference in Blacks. Recall that evidence of Black self-hatred was reported between 1939 and 1967, while the trend toward positive Black group identification was said to be demonstrated in studies conducted after 1967. If Banks's assertion is correct, then the trend of the studies conducted from 1939 to 1967 should be identical to the trend for 1968 to the present. Now, let us develop a frequency table that shows when a study was conducted (before or after 1968) and how it was classified (white, chance, Black); this has been done in Table 5. As can be seen, the addition of a time perspective clearly reveals a trend toward change. In the past, most of the studies fall within the chance category, with only 1 study showing a nonchance white preference, and 1 falling in the pro-Black category. For the studies conducted after 1968, 1

Table 4
Results of Banks's (1976) Classification of 21 Racial Identity Studies

Preference Held by Blacks	Study
White	Asher and Allen 1969
	Morland 1963
None/chance	Banks and Rompf 1973
	Brody 1964
	Butts 1963
	Clark and Clark 1939b, 1947, 1950
	Goodman 1952
	Helgerson 1943
	Kiesler 1971
	Kircher and Furby 1971
	Kline 1971
	Morland 1962
	Radke and Trager 1950
	Richardson and Royce 1968
	Stevenson and Stewart 1958
Black	Gregor and McPherson 1966
	Harris and Braun 1971
	Hraba and Grant 1970
	Ogletree 1969

Source: Modified version of table reported by Banks (1976).

Table 5
Black Identity Studies Classified by Overall Preference
and Time Conducted

	White	Chance	Black
1939–1967	1	10	1
1968–present	1 $(5)^a$	5 $(9)^a$	3 $(10)^a$

Source: Cross 1990.
[a]Numbers outside parentheses are from the Banks (1976) study; numbers within parentheses are combined totals for studies from Banks (1976) and Aboud and Skerry (1984).

study falls in the white category, 5 in the chance slot, and 3 show a Black preference for Black (x^2 value of 6.29 [$p < .05$]). Aboud and Skerry (1984) expanded Banks's analysis, and when their data is included, the *change* trend for RGO studies conducted after 1968 is all the more evident.

What, then, can one make of Banks's work? While Banks's challenge to the change trend does falter, his work, more so than any other, underscores the presence of texture in the RGO data. Whether in the past or present, Black children have displayed a variety of preference patterns, but researchers have tended to treat Black RGO data "as if" it were monotonic. In Chapter 1 we saw how the Clark and Clark (1950) data revealed several themes, not one, although a monadic theme has been the impression associated with their study and others like it. Banks's discovery of the degree to which Black children showed and continue to show an attraction to *both* Black and white symbols—for, ultimately, this is the significance of his "chance" or no-preference category—will become an important factor in our discussion of the bicultural nature of Black identity in commentary to follow.

For the time being, we can conclude that even when Banks's challenge is considered, there does seem to be a change trend in the pattern of the RGO studies across time, a change that is consistent with the concept of a new Black identity. Over time, RGO$_{(-)}$ changed to RGO$_{(+)}$.

ROSENBERG'S AND SIMMONS'S CHALLENGE TO THE PI TREND

In the spring of 1968, Morris Rosenberg and Roberta Simmons conducted a study in Baltimore of 1,988 Black and white children in grades 3 through 12; several years later, they published their findings in *Black and White Self-Esteem: The Urban School Child* (Rosenberg and Simmons 1971).

Their results indicated that Blacks had higher self-esteem than whites, a finding that held even when controlling for age and social class. Rather than suggest that their results reflected a *change trend* associated with the Black Power movement, Rosenberg and Simmons pointed to the possibility that Blacks have always had adequate self-esteem. The time frame for their argument is crucial. During the period between the confirmation of Negro self-hatred (1960) and the rise of Black Power (1968), the use of self-esteem scales became popular. In Chapter 2 of their monograph, Rosenberg and Simmons (1971) reviewed other large-scale studies that controlled for a variety of factors and reported average levels of self-esteem in Blacks. A number of these studies were clearly conducted *after* the self-hatred syndrome had been established but before the Black identity movement became current. The handful of PI studies that showed high Black self-esteem *before* nigrescence, when linked with numerous PI studies showing high Black self-esteem *after* nigrescence, produced not a trend toward a change, but one of continuity.

The implications of their work were startling, and researchers rushed to examine and reexamine the monograph, as well as the cluster of unpublished studies cited by Rosenberg and Simmons in support of the continuity argument. In the flurry of publications that followed, none was able to mount a serious challenge to Rosenberg and Simmons; in fact, additional evidence was uncovered that gave further credence to the continuity thesis (Edwards 1970; McCarthy and Yancey 1971; Taylor 1976). For example, the Rosenberg and Simmons thesis found confirmation in evaluative studies of Head Start. Head Start, although a program of hope and progress, was theoretically grounded in a deficit perspective on Negro life. This included the view that Negro children were likely to enter Head Start programs with poorly developed self-concepts. Program evaluators predicted that besides changes in school attitudes and reading and math readiness, one outcome of participation in preschool programs for Black children would be higher self-esteem. Several such studies conducted *before* the nigrescence period showed that there was no difference in self-esteem between Head Start and non–Head Start participants. Moreover, Black children in or out of the program had average levels of self-esteem (see Fox, Stewart, and Pitts 1968; Mediax Report 1980; St. John 1975). Commenting on such evidence, as well as on the Rosenberg and Simmons (1971) study, Taylor (1976) concluded: "Thus these findings argue strongly against the notion of low-self-esteem for contemporary Black children and youth. In fact, these data raise serious doubts as to whether this conclusion was ever warranted" (p. 15).

By the mid 1970s, the empirical evidence converging to form a PI trend of continuity, in which the level of Black self-esteem was average both before and after the Black Power movement, became an established, if controversial, fact. $PI_{(-)}$ did not become $PI_{(+)}$; instead, it was suggested that at least in terms of self-esteem, $PI_{(+)}$ remained $PI_{(+)}$.

Direct and Indirect Measures of SC

At the same time (1970–1976) that the Rosenberg and Simmons perspective on the PI continuity trend was being expounded (McCarthy and Yancey 1971; Rosenberg and Simmons 1971; Taylor 1976), the evidence for a RGO change trend was mounting. In a sense, the inherent distinctiveness of the PI and RGO sectors was becoming more apparent because, unlike the 1939–1960 period, when only racial preference was studied, the 1970s saw the completion of both kinds of research. Had the next order of business been PI × RGO correlation studies, the isolation and meaning of the two domains would have been complete, but this was not to occur. True, PI × RGO correlational studies began to appear (McAdoo 1970), and a significant number of unpublished dissertations with this focus had accumulated by 1980, but mainstream studies of Black identity, with a few exceptions (Butts 1963; Porter 1971), were sidetracked by a debate over whether some newly devised objective measures were more direct measures of self-esteem than measures of racial preference were. When the application of such self-esteem scales widened, the debate evolved to another level, in some ways to its logical extension, and it was wondered whether self-esteem was a more direct measure of *self-concept*. Thus, instead of clarifying that self-concept incorporated both personal (PI) and group identity (RGO), as in the formula $SC = PI + RGO$, the debate over direct and indirect measures of self-esteem moved many observers to suggest that the "self" and "personal identity" were one and the same ($SC = PI$), with RGO, the group identity factor, dropped from the equation altogether!

To comprehend this turn of events, we should recall that neither Ruth Horowitz (1939) nor Clark and Clark (1939a, 1947, 1950) codified the results of their group identity or racial-preference studies with the constructs self-esteem and self-hatred. These terms were transported from Europe, where they had been the nexus of a debate on Jewish identity, to the United States through an essay by Kurt Lewin (1941); again, when the focus was (American) Jewish identity. Lewin's essay, reprinted in 1948, became a source of inspiration for the Kardiner and Ovesey (1951) work on Negro personality—the constructs self-esteem and self-hatred appear thirty-nine times in their *Mark of Oppression*. Kardiner and Ovesey claimed to identify both group and self-hatred trends, and they argued that Negro group hatred was the root cause of Negro self-hatred. Taking his cue from Lewin, and from Kardiner and Ovesey, Kenneth Clark first applied the two constructs in his unpublished paper presented at the 1950 White House Conference on Children and Youth, which later became the basis for his *Prejudice and Your Child*. Here, Clark applied self-esteem freely to the interpretation of his group identity measures, as seen in the following: "The preferences and identification of these Negro children were interpreted in terms of conflicts in self-esteem and types of ego pressures which result when the attitudes of a larger society negate the normal self-esteem needs of human beings" (Clark 1955, 103).

Taken out of historical context, it is of course possible to suggest that Clark's work centered on the indirect measure of self-esteem; a more accurate presentation would note that Horowitz and Clark worked with a *direct measure* of the group identity component of the self, and they came to believe that their group identity measure was an indirect measure of a second component of self: one's personality, or level of self-esteem.

In their monograph, Rosenberg and Simmons (1971, 2) note Clark's concern with self-hatred and group hatred, and that self-esteem is a key construct in Clark's discourse on Negro identity. But the focus shifts almost exclusively to self-esteem:

> Much of the evidence behind the assumption of low Black self-esteem has come from studies showing that Black children prefer light-skinned dolls, pictures, or puppets to those with brown skin (Clark and Clark 1947; Goodman 1952; Landreth and Johnson 1953; Morland 1958; Stevenson and Stewart 1958) or that they show problems of self-esteem in psychotherapeutic sessions (Kardiner and Ovesey 1951; Brody 1964). While many of these studies are of a high order of excellence, they characteristically suffer from certain limitations with regard to method: (1) self-esteem has almost invariably been inferred by the investigator from indirect evidence rather than direct examination; (2) the samples have rarely been represented so that it is difficult to know to what populations they properly apply.
>
> As a result of these considerations, we undertook a study of self-esteem among Black and White children in Baltimore during the Spring of 1968. In contrast to some of the earlier in-

vestigations, ours attempted to obtain a reasonably large and representative sample of a public school population and to measure self-esteem in a *direct fashion*. (p. 3; italics added)

In fairness to Rosenberg and Simmons, they return to group identity issues in subsequent chapters of their monograph, and in another work Rosenberg (1979a) explores the $SC = PI + RGO$ formulation. But as Adam (1978) has noted, the "indirect versus direct" issue, which is methodologically centered (i.e., how best to measure self-esteem), gives way to a theoretical distortion that says self-esteem is perhaps a more direct route to understanding self-concept (i.e., racial-preference or RGO measures are invalid or, at least, of little value). In other words, $SC = PI + RGO$ is replaced by $SC = PI$, where PI is assessed by direct measures of self-esteem. The shift in focus reflects the way the methodological conflict is codified. "Traditional and indirect" implies that which is speculative and antiquated; "new and direct" suggests the modern, accurate, reliable, complete, and insightful.

Of course, Clark and his associates led the way to this confusion by putting all their eggs in one basket: self-esteem. Recall that Eugene Horowitz saw racial preference as a measure of values, norms, perspective taking, and *ideology*. Had Clark pursued this line along with his interests in Ruth Horowitz's ideas about depth psychology, perhaps Rosenberg and Simmons would have shown racial preference to be an indirect and poor measure of self-esteem but a more than effective measure of racial frame of reference, ideology, or whatever. But since the advocates of racial preference locked themselves into a narrow interpretive scheme in which their methodology, clearly understood by all to be concerned with the direct assessment of group identity, was valued only insofar as it helped to *infer* self-esteem, the resulting theoretical stance, with its either/or mentality, went beyond the pale of revision (Gordon 1976; McCarthy and Yancey 1971; Taylor 1976).

The self-hatred, or traditional, perspective further set the stage for its demise by being pejorative in the extreme. *Everything* Negro, living or dead, was defined in pathological terms. Subsequently, when the social history of Black America was revised by works that appeared between 1970 and 1980, white and Black historians did not romanticize the Black experience, they simply noted that despite the brutality and oppression of the Black experience, a series of Black figures emerge. The self-hating "Sambo" was one of them, but was not typical. Their discovery of texture in the Black experience called for explanatory models that allowed for texture. The categorical self-hating perspective did not predict (or even permit) texture; consequently, when the preponderance of revisionist sociological, psychological, and historical evidence on the Black experience demanded that texture and variability be taken into account, the self-hatred thesis seemed woefully inadequate.

Throughout the 1970s and up to the present, the assault on the self-hatred thesis has been relentless and thorough, covering a range of analyses from sophomoric nit-picking to insight and occasional profundity (Baldwin 1979; Banks 1976; Christmas 1973; Cross 1981, 1985; Gordon 1980; McCarthy and Yancey 1971; Porter and Washington 1979; Taylor 1976; Teplin 1977; Williams and Morland 1976). In a Kuhnian sense, a paradigmatic shift has occurred. Each new article has sought to demonstrate, in one way or another, the inability of the traditional perspective to explain research findings. As Christmas (1973) and Taylor (1976) have noted, nothing has seemed to "fit":

> The use of ambiguous and poorly defined terms is a basic weakness in all but a few of the many studies devoted to the issue of self esteem among Black and White children and youth. Self-esteem, self-image, self-regard are all used as if synonymous with each other and with self-concept, and often reflect underlying differences in theoretical perspective and basic assumptions. (Taylor 1976, 11)

Gordon (1980) has tried to make things "fit" again by reintegrating PI and RGO studies in an analysis somewhat connected to the direct–indirect debate. She attributes conflicting findings about Black self-concept based on doll (RGO) or self-esteem (PI) studies to the complexity level of the theories implicit in each study. She notes that many self-esteem inventories have numerous subscales, underscoring a complex, or multidimensional, approach to self-concept. In contrast, doll (RGO) studies concentrate on the elicitation of limited information (racial preference or race awareness), thus apparently revealing a monadic, unitary concept of self. Baldwin (1979) also favors this interpretation.

Such a conclusion fails to consider the confounding of *age* with task and stimulus complexity. Many important RGO studies have been conducted with very young children; consequently, the level of cognitive complexity demanded by the doll or other RGO task has been low. In contrast, self-esteem studies have made use of paper-and-pencil inventories that require a number of complex competencies to complete. Not surprisingly, most self-esteem studies have been administered to subjects who, on average, were considerably older than the subjects included in the typical doll study. When the "complex" self-esteem scales have been administered (orally) to young children, the results have generally been far less reliable than when these studies are administered to older children. Semaj (1979) has shown that older children exhibit more reliable, complex, and stable preference behavior than young children do. Thus both constructs face the same reliability and complexity issues when the subjects are young children. Along this line, a number of experts in child development have argued that only direct observation techniques can be counted on to provide valid and reliable information about social–emotional aspects of early childhood behavior, whether PI or RGO related.

This leads to the conclusion that RGO studies have produced "limited" information because the construct has been explored far too frequently with children of an age when RGO patterns are just beginning to emerge; similarly, the self-esteem literature is rich in complexity because the assessment devices have been able to take advantage of the complex adult mind. I would not take issue with a call to conduct fewer RGO studies with children, except in exploring the *ontogeny* of RGO at an early age. But rather than throw out the entire RGO paradigm, researchers should explore this extremely important component of self with older children, young adults, and adults. The truth is that RGO theory has been used to help account for the origin of social movements and revolutions (Urry 1973), let alone the preference behavior of young children. Questions of values; philosophic orientations; concepts of beauty, art, or literature; musical preferences; sex-role constructs; political behavior—these are all subtopics in the complex field of reference group theory.

Old theories die hard, and in 1978 Barry Adam wrote an article for *Social Psychology Quarterly* titled "Inferiorization and Self-Esteem" in which he attempted to trivialize the recent findings on Black self-esteem while reaffirming the relevance of racial-preference studies. Here, racial-preference tasks were viewed as more direct measures of self-esteem than self-esteem scales. Adam, whose work has focused on a phenomenological or Goffmanian analysis of the way minority groups deal with oppression (what Adam calls "inferiorization"), favors studies that show oppressed groups to be psychological basket cases and is more than a little suspicious of studies that do not fit his textureless either/or framework on the consequences of oppression. Quite predictably, his article begins with a summary of the "classical" position on Negro identity through reference to about ten studies that "all confirmed the basic discovery of lowered self-esteem in Black children" (Adam 1978, 47). All the studies he cites are racial-preference or RGO studies, not self-esteem or PI studies. Adam is unable to reference a single empirical study from his so-called classical period in which racial preference and self-esteem are shown to be correlated, since no such studies were conducted between 1939 and 1960. Instead, he offers two essays that "affirm" the connection; one is Kurt Lewin's essay on *Jewish* self-hatred.

Having established the "true" interpretation of "classic Negro identity," Adam proceeds to argue that the past is being rewritten by people whose ideology lends itself to the goals of revisionism in Black history. Thus, according to Adam, it is bias and ideology, not empirical evidence, that is reshaping the self-hatred thesis. Setting aside the question of how a researcher could bias the scoring of objectively scored self-esteem tests, let us grant that especially *after* nigrescence, we should expect to find a more romantic bias in some studies on Black identity. But one finds healthy PI levels in Negroes *before* nigrescence (i.e., before there might be social pressure to find "positive" traits in the Black psyche) from researchers who, if anything, had a stake in proving self-hatred. Typical was the mind set and response of Colleen Stewart. Stewart worked with David J. Fox and Vera Pitts on one of the first large-scale Title 1 evaluation projects involving a sample (program subjects and comparison groups) of more than 2,800 children (Fox, Stewart, and Pitts 1968). None of the three researchers was an ideologue; each was a progressive who hoped that ways could be found to educate poor children better. It was certainly their expectation that should the program show no effect, the primary outcome for program and nonprogram Black children would be low self-esteem. So stunned was Stewart by the failure of the evaluation to show low self-concept in the children, in or out of the program, let alone failure to show enhanced self-esteem accompanying program completion, she focused her doctoral dissertation on the history of the study of Black identity (Stewart 1975). In part, she sought an explanation as to why traditional theory made one so ill prepared for the discovery and analysis of Black strengths. In like manner, Roberta Simmons (1978) commented:

> Many of us measuring self-esteem of Black and White children
> in the last 1960's fully expected to find the Black self-hatred
> that was taken for granted throughout the literature. In fact, several studies that were privately circulated were unpublished because their authors didn't believe their findings in this regard.

. . . It was only when more than 12 of these studies using different self-esteem measures were brought together that it became clear that the black self-hatred theory had been seriously
challenged. (p. 56)

Evidence to counter Adam's assertion of bias is fairly easy to come by, and
stands as a commentary on how well Adam researched this point. It also
makes rather curious Pettigrew's (1978, 1983) support for the bias argument, since Pettigrew is generally associated with a more careful reading of
the Black identity literature.

At another point in the article, Adam suggests that studies of self-esteem that show no difference between Blacks and whites obliterate the consequences of oppression. The implication of this observation stands history
on its head. Between 1939 and 1960, the pejorative tradition obliterated the
humanity of Negroes by framing the Negro psyche in a caricature of pathology. The "classical tradition" made little effort or provided no room to
include Black strengths—strengths that have always existed and are now
being described by Black and white revisionists. When the slightest demonstration of texture and balance results in cries of romanticism and distortion, this makes the limitations, if not intellectual bankruptcy, of the traditional perspective all the more apparent.

Finally, having painted a false picture of racial-preference literature as
presenting unequivocal evidence of low self-esteem and personality damage, Adam discusses findings that show Blacks exhibit greater variability on
self-esteem tests than do whites. Adam contends that the "average self-esteem" finding is a fairly recent phenomenon and that had modern self-esteem devices been used in the distant past, low self-esteem in Negroes
would have been revealed by both the doll and the self-esteem scales. In the
era of Black identity change, Adam believes Blacks may be leaping from one
mode of coping with oppression (subordination, compliance, subservience,
and low self-esteem) to another (rebellion, innovative actions, militancy,
and high self-esteem) and that the two profiles cancel each other, making it
appear that the fluctuating and volatile Black group has the same self-esteem
profile as that of its oppressor, that is, average and stable:

"Nonsignificant" differences may appear where subordination
produces both compliant and militant behavior strategies, as if
the self-esteem of both dominant and subordinate group members were the same. Crain and Weisman (1972) found two

modes of either low or high measures in the inferiorized
group. . . . This raises the interesting issue of how people
"leap" from one mode of coping to another, i.e., "low-profile,"
accommodative means of getting by, develop rebellious, innovative actions aimed toward change. (Adam 1978, 51)

Here, of course, Adam has not done his homework. Monotonicity and
negativity do not characterize "self-esteem" studies of the past (doll studies),
nor do variability and bimodalism characterize self-esteem studies of the
present (self-esteem scales), for, as was clearly made evident in our earlier
reexamination of the racial-preference studies, especially as revealed by
Banks (1976) and Aboud and Skerry (1984), variability has been very much
a factor in racial-preference studies conducted from 1939 onward. The monotonic or categorical pattern associated with RGO studies is a myth. Thus
both kinds of studies reflect variability or texture; when they are juxtaposed,
it is simply not clear whether evidence of strength is always to be causally
linked to evidence of identity change. Pinpointing such a causal link would
require an examination of PI × RGO correlation studies that Adam, with the
exception of his reference to the study of Porter (1971), did not do.

Adam's notion that the contemporary Black movement glossed over
and did not completely "heal" the long-standing self-hatred "so evident in
Blacks" in the past was given a rather thorough exploration in a dissertation
(Smith 1980) published several years after the appearance of Adam's critique. Smith began her work by presupposing that reports in the literature
of adequate self-esteem in Blacks reflected a recent shift from self-hatred to
self-acceptance. She then speculated that important elements of self-hatred
"lurk" within the unconscious of Blacks, even though, at the conscious or
surface level, Blacks may exhibit a commitment to "Black is beautiful." More
specifically, Smith predicted that (1) race would be more salient to Blacks
than whites as an indicator of identity; (2) both Blacks and whites would
show a pattern of more positive connotations to the color white than Black;
(3) each group would hold mostly positive white racial stereotypes and
mostly negative Black stereotypes; (4) more Blacks than whites would show
lower levels of self-acceptance of their body image; and (5) besides having
lower global self-esteem, what positive self-esteem Blacks exhibit would be
more overt than covert. Smith employed three conscious and three unconscious measures with a sample of 30 Black and 30 white adults that included
a mixture of males and females. Smith found that at the conscious level, race
was more salient as an indicator of identity for Blacks than whites, but,

contrary to Smith's prediction, Blacks were no less accepting of their body image than were whites. At the unconscious level, Black self-esteem equaled that found in whites, and this held for global self-esteem, consistency of esteem across certain measures, and for the distinction Smith tried to make between overt and covert levels of self-esteem.

One by one, Smith's predictions of negativity in the psychodynamics of Blacks failed to materialize. For two unconscious variables, color bias and racial stereotype, Smith's interpretations took on an *Alice in Wonderland* quality—up becomes down, round becomes square, and evidence of positive mental health in Blacks becomes pathology. On the color-bias measure, Blacks did *not* register a bias for either white or Black, and they held more positive than negative racial stereotypes of Blacks as well as whites. In effect, at the unconscious level, Blacks seemed to show evidence of positive to neutral attitudes toward both races, suggesting the operation of a positively oriented bicultural frame of reference. (Black biculturality is discussed in later chapters.) Whites, in contrast, showed a decided white color bias and a tendency to depict Black racial stereotypes negatively and white racial stereotypes positively.

Perhaps out of frustration at not finding evidence to support any of her negative predictions, Smith did an amazing thing. She aggregated the racial-stereotype data and found that, for all subjects, more positive themes were made for white than Black racial stereotypes, which is to say that aggregation skewed the total scores toward the pattern of the white subjects' pro-white, anti-Black bias. This process was repeated for the color-bias data, and again the results were skewed by the pro-white, anti-Black perceptions of whites. For example, Blacks produced racial images of themselves (Black racial images or stereotypes of Blacks) that judges agreed contained 15 positive and 12 negative themes. This fit the pattern for whites, who produced racial images of themselves (white racial images/stereotypes of whites) that contained 16 positive and 12 negative themes. But opposite-race images revealed a conflict in whites because, compared to Black images of whites, which contained 17 positive and 10 negative themes, white images of Blacks contained only 8 positive and a whopping 22 negative themes. This meant that the two groups combined produced Black images that had 23 positive and 34 negative themes, and white images that incorporated 33 positive and 22 negative themes. Thus, while Blacks produced images of themselves that were no less positive than the white images whites produced of themselves, and although Black images of whites revealed a certain halo effect, *the extreme anti-Black bias of whites skewed the data.* For instance, had whites produced Black images containing 8 more positive and a 8 fewer negative themes, the totals for each racial image would have been nearly the same. Smith ran separate analyses of variance on the color-bias and racial-image scores; in each instance, the results showed the overall pattern was heavily influenced by the anti-Black bias of the white subjects, not the bias of Blacks, which, if anything, tended to be both pro-Black and pro-white. Nonetheless, in the abstract and in the conclusion, Smith emphasized the almost meaningless "total" scores, her remarks making it appear that Blacks shared a pro-white and anti-Black bias! In fact, the overall wording and tone of the abstract would lead the reader to conclude that all of Smith's original hypotheses were either confirmed or "partially" supported! Adam (1978), of course, has made much to do about "the politics of finding average self-esteem in Blacks," and in this study by Smith, which sought to confirm a negative perspective of Black psychological functioning that complements the views held by Adam, bias is very much in evidence. Ironically, however, it is a bias that, in the tradition of the "signifying monkey," exposes rather than supports Adam's bias. Smith, like Adam, cannot "explain" Black mental health, so when she discovers it, she acts "as if" it is not there and introduces an "interpretive bias" that transforms mental health into pathology.

Returning to the article by Adam, we find he almost gets it right when he questions the limitations of "global measures" of self-esteem, but here again his critique is in need of revision. People have been employing global measures in part because they have assumed that the problems Black people confront should lead to "global malfunctioning." Barnes (1972) has offered an alternative model to the culture-of-poverty thesis that suggests that the Black community, at least until the more recent advent of the Black underclass (the last decade or so), provided an ecology of human development that resulted in adequate, and in many instances, positive and enhanced, mental health. Positive, global self-esteem may reflect the general outcome of this socialization. But findings of adequate, global self-esteem need not preclude the discovery of specific deficits. For example, a national panel on Head Start, consisting of experts on Black, Asian, Mexican, and American Indian family life, found that minority status does not result in automatic inferiorization; on the contrary, it appears that young minority children enter school with a strong and positive global self-concept (Chang 1975; McKinney 1977, Mediax 1980). Nevertheless, the stigma of racism, ethnocentrism, and poverty may negatively affect the ability of minority children to refine and enhance their self-concept through incorporation of a "self-as-student" or "self-as-learner" component that facilitates successful performance in traditional middle-class academic contexts (Lassiter 1976; Picou, Cosby, Curry, and Wells 1977). This suggests that global self-esteem and context-specific academic self-esteem may not be related (Gordon 1980). Such context-specific failure may lead to *alienation*, not a generalized drop in self-esteem. This, in turn, may account for the fact that Hare and Castenell (1985) and others (e.g., Ogbu 1985) report that, though often extremely alienated from various mainstream institutions, Black youth failing in school or dropping out frequently show signs of adequate global functioning and even extreme confidence and competence for the challenges of street life. In effect, "Black rage," as a case in point, may be a symptom of Blacks who are angry because they have been made to feel inferior, or it may be an expression of the frustration of a person who discovers that his personal sense of psychological well-being has little meaning in his or her daily interactions with white society (Brown 1974). To repeat this last point in a slightly different manner, Black rage can result from perfectly normal Black people having to endure negotiations with white people (and racist institutions) who seem determined to challenge, rather than authenticate and build on, the psychological strengths Black people possess. As an aside, my father, though he attended college, had to settle for lifelong employment as a Pullman porter. On occasion he would describe episodes in which he had to "disguise" his level of education in order to "better service" less educated whites for whom, in many instances, he actually had contempt ("white trash"). His anger stemmed, not in feeling inferior to such whites, but in having to pretend to be of lesser status.

The side-by-side existence of evidence of global functioning and particularistic deficits may not constitute a contradiction; instead, it may reflect the clash that occurs when society's institutions fail to recognize and build on the strengths that the Black community has been able to fashion under conditions of oppression. Adam is correct in suggesting that there is more to the psychology of Black people than "average, global self-esteem," but he is profoundly in error when he attempts to trivialize such findings. It is my opinion that Black or minority performance on global PI measures may not predict role-specific performance; likewise, Black or minority performance on context-specific PI measures may give limited insight into global functioning. Perhaps a well-planned research program that combines global PI measures with context-specific PI measures will produce results that support neither a pejorative nor a romantic view of Black children and Black adults, yielding instead a highly differentiated, complex, and realistic picture that juxtaposes strengths and vulnerabilities.

If Adam set out to reestablish the primacy of the traditional perspective, he failed. But at least at the symbolic level, his article acts as a strong reminder that any theory of Black identity must be able to account for the findings of both PI and RGO studies. The 1970s were the heyday of the application of self-esteem scales in the study of Black identity, and this led to brilliant presentations on the PI sector of Black identity, such as the one by Taylor (1976). Nevertheless, in explaining that racial preference is not as direct a measure of self-esteem as are various self-concept scales, a void was created, for it was seldom explained what racial preference and other RGO devices do measure. And to the extent that Rosenberg and Simmons, Taylor, and others have empirically shown that the PI sector of Black identity did not change over time, the trend of the empirical studies of RGO has been equally emphatic in demonstrating that something about the Negro identity *did* change. Of course, to accept the possibility that one sector of the self-concept can change radically (i.e., group identity), while another dimension does not (i.e., personal identity), one must confront and, in effect, disprove, the central relational hypothesis that undergirds the traditional perspective on Negro identity, that is, the presumption of an overall positive linear relationship between self-esteem and racial preference or, in a more generic sense, between personal identity and reference group orientation. This presupposition can best be explored by a review of PI × RGO correlational studies. Before we begin, however, let us bring some clarity to the debate on indirect and direct measures of self-esteem because, in a very real sense, this argument has delayed the recognition and differentiation of PI and RGO.

In theory, the idea that group identity is an indirect measure of self-esteem should carry no more weight than the notion that self-esteem is an indirect measure of group identity. Both statements say the same thing; each factor is posited to be an indirect measure of the other. In the 1970s, however, self-esteem was given more favored status in the analysis of self-concept (SC), and the accumulated evidence that racial preference (RGO) may well be a rather poor predictor of self-esteem was interpreted by some to mean that RGO is an ineffectual measure of SC. Such a conclusion presupposes that (1) self-esteem is *the* primary variable in self-concept theory; and (2) for additional factors to be included in the self-concept matrix, each must first be shown to be a correlate of self-esteem. In effect, we are back to the old theory that *all* dimensions of SC are presumed to be correlated.

For whatever reason, let us suppose that RGO is discarded from the analysis of self-concept (SC). What information, if any, would be lost? The answer: any and all data regarding values, attitudes, world view, ideology, religious preference, racial preference, salience of ethnicity, or the influence of nationalism. To paraphrase Adam (1978), it would be like studying Jewish identity without studying Jewishness, Black identity without exploring Blackness, or gayness without determining what it means to be gay. In developing a holistic picture of a person, one needs both PI and RGO information. A PI exploration of the self reticulates a person's psychodynamic characteristics (one's PI profile for such factors as level of self-esteem, figure vs. field dependence, locus of control, IQ, and level of assertiveness). RGO data may tell whether the same person's reference group is Jewish, gay, Black, Palestinian, American, or some combination thereof. Each construct seeks to delineate an equally important component of SC.

My understanding of the theory implicit in studies of Black identity is that RGO is no less a direct measure of SC than is PI, for while each factor is viewed as an indirect measure of the other, each is also directly associated with separate and distinct features of the "self." The actual relationship between PI and RGO is an empirical question; speaking hypothetically, a finding of no relationship would not provide a basis for invalidating either variable as a direct measure of distinctive features of SC. Instead, it would be to discover that the respective self-concept domains to which PI and RGO are related operate more independently and are more highly differentiated than has heretofore been theorized.

Summary

Given the denseness of this chapter, perhaps a summary is in order. Research on Negro and Black identity has and continues to be driven by a two-factor model of the self-concept, involving both a multidimensional personal identity, or general personality, domain (PI), and multifaceted group identity, or reference group orientation, (RGO) domain. A review of the empirical literature on Negro or Black identity conducted between 1939 and 1980 has shown that, until recently, most have been *univariate studies* that explored either the PI or RGO dimension of Negro or Black identity.

We have traced the PI and RGO patterns across two time periods to determine what kinds of studies were used to document Negro self-hatred from 1939 to 1960 and the "new" Black identity thesis from 1968 to 1980.

Between 1939 and 1960, findings based almost entirely on RGO research showed Black children to be out-group oriented in that they exhibited a considerable attraction to symbols representative of the white perspective. Although seldom mentioned by investigators or stressed in secondary reports on these studies, a considerable amount of variance attributable to Black in-group preference usually accompanied the tendency of Blacks to select white symbols. In fact, recalling our analysis in Chapter 1 of the Clark studies, we know that as they grew older, the Black children increasingly preferred Black. Nevertheless, the lasting impression of this research has been the theme of a Black preference for white. Aside from easily biased "clinical" studies, no significant number of PI studies were conducted between 1939 and 1960; consequently, conclusions about the negative or positive nature of the personal identity or general personality of Blacks during this period is based on myth, not empirical documentation. Furthermore, reference to "indirect" evidence of self-hatred, a PI variable, was misleading because empirical support linking PI with RGO was not forthcoming between 1939 and 1960.

During the period of nigrescence, or the emergence of the "new" Black identity (1968–1980), evidence from a large cluster of PI and RGO studies seemed to suggest that Blacks experienced identity change at both the PI and RGO levels of their self-concept. But further analysis revealed that while various dimensions of the RGO component of Black identity changed with nigrescence, Black PI characteristics went unchanged, registering at average or normal levels before and after nigrescence. In other words, Blacks entered the period of nigrescence with a number of PI-related psychological strengths—strengths that went unchanged over time—but their RGO factor was affected by nigrescence in that it took on a more nationalistic and in-group orientation. This nationalistic orientation was far from categorical because the overall RGO pattern was dualistic, suggesting not so much identity confusion as biculturalism.

The finding that perhaps nigrescence affected one but not both levels of Black identity represents a major challenge to our traditional thinking about Black identity in particular and identity theory in general. In identity research with white Americans (especially Jews), Asian-Americans, and African-Americans, theorists have typically assumed that measures of PI and RGO are highly correlated. The literature on PI and RGO trends for Blacks suggests otherwise. Of course, looking at PI and RGO trends from investigations in which only one factor is under scrutiny (univariate studies), positions an observer to make intelligent guesses about the relationship between PI and RGO. More precise knowledge can be gained from correlational studies, which are the focus of the next chapter.

|| █ █ || |

CHAPTER 3

Testing the Lewinian Hypothesis

Although the major theoretical orientation guiding Black identity studies would seem to have demanded it, and the prerequisite assessment devices and statistical techniques involved in correlational strategies have been readily available for some time, until the 1970s few studies administered separate measures of RGO and PI to the same sample. Unquestionably, the study of Black identity has been directed by the Lewinian tradition of positing a positive linear correlation between self-esteem and group identity (Lewin 1941), a hypothesis that has seldom, if ever, been explored empirically, let alone confirmed. Between 1939 and 1960, scholars employing reference group assessment strategies did not feel compelled also to administer measures of personality or self-esteem, for the RGO measures were viewed as offering accurate if indirect insight into the level of one's self-esteem or general personality. Studies of personal identity did not incorporate RGO measures because such information was assumed to be redundant. What we have, then, for most of the history of the study of Black identity, are *univariate* studies of either PI or RGO, conducted by scholars who, while interested in the relationship between PI and RGO, ended up viewing that relationship through the prism of presupposition.

The early 1970s saw an important shift away from univariate to correlational studies, though the magnitude of this shift has been distorted in mainstream publications by the exaggerated significance accorded the work of Porter (1971) by Adam (1978), Porter and Washington (1979), and Pettigrew (1978, 1983). Porter was but one of five scholars who, in the course of completing their doctorates between 1966 and 1970, arrived at essentially the same theoretical perspective. The simultaneous and independent discovery of the need to explore empirically the relationship between PI and RGO by five different persons in five different graduate programs (University of Michigan, Harvard, Columbia–Teacher's College, University of Maryland, University of Chicago) was not coincidental but the natural outgrowth of increased interest in the study of Black life that paralleled the Black Social Movement. As I have labored to demonstrate, the PI and RGO distinction is easily (re)discovered by anyone who carefully reads the original doll studies, and the 1960s produced a cadre of such attentive readers in Harriette McAdoo, Edna Meyers, Penelope Storm, Margaret Spencer, and, of course, Judith Porter. (One might well add Reginald Butts who, while believing that PI and RGO were correlated, nonetheless differentiated the two constructs in an article published in 1963, three years before Meyers or Porter had completed their dissertations.)[1] Since the mainstream literature, including the important review article by Porter and Washington (1979), has totally neglected the contribution of these other scholars, and as a way of placing Porter's accomplishment in perspective, let us explore the ease by which each of the five observers came to view the same reality.

In the opening pages of her dissertation, Edna O. Meyers (1966) remarks that "the role that self-esteem and racial identity play in the achievement behavior of Negro children is a problem of deep interest to this investigator, who has been working as a psychologist with parents and children in an East Harlem psychiatric clinic. Specifically, therefore, the following study will attempt an exploration of these two variables" (p. 8). Shortly thereafter, she mentions "self-esteem" and "self-image" again, and then again ("a positive attitude towards himself, reinforced by a positive attitude toward his racial identity "). She discusses the need for a Black child to have "a sense of self-esteem as well as positive acceptance of his racial or ethnic origins." While explicating her methodology, Meyers states that as part of her study she "explored the extent of co-relationship between positive self-concept and positive attitudes towards the Negro." After demarcating the

---

1. Morris Rosenberg and Robert Simmons may also qualify for this list.

dynamics of high self-esteem that she found in a segment of her sample, Meyers asks the following question as a lead-in to the results of her racial attitude measure: "Was this feeling of self-acceptance part of, or separate from, acceptance of racial identity?" (p. 43). If one needed still further evidence that Meyers was operating with a differential perspective of PI and RGO, we find her stating that, within her study, "there were some [children] with a low self-concept, but a positive attitude towards the Negro, and some with a high self-concept, but a negative attitude towards their race. For this reason, it seemed valuable to ascertain whether there was a correlation between self-concept and racial attitudes" (p. 61). Given this statement, it should come as no surprise that although Meyers reports a positive linear correlation between her measure of self-esteem and group identity, it accounts for very little variance and is barely significant.

The ease with which Meyers handles the PI and RGO constructs can be explained in part by the fact that two of the people who guided her dissertation were Mamie and Kenneth Clark. In his major works on the topic that were in print at the time Meyers conducted her study (Clark 1955, 1965; HARYOU Report 1964), Kenneth Clark was very clear about differentiating between PI and RGO, as well as the *assumption* that the two variables were highly correlated. Meyers repeatedly cites Clark's book *Dark Ghetto*, in which the following can be found:

> Human beings who are forced to live under ghetto conditions and whose daily experience tells them that almost nowhere in society are they respected and granted the ordinary dignity and courtesy accorded to others will, as a matter of course, begin to doubt their own worth. Since every human being depends upon his cumulative experiences with others for clues as to how he should view and value himself, children who are consistently rejected understandably begin to question and doubt whether they, their family, and their group really deserve no more respect from the larger society than they receive. These doubts become the seeds of a pernicious self- and group-hatred, the Negro's complex and debilitating prejudice against himself. (Clark 1965, 63–64).

Even a cursory analysis of the dissertation by Harriette McAdoo, completed in 1970 at the University of Michigan, shows she was systematically isolating and studying the relationship between separate measures of self-esteem and group identity. According to McAdoo,[2] she arrived at her perspective on the difference between PI and RGO from a combination of her knowledge of the traditional literature and a personal encounter with one of her children:

> John [McAdoo][3] and I came to Ann Arbor in the Fall of 1966 and our youngest, Anna, was preschool age. Whenever it seemed natural and playful, we always made it a point to reinforce a positive attitude about our children's racial image and it was no different with Anna. Sometimes when giving her a bath, I would let the rinse water slowly ring from the washcloth so we could trace a stream from her shoulders to her toes. Our eyes followed the stream, and we would laugh and play and I would sometimes say something like, "Look at Mommy's pretty brown girl." Shortly after arriving in Ann Arbor, Anna entered a pre-school program. One evening John and I were sitting on our bed watching television while Anna was taking a bath. Soon she rushed into the room and climbed into bed between us while saying, "Mommy and Daddy I know I'm a pretty brown girl but sometimes I wish I could be a White girl." There was no alarm, sadness or tension in her voice, but it was clear to John and me that our little one, who by every indication was a strong and healthy and happy child, was taking on racial attitudes that were far removed from how she saw herself personally—you know, her sense of self-worth. Shortly thereafter I completed my first year paper and spelled out what was to become my major focus at Michigan—the study of identity development in children, especially Black children, and more particularly, the study of self-esteem and racial attitudes.

Since Porter (1971) used only descriptive data to infer the independence of PI and RGO, Harriette McAdoo's dissertation represented one of the first studies employing continuous data to report no overall correlation between the two constructs. Later, she collected longitudinal data on her original sample and expanded her study to include children from the North and South (McAdoo 1977, 1985). At the end of the longitudinal study, she

---

2. Phone conversation with Harriette McAdoo, August 21, 1986. "Anna" is a pseudonym.
3. John McAdoo also went on to study racial attitude change at the same university (J. McAdoo 1970).

again found no overall correlation between PI and RGO, although an association was linked to various subgroups in her sample, as was also true for the first data set.

In summarizing her doctoral dissertation, which she completed at the University of Maryland, Penelope A. Storm (1970) described a study involving "the measurement of the dependent variables: self-concept, race image, and race preference; and the observation of their interrelationships by racial group, and of their relationship and interaction with the independent variables: sex and socio-economic status" (p. 6).

Within this study, perhaps the most well designed and carefully executed early study of PI and RGO, Storm demonstrates that in the absence of a connection to someone like Kenneth Clark or a family encounter (such as happened to the McAdoos), a systematic and detailed review of the Black identity literature "naturally" leads one to a differentiation of PI and RGO. In a methodical and detached fashion, Storm shows the reader that both the generic and particularistic literature on identity development is premised on an assumed positive linear correlation between self-esteem and body image, in the case of the general population, or Black self-esteem and Black group identity, as a case in point of general theory:

> The centrality of body image in self-concept has been suggested by Allport, Ausbel, and Jerslid. As the initial development of self-awareness or self-differentiation is partially initiated by the infant's exploration of his body and his discovery that his physical needs are not necessarily needs of his environment, body image is a fundamental layer of self-concept. Race image, part of the body image, involves a recognition of the societal value system regarding certain physical and racially distinctive characteristics. However, the importance of body image or race image to self-concept may be a function of the importance of the body image or race image to the individual and his society. The child of a racial minority frequently learns that his physical person is devalued by the general society; thus, he should, theoretically, have low self-regard or a negative self-concept.
>
> In summary, self-concept and personality theorists have postulated that: (1) Social experience or environmental factors influence self-concept development. (2) Body image, of which the physical aspects of race image are a part, is one of the first aspects of self-concept to develop. (3) Self-acceptance is necessary for the development of a positive self-concept. (pp. 13–14).

Shortly before this passage, she defines self-concept as a "subjective and *personal* [emphasis added] image of self which is positive or negative in varying degrees" (p. 6). Several pages later, she says, "Race image is defined as a system of values and attitudes derived from: (1) awareness of the differentiating physical characteristics between the races, primarily color; (2) identification of the *racial group* [emphasis added] to which the 'self' belongs; (3) acceptance or rejection of the identification of the racial group to which the 'self' belongs" (p. 8). Anyone familiar with the literature will note that the key descriptors in Storm's defintions (i.e., personal self and group identity) are the same as those used by Porter (1971) to codify her constructs, although each scholar is unaware of the work of the other. This is possible because these terms "leap" from the pages of the traditional literature and do not necessitate interpretive skills. Unlike Meyers (1966), who practically bled her data in order to find some sort of connection between PI and RGO, Storm, while hypothesizing a relationship between the variables, calmly reports that she found no overall correlation between PI and RGO and that "race image and certain areas of self-concept were discontinuously related" (p. 97).

Margaret Spencer came to see PI and RGO as different features of the self through a personal encounter. Spencer[4] has noted that her perspective on Negro identity was totally in line with the pejorative tradition when she was working on her master's thesis in psychology in the late 1960s at the University of Kansas (Spencer and Horowitz 1973). After a lecture at Kansas by Thomas Pettigrew, however, she began to see "for the first time" that the pejorative perspective had an unreal "ring" to it. She found it hard to believe that anyone could be as negative and pathogenic as Pettigrew and the traditionalists depicted. For a while, she escaped from "theory and research" and began simply to observe and listen to children in natural settings. As predicted by the traditionalists, she heard Black children saying things that suggested "low racial self-image," but their actions, playmate preferences, and academic performance often seemed "disjointed" from their cognitions about race. In formalizing her observations while completing a doctorate at the University of Chicago (her basic concepts were developed between 1970 and 1971, although her dissertation was not completed until 1976), Spencer, along with Semaj (1979), Markovics (1974), and Alejandro-Wright (1985),

---

4. Phone interview with M. Spencer, August 1986.

helped explore the role of cognitive development as a mediating factor in studies of PI and RGO. With regard to the PI–RGO debate, Spencer did not find a positive linear relationship; instead, she reported an inverse (negative) quadratic trend. She had no difficulty in classifying the research literature along the PI and RGO dimensions, with her preferred labels being studies of personal identity, or self-esteem, and studies of racial attitudes.

Finally, we come to Judith Porter's doctoral dissertation, which was completed at Harvard University in 1967 under the supervision of Thomas Pettigrew. Since access to the dissertation is limited, most of the comments that follow are based on the published version of the dissertation (Porter 1971).[5]

In her work, Porter equates self-esteem with self-concept and suggests that self-esteem may have two components, racial self-esteem (or group identity) and personal self-esteem:

> The cultural evaluations of race that some Black children are learning unfavorably affect their self-esteem. We have just discussed the effects of prejudice on the child's group identity or racial self-concept. Group identity refers to how the individual feels about himself *as a member of a racial group*, whether he accepts or rejects his racial membership, but other theorists have suggested that self-concept is not unidimensional. This chapter deals with one other component of self-concept, which I call the "personal identity" dimension. Personal identity means one's esteem for himself as *an individual*, how he feels about himself on a deep, personal level. In other words, it is one's *basic sense of personal worth and adequacy*.
>
> Devaluation of one's racial group can create not only a negative group identity but feelings of inadequacy and insecurity on a deeper level as well. My data showed that the group identity component of self-concept is indeed lower among Blacks than among Whites: many Black children reject themselves on a racial basis and dislike or are ambivalent toward the fact that they are Black. I felt that because of prejudice and its social concomitants, the *personal identity* dimension of self-esteem might also be less favorable for Black youngsters. (Porter 1971, 141)

---

5. Porter's (1967) dissertation is not available through interlibrary loan or the University of Michigan Microfilm Service.

Throughout the remainder of her book, the two constructs, personal identity and group identity, are central to her commentary.

Unlike Meyers, McAdoo, Spencer, and Storm, who showed that the PI
and RGO constructs were transparently embedded in the traditional racial
identity literature, and Storm's location of the constructs in the generic human development literature as well, Porter, focusing on the same literature,
imputes an unwanted sense of ownership in the "discovery" and "labeling"
of "her" constructs. She gives no hint in her review of the traditional literature that Ruth Horowitz, the Clarks, and Kardiner and Ovesey were wrestling with the formula $SC = PI + RGO$. The best Porter can do to show that
these constructs were operative in the thinking of other scholars is to cite a
latecomer to the discourse on Black identity, Erik Erikson, and the distinction he made between individual identity and communal identity (Erikson
1968). This distracting sense of ownership and the use of Erikson to validate
PI and RGO constructs seem odd given the attention Porter devotes to the
work of the Clarks in an earlier section of her book. Porter (1971, 71) cites
Kenneth Clark's *Prejudice and Your Child* (1963 ed., p. 43). It so happens
that this citation is taken from the same chapter in which Clark wrote the
following:

> As minority-group children learn the inferior status to which
> they are assigned and observe that they are usually segregated
> and isolated from the more privileged members of their soci-
> ety, they react with deep feelings of inferiority and with a sense
> of *personal humiliation.* Many of them become confused about
> their own *personal worth.* Like all other human beings, they re-
> quire a sense of *personal dignity* and social support for *positive
> self-esteem.* Almost nowhere in the larger society, however, do
> they find their own *dignity as human beings* respected or pro-
> tected. Under these conditions, minority-group children de-
> velop conflicts with regard to *their feelings about themselves*
> and about the value of the *group* with which they are identi-
> fied. Understandably they begin to question whether they them-
> selves and their group are worthy of no more respect from the
> larger society than they receive. These conflicts, confusions, and
> doubts give rise under certain circumstances to self-hatred and
> rejection of their own group. (pp. 63–64; italics added)

This quote can also be found in Clark's 1964 report on HARYOU (p. 7), and
as noted earlier, PI and RGO are pivotal themes in *Dark Ghetto,* which Clark
published in 1965.

Thus, for the record, Porter's PI and RGO constructs are not unique, nor was she the first to test the extent of the relationship between personal and group identity. Instead, along with those listed above, she shared the distinction of conducting the kind of Black identity investigation that had eluded the field for some time: a correlational study incorporating separate measures for two hypothetical constructs omnipresent in the Black identity literature—PI and RGO. The Clark's knew they had only one measure, but they saw their results in terms of two data sets, 'with doll choice equaling RGO data and the spontaneous remarks of children, noted during the test administration, representing the personal level of self-esteem. Kardiner and Ovesey (1951) also administered one device (the inkblot test), but they organized their "evidence" along the lines of individual, group, and community dynamics, inclusive of class distinctions—all from a sample of 25 subjects! After the traditionalists repeated the self-hatred thesis over and over again, the false impression that both PI and RGO had been tested adequately was taken for granted, as reflected by literature reviews in the early 1960s such as the one by Pettigrew (1964). Eventually, the Black community called attention to itself through the Black Social Movement, and scholars, especially young scholars, took note of the failure of early writers to test the relationship between self-identity and group identity adequately. Porter, Meyers, McAdoo, Storm, and Spencer were among the first scholars to do so, each independently of the other and all between 1966 and 1970.

Aside from its place in this historical commentary, the published version of Porter's (1971) dissertation is frequently cited as one of the more important studies in the area of race, class, and identity. Closer scrutiny suggests a reputation only partially deserved.

As a study of RGO, the significance of Porter's study is uncontestable. She explored the ontology and meaning of racial preference and self-identification (Chapters 1–6 of her text) in a large sample of preschoolers ($N = 387$) stratified by race, gender, socioeconomic status, age, and, in the case of the Black children, skin color. But the section on personal identity (Chapter 7), and its relationship to class and RGO, is as weak as the earlier chapters are strong. The RGO material is a carefully designed and well-executed investigation; the PI chapter has the quality of a pilot study, which is exactly what it represents. The material in Chapter 7 appeared in her dissertation as an epilogue (Porter 1967). Porter came upon the need to study PI very late in her collection of RGO data, and the epilogue constituted an exploratory investigation. To study PI, she experimented with a set of child-oriented Thematic Apperception Test (TAT) cards, which might explain why she found lower levels of PI in Black as compared to white children, despite controlling for social class. Williams (1981) and his associates have shown that when administered to Blacks, TAT cards with white figures produce more negative protocols than occurs with similar cards incorporating Black figures. Porter, who is white, administered the test, although this in itself may not have had a bearing on the the Black children's performance, especially in view of the level of rapport she reported achieving when testing the same children for RGO. Yet, as revealed by her dissertation more so than her text, her perspective concerning the effects of social class and personal identity evolved during the process of preparing her literature review and before she had collected the PI data. Given that she started the PI study with certain expectations, and given that it is easier for experimenter bias to play an unintended role in the administration and scoring of a nonobjective personality test (e.g., the TAT), it would have been far better had she not acted as the examiner.

But aside from considerations of possible experimenter bias and the nature of the PI test she employed, the size of the subsample on which the PI and PI × RGO correlational analyses were based was far too small for the production of anything other than suggestive trends. It certainly did not provide a platform from which to launch generalizations about the dynamics of the Black psyche. Of the 387 preschoolers originally tested for RGO, she studied PI with a subsample of 57 five year olds, 38 of whom were Black and 19 white. When she analyzed the PI data by race (two levels), socioeconomic status (three levels), and self-esteem (two levels), six of the twelve cells had Ns of 3 or less (see Porter 1971, 150, table 20).

According to her dissertation, this subsample also provided the data for her discovery that PI and RGO may not be related. But this is reported in a very confusing manner. On page 144 of her text, the subsample of 57 children is noted. Three pages later, the text reads as if the subsample has been expanded by 143 children to a figure of 200 (100 white and 100 Black preschoolers). On the basis of this expanded subsample, Porter reports that PI and RGO "are in fact distinct" (Porter 1971, 147). But this subsample is documented neither with footnote nor endnote, and in the absence of additional information, the PI and RGO data attributable to this expanded group are difficult to comprehend. For example, earlier in the text, on page 119, the total number of Blacks who scored low on racial self-identification is recorded as 38, but on page 147 the number somehow jumps to 62. More confusing is what happens after the subsample of 200 is introduced. With a subsample of 200, Porter seems positioned to make a very powerful statement about the way socioeconomic status (SES) mediates PI and RGO (she had SES data on 359 of the original 387 subjects). Having made brief reference to the subsample of 200 on page 147, however, her subsequent analysis of personal identity and SES (pp. 148–161) is based on the original subsample of 57 and has cell counts that preclude any meaningful interpretation. Consequently, given the problems with her PI measure, possible experimenter bias, and the size of her subsample, most, if not all, of what Porter has to say about PI, SES, and the relationship between these two variables and RGO should be taken with a grain of salt. An extraordinary study of RGO it is; a seminal study of the relationship between PI and RGO it is not.

Finally, one might be critical of another work with which Porter is associated. In 1979, Porter and Robert Washington published what appears to be a comprehensive review of empirical studies on Black identity conducted between 1968 and 1978 (Porter and Washington 1979). They open the article by differentiating PI from RGO studies of Black identity. There follows a review of the univariate studies of RGO, then a section on univariate studies of PI, and finally a review of studies of association between PI and RGO. The bibliography consists of 146 references, yet the section on the "relationship between racial and personal self-esteem" reviews only 5 studies of association (Evans and Alexander 1970; Gurin and Epps 1975; Porter 1971; Rosenberg and Simmons 1971; Ward and Braun 1972). Keep in mind that others (Adam 1978; Harrison 1985; Pettigrew 1978) will cite the Porter and Washington piece as having found a *trend* in the empirical literature supportive of the independence of PI and RGO; in point of fact, no such trend is revealed. Aside from the study by Rosenberg and Simmons (1971), the only work cited in support of the independence of PI and RGO is Porter's (1971). The other references point in the opposite direction. In what must be an editorial error, one of these studies is incorrectly classified as a study of "Black militancy"; in actuality, the Ward and Braun (1972) experiment focuses on self-esteem and racial preference in young children, in a fashion similar to that found in Porter's (1971) study. Thus, of the five studies cited by Porter and Washington that explore the relationship between PI and RGO in Blacks, the two that focus on young children (Porter 1971; Ward and Braun 1972) come to opposite conclusions, and of the remaining three, each of which focuses on adolescents and young adults, one argues for no relationship (Rosenberg and Simmons, 1971) and two are supportive of an overall positive linear relationship (Evans and Alexander, 1970; Gurin and Epps, 1975). Such evidence hardly puts one in a position to affirm the independence of PI from RGO. By placing undue emphasis on Porter's work and overlooking the studies by McAdoo, Storm, and others, their review is revealed to be of limited value on the issue of the dynamics and relationship between PI and RGO in Blacks, although their sections reviewing univariate PI and RGO studies are excellent.

PI × RGO Correlational Studies: 1939–1987

Given the methodological limitations of any one or two studies, the scientific consensus on the nature of the relationship between PI and RGO in Blacks is more likely to result from an examination of a large body of research. Such has been the concern of Cross (1978a, 1981, 1985) and his students (Little 1983) at Cornell University. Thus the following review of PI × RGO correlational studies builds on the earlier work of Cross and Little.

It is now possible to identify forty-five studies that have empirically explored the relationship between PI and RGO in the dynamics of Black identity across the life span. Table 6 lists these studies and in the Appendix can be found information that summarizes each study in terms of authorship, sample size, methodology, and significant findings. Turning to Table 6, we note that of the forty-five studies, sixteen (35.55 percent) found an overall positive linear correlation between PI and RGO in Blacks, while twenty-nine (64.44 percent) reported no overall relationship. Thus the first impression is one of a "mixed bag," for although a clear majority call the presumed relationship into question, a significant proportion stand in confirmation of the relationship. As it turns out, the trend is much more in favor of the null hypothesis.

In classifying studies for inclusion in Table 6, weight was given not only to the statistical results reported but also to the interpretations and conclusions reached by a study's author. In the vast majority of cases, they were the same, that is, when an insignificant relationship was recorded, the experimenter reported a finding of no relationship. The reverse was true with a significant relationship. In a number of instances, almost all from studies supportive of the PI and RGO relationship, the conclusions stressed by researchers were slightly or greatly different from the actual statistical results recorded. That this tendency should be evident only in studies affirming the relationship between PI and RGO should come as no surprise; there has been more social pressure to confirm than disconfirm this hypothesis.

Of the sixteen studies noted in Table 6 that found a positive linear

Table 6
Classification of 45 PI and RGO Correlational Studies

Found No Overall Positive Linear Correlation between PI and RGO	Reported an Overall Positive Linear Correlation between PI and RGO
Bennett and Lundgren 1976	Brown 1979
M. L. Clark 1979	*Butts 1963
Cole 1979	Enty 1979
Cummings and Carrere 1975	*Fouther-Austin 1978
Dulan 1975	Hendrix 1977
Garner 1983	*E. King 1981
Grossman 1981	Maish 1978
Hall 1980	Meyers 1966
Hernandez 1984	*Mobley 1973
Horton 1973	Paul and Fisher 1980
Hughbanks 1977	*Penn 1980
Jacques 1976	*Rasheed 1981
Jarrett 1980	Schmults 1975
J.M. Johnson 1981	Stephen and Rosenfield 1979
H. McAdoo 1970, 1977	*Vaughan 1977
McWhorter 1984	Ward and Braun 1972
Markovics 1974	
Porter 1971	
J. Robinson 1977	
Rosenberg 1979a	
Sacks 1973	
Slade 1977	
Spencer 1976, 1982	
Storm 1970	
I. Williams 1975	
Williams-Burns 1976	
Wilson 1981	

*Reanalysis shows that each of these studies should actually be included in the first column.

correlation between PI and RGO in Blacks, five (Fouther-Austin 1978; King 1981; Maish 1978; Rasheed 1981; Vaughan 1977), reported an overall correlation when, in fact, only higher-order interactions were recorded; one (Penn 1980) found mixed to insignificant results, although the abstract and summary sections gave the impression of finding an overall relationship; and in two additional investigations (Butts 1963; Mobley 1973), the statistical evidence completely contradicted the conclusions stressed by the experimenter.

1. *Overall Trend Linked to Interaction*. Five studies fall into this category. Fouther-Austin (1978) administered a self-esteem scale (Tennessee Self-Concept Scale [TSCS]) and a race-awareness scale (Banks Black Consciousness Scale) to 392 Black tenth-grade students across six test sites and reported a significantly high correlation ($r = .32$) between PI and RGO for all subjects. The correlation fluctuated greatly (.07 to .50) from test site to test site and was significant only in three of the six cities; in effect, her data showed support for a PI/RGO relationship under certain circumstances, but not as an overall trend. The same can be said of a study by King (1981). She administered the Piers-Harris Self-Concept Scale and a Black identity scale to 117 fifth- and sixth-grade Black children from three predominantly Black schools in Los Angeles. King reported an overall correlation between the two measures ($r = .30$); in one school, however, the relationship was practically nonexistent, even as a trend ($r = .05$), while the other two schools showed a highly significant association ($r = .45$ and $r = .46$). King had problems with social desirability on her RGO measure, and in the two schools for which an association between PI and RGO were found, students may have been systematically exposed to Black cultural activities shortly before King collected her data. Furthermore, students at all three schools could not be differentiated by level of self-esteem. Clearly this is another instance of an overall trend that more correctly should be recorded as an interaction. Vaughan (1977) investigated the PI/RGO association with 33 third-grade and 42 seventh-grade Black children from predominantly low-income working-class families, making use of the Piers-Harris Self-Concept Scale and the Cheek Scale (race awareness). The correlation between the two instruments across all subjects approached significance ($r = .22$, $p = .065$), but was insignificant at each grade level. The self-esteem/race-esteem correlation for girls (but not for boys) was significant ($p = .02$), again pointing to an interaction effect. The pattern of the Vaughan, King, and Fouther-Austin studies was repeated by Rasheed (1981). Rasheed studied PI and RGO in 66 Black third-graders assigned to six different groups. As in the Vaughan study, Rasheed operationalized RGO through the Cheek Scale, and she employed two self-esteem measures: Piers-Harris and Coopersmith. She found no correlation between PI and RGO using Piers-Harris; results with Coopersmith and Cheek approached significance ($r = .47, p > .10$). Further exploration reveals that even this association was limited to two of her six subgroups, in which case we are discussing still another interaction, not a

main effect. Finally, in a study of adult Black identity, Maish's (1978) finding of a significant overall correlation ($r = .14$) between the TSCS and a multi-dimensional Black identity scale was readily accounted for by several lower-order cells in his sample. This pattern also held for Maish's Black Identity Scale and a second mental health measure. Consequently, each of these five studies did not find an overall correlation, although evidence was found that the two variables may interact under circumscribed conditions. When rein-terpreted, each begins to "look like" the studies found in category 1 of Table 6; that is, several studies reporting no overall correlation did report interac-tions (McAdoo 1977; Porter 1971).

2. *Overall Trend Incorrectly Reported.* On first examination, a study of PI and RGO in a group of Black children by Penn (1980) seemed to show an overall correlation ($r = .31, p > .06$) between her carefully constructed cul-tural identity scale and the Branden Self-Concept and Motivation Inventory. But the Branden scale has two parts; one measures achievement motivation and the other, self-esteem. The correlation Penn reported pertained only to the relationship between cultural awareness and achievement motivation, not self-esteem. In fact, the correlation between self-esteem and cultural identity was practically zero (Penn 1980, 104, table 1).

3. *Statistical Findings Contradict Conclusion Stressed by the Author.* Since almost any social scientific effort is subject to criticisms and limita-tions, our purpose here is not to "nitpick" but to point out two works in which the statistical results are clearly at odds with the interpretation of-fered by the experimenters. One must question whether the studies by Mobley (1973) and Butts (1963) present evidence supportive of the PI/RGO relationship, either as a main effect or an interaction. The Butts (1963) study, perhaps the first to administer separate PI and RGO measures to the same sample, applied a self-esteem and two-factor race-awareness measure (racial preference and racial self-identification) to 50 children. But the actual analysis was conducted only on 14 students who misidentified on the race-awareness measure. Of the 14, 6 scored high and 8 scored low on the PI measure. Even without conducting a reanalysis, it should be obvious that an 8 to 6 split for 14 cases is well within chance expectations; consequently, the data actually showed that one could *not* predict, beyond chance, the PI level for an associated RGO level. Butts also had direct observation ratings as another measure of PI; when the observation data failed to show a signifi-cant relationship to the misidentification data (again, $N = 14$), Butts sug-gested that his observers were probably not very reliable. Finally, Butts did not analyze his self-esteem by racial-preference data, yet he considered it

obvious that, for the other 36 subjects, many children with high self-esteem were demonstrating an "out-group" preference. Mobley (1973) also inappropriately interprets her data as demonstrating a PI/RGO relationship for a study conducted with 163 college students. The TSCS and a 101-item Black identity index were applied to the sample. Mobley failed to report the overall correlation coefficient for the relationship between the instruments; what she did show was that 9 of 101 items were statistically correlated with various TSCS subscales. In other words, 91 of the items failed to show a relationship. By chance alone, one might expect some of the 101 items to show a relationship with some of the TSCS subscales, but to report such findings as support for the PI/RGO relationship is simply not acceptable. Based on statistical results, both Butts and Mobley actually confirmed the null hypothesis and should be included in category 1 of Table 6.

Thus the studies by Butts, Mobley, Rasheed, Penn, King, Maish, Vaughan, and Fouther-Austin should be removed from category 2 in Table 6 to category 1. Doing so, we arrive at thirty-seven (82 percent) of the studies reporting no overall correlation between PI and RGO and only eight (18 percent) presenting evidence to the contrary. As shown in Table 7, this pattern of no overall relationship holds regardless of whether the studies were conducted with children, adolescents, or adults.

IDEOLOGICAL BIAS

Some observers may want to determine whether an ideological bias that lends itself to a finding of "no relationship" is operating among those conducting PI × RGO correlational studies. To the extent that a major bias or ideological slant has existed, it has been in the direction of presupposing a PI and RGO relationship. Both the advocates of the traditional pejorative perspective and those mapping Black identity change have, for the most part, taken for granted that PI and RGO are positively correlated. If anything, the bias in favor of the relationship has tended to delay the discovery of evidence that argues against an overall relationship (see, for example, Butts 1964; Meyers 1966; Mobley 1973). In an unpublished review of twenty PI and RGO studies of association, Little (1981) found that 66 percent of the studies reporting no overall relationship between PI and RGO were conducted by researchers who began their studies "firmly committed to the traditional notion of the relationship" (p. 20).

QUALITY OF THE STUDIES

Another factor to consider is the quality of the studies on either side of the ledger; perhaps the overall quality of the eight studies supportive of a PI

Table 7
PI and RGO Studies of Association Classified by Sample and Findings

Children		Teens		Adults	
No[a]	Yes[b]	No[a]	Yes[b]	No[a]	Yes[b]
*Bennett and Lundgren 1976	Meyers 1966	*Cummings and Carrere 1975	*Hendrix 1977	*Cole 1979	*Brown 1979
Butts 1963	*Stephen and Rosenfield 1979	*Fouther-Austin 1978	*Paul and Fisher 1980	Hall 1980	*Enty 1979
*M.L. Clark 1979	*Ward and Braun 1972	Grossman 1981		*Jacques 1976	Schmults 1975
*Dulan 1975		*Hughbanks 1977		*J.M. Johnson 1981	
Garner 1983		*Maish 1978		Mobley 1973	
Hernandez 1984		*Rosenberg 1979a		*J. Robinson 1977	
Horton 1973		*Slade 1977		*I. Williams 1975	
*Jarrett 1980				*Wilson 1981	
E. King 1981					
H. McAdoo 1970, 1977*					
*McWhorter 1984					
*Markovics 1974					
Penn 1980					
*Porter 1971					
*Rasheed 1981					
*Sacks 1973					
Spencer 1976, 1982*					
*Storm 1971					
Vaughan 1977					
Williams-Burns 1976					

[a]No = study in which no overall relationship was found between PI and RGO.
[b]Yes = study in which a significant overall relationship was found between PI and RGO.
*In terms of methodology and theory, these studies tended to be of a higher quality than those not starred.

and RGO correlation is superior to the average of the thirty-seven studies finding no relationship. Studies of higher methodological quality (e.g., sample selection and sample size, quality of measurement scales and techniques, statistical analysis, theroretical clarity, discussion of results) are identified in Table 7 with an asterisk. Twenty-four (65 percent) of the studies that found no overall relationship and six (75 percent) of the studies that found an overall relationship would seem to be capable of passing a quality-control inspection. Given my bias, a more neutral party may well have found fewer studies in support of the null hypothesis worthy of consideration. Still, I have been more than generous in labeling 75 percent of the studies in support of a relationship "quality studies," for most suffer from crucial methodological flaws. To begin with, the dissertations by Meyers (1966) and Schmults (1975), are weak studies by anyone's standards. Of the remaining six, four (Hendrix 1977; Paul and Fischer 1980; Stephen and Rosenfield 1979; Ward and Braun 1972) incorporate methodological weaknesses that put in doubt their major conclusions.

Ward and Braun (1972) studied the PI/RGO relationship among 60 Black boys and girls between the ages of seven and eight, making use of the Piers-Harris Children's Self-Concept Scale and a modified Clark and Clark doll task. Apparently the authors found so few subjects with either low self-esteem scores or low doll-task scores that the chi-square statistic was not applied, and a nonparametric statistic was used instead. The results of a Mann-Whitney U Test indicated that those subjects who made more (score of 3 or 4) Black color preferences had higher self-concept scores than those who made fewer (score of 2 or 1) Black preferences. The number of subjects with low doll-task scores was, in fact, very small; 70 to 82 percent made Black preferences on 3 of the 4 doll-task questions (the percentage for the fourth task was not reported). Consequently, the reader should note that an oft-cited study in support of a general relationship between PI and RGO had problems with constricted variance on one, if not both, dependent measures.

As Little (1981) has pointed out, Hendrix's (1977) finding of a high correlation between PI and RGO is probably related to the confounding of her measures. Hendrix applied what she thought were three independent paper-and-pencil measures to 240 Black high school seniors. She found that her measure of locus of control was highly correlated to the Backman Self-Esteem Test, and the Backman, in turn, was highly correlated with racial identity. Thus, both locus of control and racial identity seemed to correlate with self-concept. Nevertheless, inspection of the Noel Group Identification Scale, her RGO measure, shows that 3 of 6 items on the scale are measuring *locus of control*, not RGO; consequently, one cannot be certain that her self-concept and RGO correlation was anything more than another instance of self-concept showing a relationship to locus of control.

In an otherwise beautifully designed study, Stephen and Rosenfield (1979) made a critical error in the calculation of RGO. The authors applied the Rosenberg Self-Esteem Scale to a group of 51 Black, 192 white and, 103 Mexican-American fourth graders, and repeated measures of a 10-item semantic differential (describe what Black people are like, what white people are like, what Mexican-Americans are like). Instead of calculating the correlation between a subject's score on the Rosenberg with his semantic differential score depicting his group (i.e., a Black subject's depiction of Black people), Stephen and Rosenfield (1979) did the following:

> For each ethnic group being evaluated, the sum of the evaluations across the 10 adjective pairs was calculated. This yielded three summary attitudinal indices, one expressing attitudes toward ingroup members and two expressing attitudes toward outgroups. . . . To obtain a measure of ethnocentric attitudes, the average of the two outgroup evaluations was subtracted from the ingroup evaluation. (p. 710)

Their manipulation failed to take account of the fact that Blacks are fundamentally *bicultural* in perspective, while whites are primarily monocultural. Thus their procedure systematically reduced the magnitude of the Black in-group score, and possibly exaggerated the score for whites. At least for the Black subjects, one cannot be certain how to interpret the results. Since Stephen and Rosenfeld (1979) did not report the correlation between the Rosenberg test and the unadulterated Black perception of Blacks score, their study does not clarify the relationship between PI and RGO. It is regrettable that they did not report the PI and RGO correlation along with their PI and ethnocentric correlation.

Finally, Paul and Fischer (1980) offer what at first appears to be one of the strongest findings in support of an overall relationship between PI and RGO. They initially tested 131 Black girls and boys from seventh- and eighth-grade classes of a middle school in northwest Indiana, an area heavily populated by Blacks. Using the national norms for the Tennessee Self-Concept Scale (TSCS), they compared 28 high self-concept students with 31 low self-concept students across measures of Black acceptance (RGO), intimacy, internality, and masculinity. Their measure of Black acceptance, the Morse Black Identity Questionnaire, showed a very significant, positive, linear correlation with the total score on the TSCS ($r = .48$, p < .001). But the Morse scale, is in all likelihood *not* measuring Black identity. It consists of six items, among them the following: "If my family were white, we would have more money." It is stretching the imagination to consider any response to such a question as evidence of Black identity. The finding of a relationship between PI and RGO is dubious in the light of the unproven construct validity of the Morse scale.

This leaves only the studies by Brown (1979) and Enty (1979) standing in support of the traditional perspective, and shortly we shall see that their findings of a significant relationship between PI and RGO may be a function of certain mediating variables. All of which is to say that the few studies purporting to show an overall relationship between PI and RGO in Blacks, when examined more closely, reveal information that casts still further doubt about the efficacy of Kurt Lewin's hypothesis. One can only conclude that the trend of the empirical evidence sustaining the null hypothesis (i.e., no overall relationship) is actually more demonstrative than that suggested by Table 6.

STUDIES EMPLOYING VALIDATED MEASURES

Somewhat related to the issue of the quality of a study is whether or not validated measures were used to operationalize the PI and RGO constructs. Of the forty-five studies reviewed here, thirty-three (73 percent) employed validated PI measures, while twelve (27 percent) did not. The figures are reversed for RGO measures: fourteen (31 percent) applied validated and thirty-one (69 percent) used nonvalidated RGO measures. Table 8 shows the kinds of measures meant. In only thirteen studies (Bennett and Lundgren 1976; Cummings and Carrere 1975; Fouther-Austin 1978; Grossman 1981; Hernandez 1984; McAdoo 1970, 1977; Penn 1980; Robinson 1977; Schmults 1975; Spencer 1976, 1982; Stephen and Rosenfield 1979) were both constructs operationalized through validated measures. As it is, the trend for this subsample is more in line with the null hypothesis than the trend of all the studies reviewed. With the exception of the findings by Schmults (1975), one of the methodologically weakest of the lot, and Stephen and Rosenfield, (1979), the study previously noted as calculating the RGO factor in a somewhat odd fashion, eleven (84.6 percent) of the studies employing validated measures found no significant overall relationship between PI and RGO.

INTERACTION EFFECTS AND MEDIATING VARIABLES

In twelve studies (Bennett and Lundgren 1976; Cole 1979; Fouther-Austin 1978; Horton 1973, Hernandez 1984; King 1981; Maish 1978; McAdoo

Table 8
Validated and Nonvalidated Measures Employed in
Correlational Studies of Black Identity

Validated Personal Identity (PI) Measures
  Thomas Self-Concept and Values Inventory
  California Test of Personality
  Rosenberg Self-Esteem Scale
  Tennessee Self-Concept Scale
  Backman Self-Esteem Test
  Piers-Harris Children's Self-Concept Scale
  Brown IDS Self-Concept Referents Test
  Elkins Adjective Checklist
  Sentence Completion Test
  Coopersmith Self-Esteem Inventory

Nonvalidated PI Measures
  Taylor Self-Esteem Scale
  M. Clark Multidimensional Self-Attitude and Self-Esteem Test
  Draw-a-Person Test

Validated Reference Group (RGO) Measures
  Preschool Racial Attitudes Measure
  Semantic Differential
  Banks Black Consciousness Scale
  Milliones Developmental Black Consciousness Scale

Nonvalidated RGO Measures
  Doll-preference tasks
  Porter doll-play task
  M. Clark measure of racial preference and racial attitude
  Maish Black Identity Scale
  Trent Racial Attitude Checklist
  Storm Race Image and Race Preference Test
  Self-Portrait coloring task
  Cheek Black Ethnic Identification Scale

1970, 1977; McWhorter 1984; Porter 1970; Spencer 1976, 1982; Vaughan 1977), significant interactions were recorded. These interactions are worthy of consideration because they were recorded in some of the more methodologically sound studies (eight, or 67 percent, were listed in Table 7 as quality studies; and six, or 50 percent, incorporated both validated PI and RGO measures). Furthermore, this small cluster of studies may direct our attention to the special circumstances in the study of Black identity where PI and RGO are related. Unfortunately, the results are scattered and contradictory. Porter (1971) found evidence suggesting social class might mediate the relationship between PI and RGO in Blacks, as her working-class subsample seemed to be more inclined to exhibit both low self-esteem and negative RGO than did Black middle-class children. But neither Storm (1970) or Mc-Whorter (1984) found social class to be a mediating factor. Likewise, Mc-Adoo (1970, 1977) reported that the PI and RGO relationship was more important to a subsample of boys than girls, yet Vaughan (1977) and Cole (1979) found the reverse to be true. Hendrix (1977) concluded locus of control was an important mediating factor, but Schmults (1975) did not. Perhaps the overall trend of these interactions is best summarized by Little (1981):

> These subject and situational indicators of a correlation be-
> tween the variables support our contention that while the vari-
> ables are uncorrelated overall, there might be conditions where
> the variables act in concert. In Cross' language, we might see
> interaction instead of main effect correlations between personal
> identity and reference group orientation. Unfortunately there is
> not enough commonality among the studies evidencing condi-
> tional interactions (i.e., interaction effects resulting from the im-
> pact of mediating variables) so that we can definitively
> conclude personal identity and reference group orientation will
> correlate given particular subject or situational variables. (p.
> 33)

Little's assessment is probably true, but there is reason to suggest that age and gender should be given priority in future studies. The McAdoo and Vaughan studies, which produced contradictory findings about the role of gender, were conducted with small samples of young children, but many Black identity (nigrescence) issues come to fruition in adult life. With this in mind, we note that in one of the best PI and RGO correlational studies to date, Cole (1979) found in a large ($N = 200$) and carefully stratified sample of Black adults that the PI and RGO interface was much more evident in the dynamics of Black identity for adult females than for adult males (females with high PI had a Black-oriented RGO, while a low PI was associated with a negative RGO). What makes the Cole findings so intriguing is that the only studies reporting an overall relationship between PI and RGO for which I can find little to fault in terms of methodology, theory, and the like, are studies in which women dominate the respective samples (Brown 1979; Enty 1979).

Using the Enty Black Identity Scale to measure RGO, and the California

Psychological Inventory Self-Acceptance Scale to measure PI, Enty (1979) collected data on 415 Black undergraduates at Morgan State University in the fall of 1973. Enty found students with higher self-concepts were more likely to be involved in the Black movement, more apt to adopt Afro fashions, and tended to wear their hair in an Afro style. At a level that was almost inconsequential, she found that students who scored high on the Black identity scale also scored high on self-concept ($r = .17, p > .001$). All of Enty's subjects were females, and in view of Cole's findings, Enty probably would have recorded gender as a mediating variable, not a main effect, had her study included an equal number of males. For example, in a study of Black adults by Wilson (1981) that included 105 males and 99 females, no overall correlation was found between PI and RGO. Unfortunately, Wilson did not discuss or report any interactions, although one could well imagine that the magnitude of the effect for gender found in the Enty study, if present at a similar level in Wilson's data set, could well have been overlooked by Wilson or considered too modest for notation. In addition to Enty, Brown (1979) found a correlation between PI and RGO; again, however, we note that of the 929 subjects in her sample, only 37.3 percent were adult males, while 62.7 percent were adult females. As we see later in this chapter, there is more to be made of Brown's results, but for the time being, the studies by Cole, Enty, and Brown give some reason to conclude that in correlational investigations of Black identity, adult females, but not males, may evidence an identity structure and dynamic in which PI and RGO are related. But the amount of variance accounted for by this tendency may approach the inconsequential.

Corroborative Evidence: Effects of Black Studies and Transracial Adoption on Self-Concept

Two sets of studies provide powerful if indirect evidence that PI and RGO are independent: studies of the effects of Black studies on self-concept, and investigations on self-concept development of Black children adopted and raised by white parents.

EFFECTS OF BLACK STUDIES

Black Studies programs began to appear in public schools in the late 1960s, and almost from the beginning, researchers have attempted to assess their effects on Black children and college students across a multitude of variables, including self-concept. The self-concept focus has produced contradictory findings, with Bennett-Powell (1976), Robinson (1976), Davis (1980), Powell-Hopson (1985), Smith (1974), and Carter (1974) suggesting exposure to Africana materials improves self-concept, while Carey and Allen (1977), Perry (1977), Curtis (1975), and Melancon (1976) found no effect on self-concept. Almost all the researchers working in this area have presumed that PI and RGO are intricately related, and in most cases only one measure was used to assess change: a PI device or an RGO strategy. Thus, although Black Studies are an attempt to manipulate RGO, the belief in a high correlation between PI and RGO has freed many experimenters to test the effects of this RGO intervention through either a PI or an RGO measure. Hypothetically, studies employing an RGO device to assess the effects of an RGO intervention should be more likely to show change in self-concept than similar studies employing a PI measure. With few exceptions (Crawford 1979; Smith 1974) this is evidently true. RGO interventions evaluated with PI devices, typically self-esteem scales, report no change in identity (Carey and Allen 1977; Curtis 1975; Melancon 1976; Perry 1977), but the same kinds of RGO instructional interventions have produced dramatic effects when evaluated with an RGO measure (Bennett-Powell 1976; Carter 1974; Davis 1980; Powell-Hopson 1985; Robinson 1976). We begin with studies employing PI measures.

Curtis (1975) studied the effects of a five-week program on 50 low-income Black adolescents, evenly divided by sex, using the Tennessee Self-Concept Scale, a PI device. His design called for the random assignment of 10 subjects (i.e., S_s) to each of the following groups:

Group 1: pretest, Black Studies, posttest

Group 2: no pretest, Black Studies, posttest

Group 3: pretest, consultation/rapping, posttest

Group 4: no pretest, consultation/rapping, posttest

Group 5: pretest, no treatment, posttest

Programmatically, his design involved three substantiative clusterings: subjects receiving Black Studies (groups 1 and 2), subjects receiving no Black Studies but provided consultation and rapping sessions (groups 3 and 4), and a no-treatment control group (group 5). Analysis of variance failed to show a difference between the three conditions, nor was there a significance for test taking. At posttesting, the mean self-concept score for subjects receiving the Black Studies module was 326.6; those receiving the consultation/rapping treatment, 330.5; and the no-treatment condition, 321.9. Since test taking showed no effects, Curtis turned his attention to the difference in scores for subjects in the three conditions for whom pretest and posttest scores were available. Here he made a critical error. He ran separate *t* tests on the pretest and posttest scores for each condition, rather than an analysis of variance of the difference scores for all three conditions. That is to say, he ran one *t* test on the pretest and posttest scores for subjects involved in the Black Studies module, another *t* test for those in the rapping session, and so on. But he never statistically compared the difference scores across conditions, thus totally obviating the function of his no-treatment control condition. As can be seen in Table 9, the no-treatment control group established the fact that in the experiment, pretest and posttest self-concept scores could be expected to fluctuate by plus or minus 8.8 points.

The mean difference (*m*) score for the Black Studies treatment was 9.0, well within chance expectations (plus or minus 8.8) and thus clearly not significant. If anything, the consultation/rapping showed a difference (*m* = 14.6). The keen observer will have noticed that the consultation/rapping treatment, as described by Curtis, represented a PI-oriented treatment (rapping about general and personal problems and challenges, or, an informal group-therapy treatment). Thus, while his PI measure did not show PI to be affected by Black Studies (an RGO intervention), it may well have shown that a PI-oriented intervention had mild effects on the PI sector of self-concept.

Perry (1977) investigated the effects of a five-week Black literature course on the self-concept and reading achievement level of 39 Black

Table 9
Pre- and Posttest Self-Concept Mean Values Based on
TSCS for Three Treatments

| | Self-Concept Scores | | |
	Pretest	Posttest	Mean Difference
Black Studies condition	308.7	317.7	+ 9.0
Consultation/rapping	315.5	330.1	+ 14.6
No treatment	330.7	321.9	− 8.8

Source: Curtis 1975.

eighth-grade boys. The youths were divided into three groups, two of which received a five-week English literature course stressing Black literature, and a control group that experienced a traditional English literature curriculum. Perry used a self-concept test based on the semantic differential; he also administered a reading test. At the end of the experiment, Perry reported no differences between the groups on reading scores or self-concept. Perry concluded that exposure to selected Black literature did not seem to have any influence on the self-concept of the eighth-grade Black males in his study. Since his design did not incorporate an RGO as well as a PI outcome, we can say only that his RGO manipulation, as measured by a PI outcome, showed no effects. But this is consistent with expectation, for given that PI cannot predict RGO, then a PI outcome would probably be insensitive to the effects of an RGO manipulation.

In one of the better-designed and well-executed PI studies, Carey and Allen (1977) explored the impact of college-level Black Studies on the self-esteem of Black students. They randomly selected 218 male and female college students from five predominantly white state universities in the Southwest. Selection of participants from the different institutions allowed them to control for quality of Black Studies program, as 42 percent of the sample attended two colleges with strong programs, 45.8 percent attended two institutions with medium-quality programs, and 11.9 percent attended a college with a very weak program. Of the 218 subjects, 118 participated in Black Studies and 100 did not. The total score on the Tennessee Self-Concept Scale was the outcome measure. A student t test showed no difference between the self-concept of participants ($m = 333.7$) and nonparticipants ($m = 340$), nor could the two groups be differentiated on achievement. Apparently, the authors had an axe to grind, for the remainder of their article is concerned with bashing Black Studies programs: "The evidence suggests that viewing Black studies as a social-psychological armor within which Blacks could protect themselves from racial oppression while on a white campus was at best a perceptual distortion and, at worst, an ideological hoax" (Carey and Allen, 816).

The conclusion of their article states:

> The study produced some new data and raised a number of
> questions with regard to the establishment of any kind of com-
> pensatory educational program to assist minority students in
> higher education. It is apparent that a multiple causation ap-
> proach is needed to appropriately conceptualize the phenom-
> ena of group identity and academic performance.

The expected positive impact of Black studies on the self-concept and achievement of Black students has been, at best, minimal. Indeed, one may seriously question the intellectual/social-psychological validity of Black studies as presently conceived and practiced on white campuses. No statistical evidence was found to justify the existence and continuance of these programs in their present state. Perhaps the content of the programs was not sufficiently different from other courses to make a difference. If this was the case, program directors and others have not fulfilled their obligations to make Black studies a viable academic experience. Simply being housed in academia was not enough to guarantee academic purity. We hasten to add, however, that the failure of this research to establish a statistically significant relationship between the aforementioned variables does not deny the existence of other types of benefits that may exist. Perhaps future programming in ethnic studies should establish a set of entrance criteria and prerequisites, and focus on aggregate benefits to be derived rather than individual participant benefits. (p. 818)

We see the same analytic error made here as in the Curtis (1975) and Perry (1977) studies, but here it is even easier to follow. From the quote above, it appears that Carey and Allen are interested in the group identity component of the self-concept, yet they conducted a study that employed measures insensitive to RGO. Consequently, although they preceive their work as comprehensively testing the effects of Black Studies on self-concept, their results provided only half an answer. We still do not know how Black Studies affect group identity.

Studies that have found that Black educational materials can have an effect on self-concept have invariably employed RGO outcome measures. Bennett-Powell (1976) examined the effects of exposure to racially relevant storybooks and learning materials on young Black children's racial attitudes and racial self-identification. Subjects of the study were 96 Black four- and five-year-old males and females attending seven Black day-care centers in the inner city of Cincinnati. The children were randomly assigned to small groups according to three treatment and one control conditions:

1. Program 1. Storybooks and materials—teachers read and discussed preschool storybooks whose main characters were Black and exposed subjects to other learning materials (puzzles, coloring books, etc.) with Black figures.

2. Program 2. Storybooks only—teachers read and discussed the same storybooks and worked with subjects on cognition activities.

3. Program 3. Attention/placebo—teachers worked with subjects on cognition activities.

4. Nontreatment Control. Subjects were not exposed to any experimental program.

Eighteen Black undergraduate females acted as teachers, with a different teacher assigned to each ongoing group. Each treatment lasted thirty minutes and was given five days a week for six weeks. The Preschool Racial Attitudes Measure II (PRAM II) was used to operationalize racial attitudes, and a modified Horowitz Portrait Series defined the index for each child's racial identification. All children were tested on the same measures at the end of the program and during a follow-up six weeks later. Multivariate analyses of racial attitudes and racial identification scores produced significant results for treatment, time, and a treatment-by-time interaction. Children in program 1 exhibited more positive racial attitudes and racial identifications immediately after completion of the program than children in the other three groups. At the time of follow-up, the high racial identification pattern of program 1 children persisted; however, the racial attitudes for the children across all groups fell within the same range. In summary, this RGO intervention produced immediate and lasting effects on the RGO component of self-concept when the RGO intervention was assessed with two sensitive RGO outcomes. But we know nothing of PI because PI was not measured.

In addition to the manipulation of storybooks and learning materials, Powell-Hopson (1985) investigated the effects of modeling, reinforcement, and color-meaning word associations on altering the racial preferences of Black and white preschool children. Her sample consisted of 155 male and female children between the ages of three years and five years eleven months, 105 of whom were Black and 50 of whom were white. A Black female experimenter and a Black male assistant conducted the intervention. Treatment involved modeling Black preferences, reading stories depicting Black children in positive situations and having positive characteristics, and reinforcing children who chose Black dolls (i.e., whenever someone played with the Black dolls, positive adjectives were ascribed to them). Pre- and postadministration of a doll-preference task constituted the dependent variable. Results showed that 64 percent of the children chose the white doll to play with in the pretest condition; the six preference-question responses also significantly favored the white doll. In the posttest, 67 percent chose the Black doll to play with, and the pattern of responses to the preference questions also favored the Black doll. Again, no PI information was produced.

In a somewhat related experiment having a more cognitive bent, Robinson (1976) employed a concept-formation framework with a verbal-correction procedure to teach young Black and white children new strategies for evaluative decision making. The children were told that evaluative decisions were to be made only in the presence of appropriate cues, such as facial expressions and pictured activities or gestures, not simply because of the race of the pictured person. Using the Preschool Racial Attitudes Measure (PRAM) as a screening device, 60 Black and white children were randomly assigned to various treatment conditions, including a no-treatment control group, and taught the new strategies. Posttest administration of the PRAM showed that the treatments effectively altered the racial bias of both Black and white children. Had Robinson or Powell-Hopson used self-esteem (PI), as opposed to RGO, outcome measures, more than likely neither would have found the effects they did find.

Such an error was made by Young (1977). We have noted that factors such as racial preference, world view, ideology, and personal values fall into the RGO sector of the self-concept. Young (1977) studied the results of values-clarification training on the self-concept of Black female students at Mississippi State University. Forty volunteers were randomly assigned to either a treatment or a control group. For a three-week period, the experimental group engaged in values-classification training sessions, meeting once a week for two hours each session. In addition, this group participated in small-group, large-group, and individual exercises selected from leading values-clarification publications. Young served as the facilitator. Unfortunately, Young chose to measure self-concept with a PI device (Tennessee Self-Concept Scale), which, of course, was insensitive to his RGO intervention; consequently, he found the intervention had no effect on self-concept.

In a handful of cases, the effects of Black Studies or related RGO interventions have been assessed across both PI and RGO outcomes (Carter 1974; Davis 1980; Horton 1973; Melancon 1976; Rasheed 1981; Roth 1969).

Rasheed (1981) attempted to settle a number of questions about the relationship between PI and RGO and the effects of PI and RGO interventions. Her research called for an intervention designed to manipulate self-esteem, another aimed at enhancing Black identity, a third condition in which both treatments were combined, and control conditions in which no treatments were applied. Groups were further divided for counterbalanced administration of treatments and measures. Subjects consisted of 66 third-grade Black children, evenly divided by sex. Both the Piers-Harris and Coopersmith self-concept tests were used to measure PI; a modified version of the Cheek Black Ethnic Identification Scale defined level of RGO. None of Rasheed's major propositions was confirmed, none of the different kinds of treatments had their intended effects, and PI and RGO showed no overall correlation. But she did report certain tendencies. The Coopersmith produced a modest positive correlation with RGO, and the Piers-Harris produced a statistically inconsequential negative trend, leading Rasheed to suggest that the relationship between the variables might be test sensitive. In contrast, recall that King (1981) used Piers-Harris in her PI and RGO study and in two schools in her study, Piers-Harris showed a strong *positive* correlation with RGO; the third school showed an inconsequential but slightly negative relationship.

Consistent with our earlier discussion about gender, Rasheed also reported interactions involving sex of the subject and treatment effects. Rasheed concluded that PI and RGO and their associated interventions may involve much more complicated patterns than heretofore considered; in some ways, however, Rasheed took her reported interactions too seriously in view of the major limitations of her study. Unlike the other programs and interventions analyzed here, which lasted anywhere from three weeks to three months, Rasheed's treatments were a one-shot deal, one hour in duration. Also, her measure of RGO left much to be desired. The Cheek Scale is not very proactive and tends to define Blackness in terms of one's level of anti-whiteness.

On a more successful note, Melancon (1976) studied the effects of multicultural education on the self-concepts and social-interaction patterns of fourth- and fifth-grade Black and white students. An ethnic education program was developed, involving the study of Black Americans, Irish-Americans, and French-Americans; the design included treatment as well as no-treatment control classes. Classes were held three times a week for twelve weeks. Self-concept was measured by Piers-Harris (pre- and posttest), a social network intervention inventory was administered three times, and general knowledge tests and essay examinations were given by each teacher at the end of the unit. Although the knowledge tests, essays, and the rest made it clear that new knowledge was absorbed by the students, the information and experience had no significant effect on self-concept as measured by

Piers-Harris (no PI effect). Statistically significant increases in transracial so-cial interactions (RGO pattern) were recorded.

Roth (1969) claimed that both self-concept and racial pride were pos-itively influenced by Black Studies programs. Roth located several school systems in Michigan around 1968; one made the study of the Negro an integral part of its curriculum, the other had no such policy. Thirty-six fifth-grade Black students attending either segregated or integrated schools within a district that emphasized Black Studies were compared to 33 Black students (17 from segregated and 6 from integrated schools) from the dis-trict with no Black Studies curriculum. A semantic differential with the stim-ulus word "Black people" was the measure of racial pride (RGO), and the Self-Concept and Motivation Inventory (SCAMIN) measured self-concept (PI). From the pre- and postadministration of his measures, Roth developed and analyzed the percentage of change scores and found that students ex-posed to a Black Studies curriculum showed greater gains on the "Black people" semantic differential than control students, with no interaction for racial composition of the schools. But a comparison of the posttest means indicated that except for the control group from the segregated school, con-trols had as positive an image of Black people as children exposed to Black Studies, calling into question whether significant change had actually tran-spired.

The pattern of the results for self-concept was equally problematic. At first, the overall analysis showed no difference in change scores for self-concept, nor was there a significant interaction. Further analysis indicated that control subjects at the integrated school could not be differentiated from any of the subjects receiving Black Studies, while the control subjects from the segregated school showed a modest decline in self-concept over time. Had Roth assumed the decline was the result of normal perturbation in self-concept scores, then his PI measure would have registered no real change for all subjects that could not be explained by chance or normal develop-ment. This is supported by his final table, which displayed the posttest self-concept means for both control and treatment groups. Both sets of subjects showed self-concept scores well within the average range for the SCAMIN (i.e., no one registered a low self-concept), and, with one exception, the means were practically indistinguishable (the treatment was not registering a meaningful effect on PI). Thus, if anything, Roth's findings were "mixed," with the change in RGO mildly more convincing than any evidence of PI change.

More convincing evidence that RGO and not PI is likely to be influenced by Black Studies programs comes from studies by Horton (1973), Davis (1980), and Carter (1974).

Horton studied the self-concepts of 70 preschool children, 54 of whom were involved in a child center that did not stress Black awareness and 16 who attended a child center in which the curriculum placed major emphasis on a child's "Black identity and African heritage." Self-concept was measured with the Thomas Self-Concept and Values Inventory. Horton added an additional factor to the Thomas test in order to assess the child's racial identity. Exclusive of the racial identity factor, Horton found no overall difference between the level of self-concept for children in either school. Nevertheless, while the children in the non–Black-oriented program evidenced a white orientation, every single child participating in the child center that stressed identity and African heritage self-identified as "Black."

Working with older subjects and a larger sample, Davis found essentially the same pattern. Combining interviews and anthropological information, Davis (1980) identified two clusters of schools (traditional and nontraditional) in the Chicago, Illinois, and Gary, Indiana, areas. Schools categorized as traditional placed little formal emphasis on Black identity, Black culture, Black history, or African heritage. The nontraditional schools, including an independent Black Nationalist school, had a strong and formalized Black cultural orientation that was an integral part of the school curriculum. Two hundred thirteen traditional school students and 91 nontraditional students, all in the sixth grade, were compared on a multidimensional (self, Black consciousness, Black identity, family expectations) identity questionnaire, and each subject drew a colored self-portrait. Interviews were conducted with students and teachers from each school, and observational notes on the dynamics of each school were compared. Analysis of the results of the questionnaire showed that students from the nontraditional school had slightly higher self-concept levels than those from the traditional school. Actually, both groups had a positive self-concept, although the difference between the two groups was statistically insignificant. From the interviews, Davis noted that in response to the question "Do you like yourself most of time as you are?," there was considerable agreement among the traditional students that they felt good about themselves.

On the questionnaire, there was no difference between the groups on the Black identity factor, but the nontraditional students registered a higher level of Black consciousness as well as a higher sense of awareness that their parents expected them to make a strong effort to integrate Black education with their general education. Correlational analysis produced results that called into question part or all of Davis's nonvalidated self-identity questionnaire. As expected, there was no correlation between the self-concept and the Black identity factors; paradoxically, however, a very high correlation was registered between self-concept and Black consciousness. When Davis ran the correlation between his Black identity and Black consciousness factors, he recorded no relationship, a finding greatly at odds with established research; consequently, all the findings on his questionnaire must be taken with a grain of salt. Yet an analysis of his interviews and field notes, in conjunction with the results of the self-portrait task, provided rather strong evidence that racial identity, more so than self-concept or personal identity, was strongly affected by the kind of school attended. Although 54 percent of the traditional school students drew portraits that differed from their personal appearance (i.e., portraits were white-looking), practically every student from the nontraditional school offered an accurate and racially realistic self-portrait:

> The non-traditional school subjects drew themselves more representative of how they actually look. All of their portraits were colored with brown crayon to appear bronze or very dark brown or were penciled in heavily. Not one of these students colored in blonde hair or blue eyes. From visual observations made by this researcher, it was apparent that most of the students in these schools wore more symbolic Afrikan attire and hair styles. Their illustrations portrayed Afrikan facial features, braids and beads, jewelry and the short and long "natural" hair cuts. They illustrated themselves pictorially with a strong perception of Afrikan descendency, as they really looked physically. (Davis 1980, 64)

Thus, while Davis's PI results, aside from the validity and reliability of his self-concept instrument, showed an almost inconsequential difference between the two groups, the self-portrait task was more than effective in showing an RGO difference between students attending schools with a strong Black Studies emphasis and those experiencing a more traditional curriculum.

Finally, in a study to be discussed in considerable detail in Chapter 5, Carter (1974) stimulated Black identity development in a group of Black college students. At the end of her study, advances in Black consciousness were registered in subjects who nevertheless showed no change in their level of personal identity; that is, their PI baseline was the same before and after change was recorded in their RGO.

In summary, studies of the effects of Black Studies programs or associated studies of RGO manipulations have produced results that are remarkably consistent with the proposition that PI and RGO are not correlated. When understood to be an RGO intervention, and when assessed with RGO outcomes, Black Studies have been shown to change or enhance the RGO factor of the self-concept. But when, for whatever reason, Black Studies or RGO manipulations have been assessed solely on PI outcomes, no effects have been registered. In the handful of studies in which both PI and RGO were assessed, the effects of Black Studies or related RGO treatments on PI have been unconvincing, inconsequential, or simply nonexistent; but the effects on RGO have been compelling. The dynamics implied by the results are as follows: Black Studies programs and related RGO manipulations have the capacity to alter, to one degree or another (including radicalization), the RGO structure and function of the self, but they are relatively *useless* in the manipulation of PI. Black students taking Black Studies enter and leave such courses with the same personality dynamics. Even when a college student becomes "militant" or "radical," the psychodynamic aspects of the militancy will be dictated by the personality processes characteristic of the person *before* entering the course, not by the course content. The overwhelming majority of cases shows that Black Studies programs may alter some *cognitive RGO dimension*, just as do college courses in the humanities, social sciences, or history (at least when students take the material seriously). Thus, neurotic Negroes taking Black Studies might become more Black oriented, but they will leave the course no less neurotic; likewise, a Negro with a healthy personality and strong self-concept will remain as such after completing an intellectually engaging Black Studies seminar or course, although his frame of reference about Black music, Black history, and the rest may be significantly altered. In most quality Black Studies programs, the emphasis is on analysis and information processing, not psychotherapy. Nevertheless, just as some white (and Black) students may radically alter their RGO (political views) after taking a seminar on advanced political theory, so no one should be surprised when a deracinated Black freshman responds with considerable passion to information received during a dispassionate and scholarly lecture by a Black Studies professor.

EFFECTS OF TRANSRACIAL ADOPTION

Perhaps nowhere does the presumption of a positive linear relationship between PI and RGO stand out in such stark relief as in the controversy over transracial adoptions. In the late 1960s and early 1970s, as Blacks re-joiced in the swirl of nigrescence, a clarity and consensus about the mean-ing of being Black helped mold Black opinion on certain social policy is-sues. Having apparently been *restored* to a state of mental health through nigrescence, Black adults sought ways to codify and institutionalize their revitalization and metamorphosis. Nothing seemed more at odds with this trend than the fact of white Americans adopting Black children. Surely such children would come to prefer white to Black, the racial-preference pattern *documented* as being at the heart of the self-hating Negro identity, and over which many Blacks had only recently triumphed. In this sense, opposition in the Black community toward the transracial adoption of Black children was as much a logical extension of traditional research literature on Negro self-hatred as the perceived effects of psychological nigrescence. Opposition was articulated by a number of scholars (Chestang 1972; Chimenzie 1975; Jones 1972), and in the early 1970s it became the official policy of the National Association of Black Social Workers (NABSW) to oppose the placement of Black children in white homes. The organized opposition resulted in a pre-cipitous decline in such adoptions, but there is more to the story. The trans-racial adoption issue provided a forum through which members of NABSW and progressive whites were able to attack, and for the most part diminish, the institutionalized policies of formal adoption agencies that inhibited, and in some cases practically made impossible, the placement of Black children in Black homes. Thus, at the same time that transracial adoption of Black children declined, inracial placement increased dramatically. Moreover, in agencies that continued to support transracial adoptions, the debate resulted in more careful placement and follow-up policies and procedures.

Although the whole affair has probably produced more positive than negative consequences, some observers were greatly concerned about the exaggerated and perhaps unfounded negative assumptions associated with transracial adoptions. Although such adoptions present unique challenges, many saw these challenges as warranting more than a categorical rejection of transracial adoption. Besides, by the mid 1970s, advances that had facili-tated inracial adoptions were still not servicing all the Black children in need of placement. Since no one on either side of the debate was in doubt about the negative effects on children of growing up in nonpermanent ar-rangements, the pressure to reopen transracial placement steadily in-creased.

Partly because of the pressure to relegitimize transracial adoptions, research on the effects of such adoptions began to be conducted more fre-quently by 1975. Those who opposed transracial adoptions predicted that research would show transracially adopted Black children with a higher incidence of pathology than those who were inracially adopted (low self-esteem, damaged personalities), as measured by PI devices (self-concept scales, personality measures); and a greater propensity to identify as, or prefer, white on racial-preference and racial-attitude measures (i.e., an out-group RGO pattern). Embedded in these negative predictions is the Lewinian notion that PI and RGO are correlated. Furthermore, opponents of transracial adoption seem to think it impossible for adoption agencies to develop screening procedures that can effectively identify white parents who can reasonably be expected to raise healthy Black children (Allen 1976).

From another vantage point, those arguing in favor of transracial adoptions believe that agencies already have efficacious screening and placement procedures and that Black children, properly placed, should show normal personality and self-esteem patterns (PI outcomes). Advocates have often neglected or been timid about RGO effects, but implied in their stance has been the notion that transracial adoption does not automatically lead to (racial) self-hatred or "in-group racial rejection" (in the heat of debate, there has been a tendency for both sides to exaggerate their positions).

For those who believe PI and RGO are one and the same, the results of studies on transracial adoption have been contradictory or confusing, with some studies claiming no overall ill effects for Black children raised in white homes and others pointing to possible damage and pathology. Yet, when one determines whether self-concept or personality was measured with a PI or an RGO outcome, the contradictions and confusions give way to plausible results that provide added weight to the notion that PI and RGO are different components of self-concept or personality.

Assessing the effects of adoption through a PI measure *only*, one of the most extensive longitudinal studies found little evidence that PI damage in Black children resulted from transracial adoption (Feigelman and Silverman 1984; Silverman and Feigelman 1981). In 1975, a large-scale survey of adopting white parents was conducted. Although the survey focused originally on transracial adoption involving foreign-born children, Silverman (1980) isolated a subsample of 153 white households, 56 of which adopted Black children and 97 that adopted white children. The data set allowed for the construction of a four-item child's maladjustment index. In their first report on the children, Silverman and Feigelman (1981) found that after controlling for the age at which a child was adopted, there was no difference in the reported incidence of maladjustment between the two groups of children. In a follow-up study conducted when many of the children were adolescents, the same results prevailed (Feigelman and Silverman 1984). As an aside, we should note that in the literature reviews for both articles, Silverman and Feigelman do a commendable job of summarizing both the PI- and RGO-related objections to transracial adoption. This is followed by the report of no ill effects on their PI-related maladjustment index. But they then discuss their results "as if" a comprehensive analysis of both the PI and RGO effects of transracial adoption had been conducted. For the record, their effort, although an important and controversial one, helps clarify the effects of transracial adoption on the PI but *not* the RGO component of the adoptee's personality or self-concept.

The findings of Feigelman and Silverman do not stand in isolation. Of the transracial adoption studies employing a clear-cut measure of one or more PI dimensions (self-esteem, behavior adjustment, level of psycho-pathology, etc.), the overall trend has been to show no difference in the PI profile for Black children involved in transracial compared to inracial adoptions (Grow and Shapiro 1974; Heacock and Cummingham 1977; McRoy 1981; McRoy et al. 1982; Shireman and Johnson 1981, 1986; Simon and Alstein 1977, 1981). The proportion of transracially adopted children showing behavioral and personality problems or deficits is apparently no higher than that to be found in all children experiencing adoption, and this holds true for young as well as adolescent adoptees.

Within the rigid framework of traditional theory on Black identity, one would expect that since transracially and inracially adopted Black children have similar PI characteristics, the same should hold for their RGO, or "level of Blackness," pattern. What has been discovered does not confirm such simple theorizing. Heacock and Cunningham (1977) found no difference in self-esteem and psychopathology between transracially and inracially adopted Black children, but the two groups did show differences on RGO, with Black children reared in white families showing a tendency to view Blackness and Black skin more negatively than Black children reared in Black families. In contrast, Simon and Altstein (1977), who also reported average PI levels in their sample, could find no evidence of a white prefer-ence and a white-oriented identity in young transracially adopted Black chil-dren. Complicating the picture still further are the results of a longitudinal study by Shireman and Johnson (1981). They found that at age four, not only did a group of transracially adopted Black children evidence positive per-sonality adjustment (PI pattern) but their RGO profile, as measured by the Clark Doll Test, was "stronger" and more "Black oriented" than that of peers being reared in Black homes! The children were again tested at age eight (Shireman and Johnson 1986); as before, their PI profile was not a distinguishing factor, with about 78 percent of each group showing excellent-to-good adjustment. On measures of Blackness, the big change was among inracial adoptees, who moved from a white orientation at age four to a Black preference pattern at age eight. Shireman and Johnson have never reported a correlation for their PI and RGO measures; however, in analyzing the age-eight data set, they did indicate that the proportion of children experiencing adjustment problems clearly related to racial identity issues was the same for each group (20 percent of the transracial group and 19 percent of the inracial children).

Taken together, these studies play havoc with traditional assumptions about the relationship of PI and RGO in the dynamics of Black identity. If the response of the Black children gives any indication of the socialization schemes pursued by their white adopted parents, a variety of racial identity (RGO) strategies have accompanied successful methods of inculcating high levels of personal esteem (PI). Were PI and RGO highly correlated, the range of racial identity options leading to personal happiness for any Black child, let alone those in transracial circumstances, would be narrow. Yet even the identity patterns associated with inracially adopted Black children contest this assumption. Recall that on the Shireman and Johnson longitudinal study, the Black children reared in Black communities by Black parents displayed identity variability at ages four and eight that did not translate into PI variation. At age four, inracially compared to transracially reared Black children had dramatically lower Blackness scores, although the two groups did not differ in their PI profiles, both of which were positive. The inracially reared children achieved much higher identity scores at age eight, but there was no proportionate increase in the indices for their PI adjustment, as would be called for by traditional theory.

The social policy latitude suggested by these results should not be misinterpreted as an "anything goes" in transracial adoptions, for the social contract between white adopting parents and Black children extends to the Black community. The reasonable sectors of the Black community have a moral right and obligation to ask of adopting white parents that which it asks of Black parents: Bring up Black children who show no signs of extreme alienation from Black people and Black culture. As children reared in racially mixed family settings, transracially adopted children can be expected to experience some degree of estrangement from Blackness, much as currently happens to the children of the Black middle class or as seen in the attitudes and perceptions of poor Black children toward Blacks who live "outside" the community. Certainly, too, transracially adopted Black children can be expected to be more bicultural than categorically Black oriented,[6] and given the demographics of transracial adoptions, they will probably become middle class.

Being middle class, bicultural, and mildly estranged are consequences one should gladly exchange for the pathology, poverty, and lack of hope similar children might experience if left in nonpermanent-care arrangements. Nevertheless, extreme racial alienation must be avoided, and that can best be achieved if adopting white parents follow the recommendations offered by McRoy, Zurcher, Lauderdale, and Anderson (1984). They ask adopting white parents to (1) live in or near racially mixed environments; (2) encourage a good mix of opposite-and same-race friendships for their adopted Black child; (3) demonstrate on a daily basis the acceptance of Black people in general, not simply the target child; (4) sustain an interracial and bicultural lifestyle for the family as a whole; and (5) enroll the child in a racially mixed public or private school.

As for those who remain categorically opposed to transracial adoptions, it must be recognized that the theoretical basis for such opposition has been tested and found wanting. In the dynamics of Black identity, PI and RGO are not rigidly structured in such a fashion as to preclude the

---

6. Johnson, Shireman, and Watson (1987) found that the proportion of transracially adopted children receiving high Black-oriented scores on racial self-identification and racial preference was lower than that achieved by Black children adopted by parents of the same race. These patterns reflect positive and culturally functional strategies tailored to meet the needs of each group. The transracially situated children are learning to live and function in a familial and community setting that is racially mixed; consequently, their preference patterns should not be expected to be categorically Black. A healthy adjustment would be a (bicultural) neutral preference pattern that is devoid of anti-Black sentiments or extreme pro-white attitudes. But the combination of a positive Black self-image and a balanced or bicultural racial-preference pattern would mean that the proportion of transracially adopted Black children with matching high Black self-identity and racial preference scores whould be *low*. And this is exactly what the authors reported. The children raised in Black communities also must master certain bicultural skills and attitudes, and they must struggle against developing anti-white attitudes, let alone anti-Black sentiments. But their greater familiarity and intimacy with Black ethnicity should result in higher Black preferences. Thus, in addition to a high score on Black self-identification, a larger percentage of the inracially adopted Black children should produce matching high scores on Black preference measures. Again, this is what Johnson, Shireman, and Watson found. In effect, both groups were very much on target with regard to the different racial identity matrix each must develop for a healthy adjustment, although, as Watson pointed out, the continued adjustment of the transracially adopted children may be in jeopardy. Many transracial families in the study started out living in racially mixed communities, but 80 percent reported having moved to all-white locations, which could lead to alienation rather than biculturalism.

possibility of sensitive and carefully screened white parents rearing Black children, any more than there are theoretical grounds against Black parents rearing white children.[7] As the evidence continues to build, there seems to be no scientific basis for opposing transracial adoptions. What is needed is more research, such as that by McRoy et al. (1984), which strives to identify factors that differentiate successful and less successful transracial adoptions. Every attempt should be made to place all children inracially, but research, not ideology, should dictate decisions about transracial placement.

----

7. Black "nannies" raising white children is not restricted to the South. See the article on nannies in New York City by Kathy Dobie, "Black women, white kids: A tale of two worlds," *Village Voice* January 12, 1988, 20–27.

IIIIIII

CHAPTER 4

Issues of Imposition, Self-Hatred, and Celebration

In the early 1950s, Kenneth Clark and his associates announced that the average Black American suffered from low self-esteem, self-hatred, and anti-Blackness. This conclusion was based primarily on empirical evidence garnered from one kind of investigation of the Black psyche: studies of reference group orientation (RGO). Some forty years later, the scenario repeated itself. At the 1987 Convention of the American Psychological Association (APA), a young scholar who had replicated the Clark Doll Test on a group of preschool Black and white children reported that Black children continued to exhibit tendencies toward self-hatred (Powell-Hopson 1985). As in earlier studies, Powell-Hopson's study presented not one scintilla of PI information to support her contention that doll preference predicted mental health. A thorough reading of Powell-Hopson's (1985) dissertation, on which her APA presentation was based, reveals that she referenced, and thus was presumably informed about, Harriette McAdoo, Judith Porter, and others who recommended that one should avoid conducting a univariate study on the identity of Black children—especially one driven only by RGO data—since the general public is likely to misinterpret simple color preference for mental health. (Many Black as well as white Americans know of the connection between the earlier doll tests and the 1954 U.S. Supreme Court *Brown* v. *Board of Education* decision on school desegregation; consequently, it will take years of reeducation before the general public becomes aware of the limited predictive validity of color preference for self-esteem.) Nevertheless, Powell-Hopson conducted her study using only the Doll Test.

She maximized the discovery of a white preference in all children by using one of the most commercially successful dolls in the history of toy manufacturing—the Cabbage Patch Doll. Though it comes in both a Black and a white version, the doll given most prominence in the manufacturer's advertising campaigns was the white doll; thus it constituted one of the least stimulus-neutral dolls ever employed in a racial-preference study. As many Black parents have discovered, Black children, on being given the Black doll, very often come to like "it," but they often long for the "real" doll.

Powell-Hopson's discovery of a white preference in Black children exploded in the media, in part because of the fortieth anniversary of the Clarks' doll study. Besides being featured in stories in the *New York Times, Newsweek*, and *Time*, Powell-Hopson made several television appearances, including one on "Tony Brown's Journal." The Brown show played like a fantasy. Here were what appeared to be a fairly normal group of Black people driving themselves into a neurotic fit over a carefully crafted discussion of the "deeper meaning" of color preference in preschool Black and white children. The audience was told that at the beginning of the study the children preferred "white" (*gasp!*), but the story had a happy ending (*applause*) because Powell-Hopson's intervention produced a turnaround, and at the conclusion of the study, the Black children preferred the Black doll (*hurray!*). The children were described as having been brought to a better "mental state and outlook" by developing a Black preference. As in any good Ishmael Reed plot, a choice piece of information was hardly mentioned: Assuming for a moment that the mental health of the Black children was improved by the intervention, the same logic would lead us to conclude that Powell-Hopson's study was the first experimentally to induce self-hatred in whites, since the majority of the white children responded to the intervention with a Black preference! The Brown television show ended with applause and congratulations to Powell-Hopson and her associates for an informative and "important" study; the Ishmael Reed version would have ended with a cluster of white parents storming the stage to explain why they were suing Hofstra University and Dr. Powell-Hopson for having taught their (white) children to hate themselves.

The fact is, had every single Black child in the earlier Clark or the more recent Powell-Hopson study selected "white," this would be no more an automatic indication of cultural pathology or poor mental health in Black children than would the color and cultural preferences of Black adults predict their level of self-esteem. For example, is anyone willing to suggest that Debbie Thomas, the world figure skating champion, should be viewed as a self-hating Black woman because she enjoys participating in a traditionally "white" sport? Are Leontyne Price, Jessye Norman, Kathleen Battle, or Andre Watts too white oriented and thus self-hating because each excels at a European art form? Since Jesus Christ is generally depicted as "white," does being a Black Christian reflect self-hatred rather than acculturation? If color preference can mean pathology as well as evidence of acculturation or assimilation, how does one know when the former and not the latter is indicated by a white preference among Blacks? As to whites, can anyone demonstrate that color preference will help differentiate a group of self-hating, anti-Semitic, anti-Black white men from a group of white men of normal mental attributes raised in an all-white town in Wyoming? In a color-preference test, both groups will probably prefer white; with no additional information, the two groups cannot be differentiated.

Explaining the Low Correlation

At least four factors can help explain why the mental health characteristics of Blacks, including any propensity toward self-hatred, are not, and have never been, easily predicted by measures of racial identity:

1. The limited generalizability of results of racial-preference studies conducted with 3- and 4-year-old children

2. The effects of Black biculturalism, acculturation, and assimilation on Black monoracial preference trends in racial identity experiments

3. The problem of interpreting the meaning and salience of racial preference and racial identity for Black adults operating with a multiple reference group orientation

4. The historical failure of students and scholars of racial identity to differentiate between concepts and measures of ascriptive RGO and concepts and measures of self-defined RGO

Regarding point 1, I argue that researchers have been far too eager to make generalizations about the development of Black identity across the life span based on research limited to preschool children. Preschool racial preferences are extremely unreliable and provide a weak foundation for life-span projections. Points 2, 3, and 4 are interrelated in that each challenges the major premise guiding most racial identity studies, the "monoracial thesis." Researchers have attempted to study the presence or absence of an "in-group" or same-race reference group orientation in Blacks. Thus, whether in the doll preferences of children or the racial attitudes of adults, Blacks have been expected to exhibit a same-race (monoracial) preference and/or attitudinal pattern. Yet bicultural tendencies in Black children (point 2) and multiple reference group orientations in Black adults (point 3) call into question whether a monoracial thesis should ever have been the major hypothesis guiding Black identity studies. As a further extension of points 2 and 3, note in point 4 that "race" is not always the most salient dimension of the reference group orientation of mentally healthy Black people. In such instances, the monoracial thesis is clearly inappropriate.

RACIAL-PREFERENCE STUDIES AND PRESCHOOL CHILDREN

Far too much of the discourse on the mental health characteristics of Blacks across the life span has been premised on the group-identity information generated from Black preschool children. There is reason to believe that the group identity preferences of extremely young children cannot predict their future racial-preference patterns, let alone their ongoing or future general personality dynamics. This was evident even in the earliest racial-preference studies. Recall that the so-called out-group, or white orientation, that Clark and Clark (1947) recorded for their subsample of three and four year olds "disappeared" in their subsample of six and seven year olds. This pattern held for the Doll Test (Clark and Clark 1947) and the Draw-a-Person task (Clark and Clark 1950). Even if one could find evidence of a strong relationship between PI and RGO during Black adolescence and Black adulthood, the racial attitudes and preferences of Black children younger than four or five years of age would give us little insight into future trends. Studies by Alejandro-Wright (1985), Semaj (1980), Spencer (1982), and Markovics (1974) suggest that it is an intellectual absurdity to ground a discussion of Blackness across the life span on the uninformed, naive, and cognitively inconsistent and unstable racial-preference (i.e., group identity) choices of Black preschoolers.

Aside from an overreliance on information gleaned from preschoolers, students and scholars of racial identity have sought to confirm a "monoracial" conception of the "healthy Black racial identity" that seems far removed from the textured racial identity found in Black adults and, to a lesser degree, in Black children.

MONORACIAL PREFERENCE AND BICULTURAL COMPETENCE

Whether measured by doll preferences in children or various attitude scores in adults, the mentally healthy developmental pattern for Black and white racial identity across the life span has been a same-race, or monoracial, reference group orientation. This standard is generally based on the presumed mentally healthy racial attitudes found in whites; especially in racial-preference studies, white children have traditionally exhibited a white-oriented, monoracial preference pattern. Conversely, an attraction to "White" in Black children is thought to be "problematic," and Eurocentric cultural preferences in Black adults are viewed with suspicion. Judging from recent studies by Powell-Hopson and Hopson (1988) and Gopaul-McNicol (1986), the monoracial thesis first articulated by Ruth Horowitz and Kenneth and Mamie Clark is alive and well in racial-preference studies currently conducted with Black and white children.

Evidence is accumulating that Black children are reared to be *biculturally competent*. That is, they are brought up to be attracted to, appreciative of, and capable of functioning in both Black and white "worlds." White children, in contrast, are more likely to see the world in monoracial terms. Differences in socialization strategies, and the implications such strategies have for predicting racial preferences in children, were the focus of a study I conducted a few years ago (Cross 1983).

My study focused on bicultural and monoracial themes in the everyday activities of young, urban, middle- and lower-class Black and white mothers from single and couple households. Each mother in the study had at least one child, two and a half to three and a half years old, and the target children included an equal number of boys and girls. A series of in-depth interviews provided detailed information about the cultural and racial characteristics of key people (i.e., the social network) in the lives of these mothers and their children. In addition to social-network data, and as part of the study of a typical day in the life of a mother and her child, a content analysis of the everyday activities of each family was conducted to determine the extent to which white and Black mothers raised their children to be aware that the world consisted of people of different cultures and races. Each mother was asked to describe the stories told or read to her child, the magazines the child was allowed to see and play with, the radio music or records listened to when the child was playing nearby, the history behind the child's name and nickname, the events (e.g., movies, plays, church programs) recently attended with the child, what was considered before purchasing the child's toys, the child's favorite television shows, and the subjects emphasized in everyday conversations with the child. Along with the everyday activities, data were collected on the number of Black and white dolls or, with little boys, Black and white human figures found in the child's possession.

The content analysis of commonplace child-related activities suggested that white mothers did not seem to be cueing their children toward a biracial or multicultural world view. The white mothers were not explicitly white oriented or racist; the process revealed was one of omission rather than commission. The white mothers simply gave little indication that some of a child's everyday activities could be used as vehicles to increase the child's awareness that the world consists of people who are different in appearance, behavior, and culture. In the white homes, television was the primary way the white three year olds discovered the existence of people of color. In addition, it was found that the average white mother's social network consisted almost entirely of white people.

On average, 21 percent of the activities described by the Black mothers had an explicitly Black culture base, while 79 percent reflected a general American or white frame. The doll count produced a much higher Black ratio; typically, about 41 percent of the dolls found in Black homes were Black and 38 percent were white (the rest were neither black nor white). This suggested that the Black child was being steered toward becoming biculturally competent. The cultural competence emphasized depended on the specific nature of an activity. For example, religious activities and musical events had a decidedly Black orientation, the doll count showed that mothers depicted the world as consisting of both Black and white people, and the overall emphasis of Black mothers was the communication of information about the white world. This last point was somewhat misleading. While it was true that, generally speaking, the Black households stressed white cultural information (79 percent) over Black information (21 percent), both kinds of information were being communicated by *Black* people. The social network of both the single- and two-parent Black households were overwhelmingly Black, and it was unlikely that the Blacks in these networks were passing on information about the white world to the Black children without first filtering its racist content. Thus the Black three year olds in the study were probably informed about the Black and white worlds from a *Black* perspective. This is not to suggest that a Black nationalistic frame was the filter applied. Few children had African names; most of the oral bedtime stories or books used to read to the children, with the exception of magazines, were white-oriented; and few mothers stressed activities that promoted a very conscious sense of Blackness in their children.

At the conclusion of the study, I pointed out that if one used the information generated by the social-network and content analysis to predict racial-preference patterns in Black and white children, it would be reasonable to assume that the two groups of children would "play back" reality in a manner similar to the way in which reality had been presented to them. A categorical same-race preference would be predicted for whites as a group, and a "split," or dual, pattern for Blacks as a group. Such patterns would show the ontogeny of a white-oriented monoracial reference group orientation in whites, and a biracial reference group orientation or bicultural competence in Blacks.

Though it was not necessarily their intent, a study by Banks and Rompf (1973) resulted in a rather dramatic display of Black biculturalism. They asked a group of Black and white children seven to eight years old, to view the performance of two players (one Black, one white) in a ball-tossing game. Each game consisted of 5 trials for which the outcomes were controlled: (1) White wins by small margin; (2) white wins by large margin, (3) Black wins by small margin; (4) Black wins by large margin; (5) one trial ends in a tie. The trials were randomized and the race of the experimenter was balanced. After each trial, a child was instructed to reward the winner by placing from 0 (zero) to 15 pieces of candy in a container. After a game was completed, the child also indicated a choice for overall winner. Consistent with past research, white children showed a preference for the white player by rewarding him more for his performance across all trials, and by more often selecting him as the overall winner. Although Black children showed a preference for the white player by rewarding him more often after each trial, the same Black children showed a preference for the Black player by choosing him significantly more times as the overall winner. To repeat, the same Black children exhibited a Black or white preference, depending on the cultural implications of the task they were evaluating, suggesting, of course, the operation of a bicultural frame of reference.

It is sometimes overlooked that in the famous self-esteem study by Rosenberg and Simmons (1971), they noted the operation of a dual reference group orientation in Black children. They found that Black children had as high (or higher) a level of self-esteem as that found in whites, even though the Black children also showed a clear-cut preference for light skin. And yet, 73 percent of the Black children (65 percent for the whites) said that they were very good-looking or pretty good-looking. In fact, the Black children were even more enthusiastic about their looks than the white children were. In response to these findings, Rosenberg and Simmons (1971) noted the following:

> Why are Black children at least as likely as Whites to consider themselves good-looking? We have seen that Blacks show a clear preference for the White physical model, a model from which they depart obviously more than do Whites. How, then, can one explain their relatively high degree of satisfaction with their looks?
>
> It appears to us that what has been generally ignored in discussions of the matter is the point of reference, the basis of comparison. Whatever the ideal physical model, Blacks probably evaluate themselves relative to one another and not relative to Whites. Their own racial subgroup is probably their "comparison reference group," serving individuals as their standards or checkpoint for self-evaluations. Thus, the Blacks may admire the White Anglo-Saxon type and judge the attractiveness of other Blacks to the degree that they approximate this model, but it is likely that they compare their own looks with that of other Blacks. (p. 47)

Biculturalism in Blacks has extremely important implications for how one scores and interprets racial-preference tasks or tests. To the extent that monoracial trends can be expected of white children, it is equally true that Black biculturalism should act to blunt the level of monoracialism that Black children will exhibit on similar tasks. For example, Johnson (1983) found that comparing the aggregate score of Black and white children on a popular racial-preference test was very misleading. More revealing was the ratio of Black to white preferences made to positively worded forced-choice items. The white children in her sample tended to select white, resulting in a monadic white-preference set. Black children, in contrast, tended to show a split pattern, indicating a preference for both Black and white. In scoring only for the same-race pattern, the device was stacked against the Black child who tended to be bicultural. The Black child's lower aggregate score was not a function of same-race rejection; it resulted, instead, from having an attraction to both choices. It is interesting to note that this "multiple anchor point notion" corresponds to a variety of constructs used to describe the Black perspective: "double consciousness" (DuBois 1903), "double vision" (Wright 1953), "bicultural" (Valentine 1971), "diunital" (Dixon and Foster 1971), and "multidimensional" (Cross 1978b).

MONORACIAL PREFERENCE AND MULTIPLE REFERENCE GROUP ORIENTATIONS

If the unaccounted-for biculturalism of Black children can cause interpretive problems for investigators who presume that Black children should display same-race monoracial preferences, the inherent flaw in the monoracial thesis becomes even more acute when applied to Black adults. Living in a modern, urban, complex, highly technological, and stratified society, adult Black Americans, and in general most adult Americans, develop reference group orientations that are multifaceted, layered, and flexible. Different situations may call for different roles, priorities, and multiple allegiances. In the typical "racial identity" experiment, for which monoracialism is the focus, the resulting low correlation between monoracialism and self-esteem may reflect, in part, the investigator's failure to identify all the reference groups that feed into the person's self-esteem matrix. Thus some people may score low on Blackness (RGO) and low on self-esteem (PI), while other subjects from the same experiment may show a low Blackness score but high self-esteem when the high self-esteem is related to a reference group affiliation not explored in the experiment. When the investigator submits such data to correlational analysis, the scores from the two kinds of subjects cancel each other, and the result is "no correlation" between self-esteem and group identity.

EXPERIMENTER-ASCRIBED VERSUS SUBJECT-AFFIRMED GROUP IDENTITY

In discussing the finding that PI and RGO may not be correlated, my associates in the field of clinical psychology noted one implication that seemed to contradict their experiences with normal as well as highly troubled clients. On the one hand, they agreed that having a particular group identity was associated with neither high nor low levels of mental health. They could readily recall instances of people who shared a common world view but whose intrapsychic worlds were vastly different—some being conflicted and vulnerable, others being interpersonally competent and less troubled. On the other hand, no matter what a person's level of self-esteem (as a case in point), whether average or below average, that person's sense of being and meaning in life seemed to be intimately anchored with a particular group or groups. Thus the clinicians were perplexed by the implication of correlational studies of PI and RGO that suggested that social anchorage and a sense of connectedness were not a common dynamic in the group identity and general mental health of Black people and, by inference, were an unnecessary element in the general human condition.

There is a fundamental difference between the way in which clinicians and empiricists operationalize the term group identity (RGO). *In clinical settings*, the subject's RGO is the object of discovery. Acting like an anthropologist, the clinician comes to know a specific person's reference group orientation through an analysis of that person's phenomenological world view. The client's self-defined RGO is a part of his or her "interior psychological space," "cognitive map," or "mental mazeway" that is generally not apparent and must be communicated, revealed, or discovered. It is the object of inquiry, not imposition or designation, and ultimately should be viewed as a highly personal affirmation. We can refer to the person's personally affirmed group identity as the personal RGO.

In the experimental setting, just the opposite procedure is taken. Group identity, or RGO, becomes an imposed rather than self-defined entity. RGO is a societal, sociological, and often demographically derived construct that is ascribed to the subject by the experimenter. The experimenter "sees" that the subject is "physically" Black and presumes, therefore, that Blackness is, or ought to be, the subject's self-defined or personally affirmed group identity. This imposed RGO, based on the experimenter's definition of what is important, can be called ascriptive group identity, or ascriptive RGO. Most, if not all, Black group identity studies have been studies of ascriptive RGO masquerading as studies of personal RGO. In Black identity studies, the salience of race is used as a benchmark of "mental health." Blacks who make race highly salient are said to have a high and positive Black group identity; those who do not, a low and negative one.

But race *need not* be the most salient dimension of a Black person's personally affirmed group identity. Some Blacks make religion, sexual preference, social class, economic status, or being an American more salient than race (Little 1981). Such people, confronted with the limited monoracial, either/or choices of most racial identity tasks, may score "low" on Black identity as a way of trying to communicate that Blackness has low, as opposed to "no," salience to their personal RGO (i.e., their low scores reflect low salience, not anti-Blackness.)[1] Consequently, a low score on a Black identity task, may not, in and of itself, predict the absence of an identity or the operation of low self-esteem.

Elsewhere, Urry (1973) has emphasized that the concept of reference group was developed to help account for the fact that an actor may manifest attitudes generally associated with a group of which the actor is not a member. Urry has further stated that "it is because of man's ability through symbols, language and communication to take on the role of the other that he is able to orient himself to groups other than those with which he is directly and continuously implicated" (p. 18). In a similar fashion, Teeland (1971) has pointed out the following:

> The focus is no longer just on the objective affiliation or public definition of the subject as a member of a particular group or class. Consideration must also be given to the degree to which persons actually identify themselves with the social category in question. It is possible, for example, for everyone to describe a subject (ex. a Black man) as a member a certain group or culture (ex. Black society), but that group may have little effect on his attitudes or ideas. As a matter of fact, the group to which the subject aspires and from which he adopts a perspective can be a group to which few others would classify him as a member (for example White society). (p. 15)

The distinctions to be made between ascriptive RGO, personal RGO, biculturalism, and multiple reference group orientation have been captured in a brilliantly conceived and carefully executed dissertation by Johnson (1981). Johnson studied the psychological characteristics (mental health and self-esteem) and reference group orientation of 51 Black men. All the men were gay. Thirty-one of the Black homosexuals maintained primary identity in terms of their race/ethnic culture and were classified as Black identified. In effect, their self-defined and ascriptive group identities were one and the same. Twenty of the Black homosexuals shared with the first group the same ascriptive group identity in that they were Black; their primary identification, or personally affirmed group identity, however, was that of being gay. Johnson classified them as "gay identified." The two groups were fairly

---

1. For most measures of Blackness employed to date, one typically cannot determine, without additional information, whether a low score reflects lack of salience or anti-Blackness.

well matched for age, education, and income. For this in-depth study, each subject was given ten psychological measures (psychosomatic complaints, happiness, exuberance, self-acceptance, loneliness, depression, tension, paranoia, suicidal feelings and impulses, acceptance of professional help), and eight reference group or social measures (interactions with homosexuals, acceptance of homosexuality, interactions with Blacks, racial esteem [i.e., attitudes toward Blacks], interactions with whites, attitude toward whites, attitudes toward overt expressions of homosexuality in general, attitudes toward overt expressions of familial homosexuality).

Johnson found minimal mental health differences between the two groups. The Black-identified men were somewhat more likely to accept the value of professional help than were the gay-identified men. Since it would be easy to argue that this variable reflects more a social or RGO attitude than a PI variable, one could say that none of the relevant PI variables differentiated the two groups. Though statistically insignificant, the higher suicidal impulse score for the Black-identified men deserves comment. While none of the gay-identified men had, or rarely admitted having, suicidal thoughts, a modest number of Black-identified men did admit to an occasional struggle with such tendencies. Thus their higher score could suggest a more realistic attitude on that particular scale, not a higher propensity toward suicidal thoughts. In any event, on all the other measures, such as self-acceptance, happiness, depression, and loneliness, the scores for both groups were remarkably similar. In other words, having different personally affirmed group identities (personal RGO) neither enhanced nor negatively affected personal adjustment. Stated in a slightly different fashion, each personal RGO was equally efficacious in helping members of the two groups achieve comparable levels of mental health; consequently, there was no apparent relationship between *type* of personally affirmed group identity and mental health (PI). This suggests that the mentally healthy person has some reference group or groups to which he or she is anchored, but one's emotional health does not require that it be the reference group to which one is publicly ascribed. Thus, ascriptive RGO may show a weak relationship to personal identity, but perhaps personal identity and personal RGO are highly correlated.

Johnson did record important differences between the gay- and Black-identified groups on various social, or RGO, measures. The gay-identified Black men were more likely to live in the gay community, tended to have white lovers, and felt comfortable and welcomed in the gay community and uncomfortable and mildly estranged from the Black community. The gay-identified men felt less inhibited about public displays of affection toward their male friends and lovers.

A very different picture evolved for the Black-identified gays. For them, being Black was highly salient to their private and public life. They enjoyed living and partaking in the traditional aspects of the Black community; most of their friends were Black, as were their lovers; and in line with their Black allegiance, they felt estranged from the predominantly white gay community. Given the salience of Black traditionalism to their lives, it should come as no surprise that the Black-identified gays preferred private displays of affection between gays and even felt uncomfortable with public displays of affection.

In summary, then, to the extent the two personally affirmed group identities were linked to PI profiles that were indistinguishable, it was equally true that being a gay- or Black-identified person resulted in a number of important differences across an array of social, cultural, and political propensities. Johnson's results are consistent with a major literature review recently completed by Cross, Parham, and Helms (in press) in which it was found that the difference between Blacks with limited versus advanced levels of Black identity development was not in the area of PI, but in various correlates of RGO, such as racial self-image, attitudes toward one's ascriptive group, choice of organizational membership, and ideology. That is to say, Black people operating from the perspective of the traditional Negro may differ radically from Blacks guided by the "new" Black identity insofar as cultural values, artistic preferences, political propensities, social preferences, and world view are concerned, but be undifferentiated across measures of self-esteem, anxiety, personal worth, happiness, contentment, depression, and the rest. Thus the significance of reference group orientation (RGO) or ideology or nationalism or group identity may rest not so much in a capacity to create, change, or enhance elements of personality but in a capacity to bring about consensus, unity, or a sense of peoplehood among a group of people who, individually speaking, represent a broad range of personalities, self-concepts, and levels of self-esteem.

Before leaving the Johnson study, let us imagine what might have resulted had Johnson approached the two groups of Black men in a more traditional manner. He might have been content to administer either a self-esteem (PI) or a Black identity measure (RGO), but certainly not both. In administering only a Black identity device, he would have (correctly) recorded that one group was Black identified, but several of his more predictable inferences would have been incorrect. He would have suggested that the Black-identified group probably had high self-esteem, while the men scoring low on Blackness might have been labeled as suffering from low self-esteem, or self-hatred. Had he begun, instead, with a self-esteem (PI) measure, he would have (correctly) recorded that both groups had adequate levels of self-esteem, but he would have been incorrect in inferring that both were high in Black identity development. Had he administered both kinds of devices, he still would not have discovered the personally affirmed group identity of the gay-identified Black men, nor would he have recorded that being gay was also an important element in the life of the Black-identified gay men. But, of course, Johnson did not miss any of these points, for in conceptualizing the experience of Blacks as multidimensional, layered, and inherently complex, he brought us closer to the rich texture that was as true of Black life in the past as it is today.

As made clear by the Johnson study, Black people have achieved personal happiness through a variety of group identities (i.e., Blacks differ on the salience of being Black); thus, Black identity is not predictive of personal self-esteem or personal happiness, but it is predictive of a particular cultural—political propensity, frame of reference, or world view. PI, while not predictive of the content of a person's RGO, is predictive of ego strength, mental health, and interpersonal competence. One could be neurotic (PI) and have a Black or a traditional (Negro) identity; or one could be "normal" and have either identity. PI tells us something about the mental health of a person, independent of the content of his or her group identity. RGO data tell us a great deal about a person's world view, independent of the personality to which that world view is attached. Thus each sector is capable of predicting extremely important factors, but each is a very poor predictor of the other.

Forgotten Studies of Black Identity: Overlooked Themes

Many factors explain the lack of a relationship between PI and RGO in the study of Black identity, and my discussion does not exhaust the possibilities (Foster and Perry 1982; Logan 1981; Spencer, in press; Teplin 1977). If any single theme cuts across the points raised in this chapter, it is the incredible degree to which presupposition, rather than empirically driven concepts, has dominated past and present thinking. A great deal of the psychological complexity inherent in the Black condition might have been discovered as long ago as the 1940s had the pioneers of the field established a tradition of conducting PI and RGO correlational studies. Their failure to do so may be explained as much by political factors as scientific trends. Certainly Ruth

Horowitz, the Clarks, Kardiner and Ovesey, and anyone else of their era found it difficult to be anything but enchanted with psychoanalysis and the "do it all–analyze it all" capacity of "projective tests." Theirs was the heyday of Freudian psychology, and inkblot and the doll-preference tests were viewed by many as "state of the art" devices. But more so than by an over-reliance on projective theory and techniques, progress in the study of Black-ness was sidetracked by the struggle to defrock "Jim Crow." As noted at the end of Chapter 1, the selection of Kenneth Clark to be the primary "inter-preter" or "filter" of the social scientific literature on Negro identity was part of a very effective strategy aimed at destroying the legal and political system known as segregation. But the testimony one may give in a courtroom is not analogous to a discourse among scientists. Science in the laboratory permits ambiguity and a polyvocal discourse. In the courtroom, a rigid hermeneutic based on adversarial relations applies, so any evidence, scientific or other-wise, is circumscribed by a discourse in search of absolutes: yes or no, true or false, proof of damage or no proof of damage, innocence or guilt. With Clark and the thirty-four social scientists who helped prepare and/or were signatories to the social scientific brief submitted to the Court, their testi-mony and statements had to be convincing within the context of legal pro-ceedings, not a scientific conference.

Unfortunately, the effect of the 1954 Supreme Court desegregation de-cision was the intellectual canonization of the self-hatred thesis. Although based almost entirely on doll studies with preschool children (i.e., inher-ently unreliable RGO evidence), and with only one PI study (i.e., the Kar-diner and Ovesey [1951] "self-hatred" study), Clark's (1955) interpretation that Negroes were typically self-hating—a self-hatred he felt was "easily" recognizable in the youngest and oldest Blacks—became dogma, rather than an opinion subject to social scientific inquiry. As dogma, the self-hatred thesis was characterized by gaps in knowledge, blind spots, and, on occa-sion, intellectual intimidation.

In a few instances, the more normative, celebratory, or non–self-ha-tred themes of Black personality did manage to find expression in studies conducted before the 1954 desegregation decision. Kenneth Clark's mentors at Howard University were Max Meenes and Francis C. Sumner (Bayton 1975; Hentoff 1982; Ross and Bayton 1979), and shortly before Clark entered Howard, Sumner completed a study of the mental health characteristics of Negro college freshmen, the results of which led Sumner to conclude: "It appears that from the combined average symptom-frequencies of 203 Negro college freshmen or of 396 Negro college students investigated altogether that the mental health of Negro and white college students is approximately identical" (Sumner 1931, 575–576).

Max Meenes reported similar findings (Meenes and Bayton 1936), and ten years later, in an article for which Sumner was the second author (Wheatley and Sumner 1946), essentially the same results were obtained with still another group of Negro college students. The studies by Meenes and Sumner that document adequate personal identity development in Blacks were not cited by Kenneth Clark (1955) when he wrote the position paper that eventually was read by the Supreme Court justices, nor was an important racial-preference study conducted by Meltzer (1939). Almost at the same time that Ruth Horowitz was publishing the results of the racial identity study she conducted with 24 preschoolers, Meltzer (1939) was studying the racial and ethnic preferences of Black ($N = 364$) and white ($N = 1,265$) children from the fifth through eighth grades of the St. Louis public school system. A paired-comparison test was used, and 21 different races and nations were represented. The results showed that while whites ranked the Negro twentieth, or next to last, the Negro children ranked their own group first. In fact, in Clark's (1955) Supreme Court paper, one is never given the impression that six years earlier, in 1944 (Clark's first version of the paper was written in 1950), Otto Klineberg, having conducted an exhaustive review of the personality literature, remained unimpressed about any crucial personality differences between Blacks and whites empirically demonstrated in the psychological research conducted between the early 1920s and the early 1940s (Klineberg 1944).

Silencing these dissenting voices through omission had the effect of making the self-hatred theme appear to be unchallenged. It is not that researchers with a different slant stopped writing after the Court's decision (Grossack 1957). Five years after Clark published his Supreme Court brief as a text (Clark 1955), there appeared what should have been heralded as a major revisionist work on Black identity in the form of a study by John H. Rohrer and Munro S. Edmonson, *The Eighth Generation: Cultures and Personalities of New Orleans Negroes*. As the title implies, Rohrer and Edmonson did not believe in a monolithic Black culture or Black personality; rather, they felt that to study Blacks was to encounter cultural and psychological diversity. The sources of their intellectual inspiration were Allison Davids, John Dollard, and Gunnar Myrdal:

> If, as Davids & Dollard argued, the universal experience of caste frustrations cannot be construed as inevitably marking all Negroes with similarly learned psychological responses because

class factors intervene, and if, as Myrdal adds, class factors are
not the only intervening variables, we are left to conclude that
race can have no generic meaning for Negroes: their experiences are too diverse and too diversely perceived. (Rohrer and
Edmonson 1960, 71)

Not surprisingly, the work of Rohrer and Edmonson represented a
very conscious "broadside" of Kardiner and Ovesey's self-hatred thesis. Like
Kardiner and Ovesey, Rohrer and Edmonson relied on the case study
method, but from a description of their methodology, they seem to have
succeeded in controlling for experimenter bias, a factor they felt may well
have contaminated the "mark of oppression" study: "The subtle problems of
objectivity in the treatment of patterns of unconscious motivation are well
known, and constitute a particular hazard of research of the type Kardiner &
Ovesey report" (p. 72).

At the conclusion of their study, Rohrer and Edmonson reported that
the self-hatred thesis was helpful in explaining only a handful of cases. They
even went back and reanalyzed the case studies used by Kardiner and Ovesey and found that the *original* evidence for self-hatred had been exaggerated:

Among our own cases we find individuals who could be used
as evidence to support Kardiner's and Ovesey's thesis, but we
also found some who could not. We see the same picture, in
fact, in Kardiner's and Ovesey's cases: self-hatred is found in
only seven of twenty-five records; five of these were records of
patients in therapy. (p. 72)

Not content with the findings from their case studies, Rohrer and Edmonson also conducted a study of the parental attitudes and socialization
practices of 105 Black women, randomly selected and stratified by social
class. Again they reported that the self-hatred thesis had little explanatory
value.

Near the end of the Rohrer and Edmonson (1960) study, one finds a
statement that could well be used as an epigraph in this book:

One set of experiences of particular interest in our subjects is
that having to do with being Negro. The variety of patterns of
identification we have found correspond to a diversity of "racial" experiences, a great divergence in their evaluation, and a
consequent lack of any universal attitudes toward this common

yet complex experience. The meaning of being Negro for each subject is strongly conditioned by the values associated with his particular role identification, and these in turn determine, at least in part, what his racial attitudes will do to the quality and nature of his psychodynamic consequences. Some individuals may identify with the white aggressor, with a corresponding loss to self-esteem and an unconscious burden of self-hatred. . . . Others may identify with Negroes, . . . without any apparent feeling of self-depreciation. Yet others may "use" a racial identification as they might use small size or a minor illness to excuse inadequacy feelings that have their roots in other experiences. . . . The problems posed by being Negro, like the problems posed by being male or being female, are met in different ways and with differing degrees of adequacy by different individuals, depending on the broader framework of the individual's personality organization and its attendant values. (pp. 305–306)

I have spent some time reviewing Rohrer and Edmonson's work in order to make the following point: For every hundred times one is likely to see the Kardiner and Ovesey "mark of oppression" study cited, one is lucky to find a single reference to the Rohrer and Edmonson study. Kenneth Clark did not cite it in the 1963 edition of *Prejudice and Your Child*, although he did cite *Mark of Oppression*, and this pattern was repeated in the important literature review by Proshansky and Newton (1968). Thomas Pettigrew did cite Rohrer and Edmonson in his important book on the Negro published in 1964; but the paragraph devoted to their work in no way communicated to the reader that the Rohrer and Edmonson text stood as a counterthesis to the self-hatred theme (see Pettigrew 1964, 23).

There are other instances when the self-hatred thesis surely should have been refuted or contested, but authors seemed to be intimidated by the dogma of self-hatred. Thus they searched for "evidence" of self-hatred where it did not exist (see, Butts 1963; Smith 1980) or where it was of little consequence (see, esp., Meyers 1966). While the Smith, Meyers, and Butts studies are not considered to be of great significance, one of the most famous early racial-preference studies was authored by a scholar who also appeared to have been intimidated by the self-hatred dogma.

In 1952, Mary Ellen Goodman published a study that focused on the development of race awareness in young children. Even by today's standards, it remains one of the better studies on the ontogeny of group identity in young children. In almost every instance, Goodman's work has been cited as a univariate study of group identity; however, a careful reading of her text shows that she also collected detailed ratings on 30 general personality traits for each of the 61 Negro and 44 white children in her sample. The personality findings were downplayed, however, appearing only in the appendix at the end of her text. Goodman gave two reasons for discounting the self-identity data. The first was that she had some questions about the reliability and validity of the rating technique, although from the description of her procedures and results, she seems unduly self-critical. Her second reservation about the data is perhaps more revealing. Goodman hesitated to explore the self-identity data fully because, at the time of her publication (1952), the discourse on Negro identity was dominated by Kardiner and Ovesey's thesis of Negro self-hatred (their work, *Mark of Oppression*, appeared in 1951). Despite her reservations, Goodman's data set was superior to the one presented by Kardiner and Ovesey and showed Negro children with self-identity characteristics (general personality traits) that were a far cry from any "self-hatred" model, a model she somewhat signifyingly refers to in the last sentence of her book as the "distinctive personality traits of Negro adults."

> We must conclude that this study does not *establish* significant personality differences between the members of the two racial groups. However, our data do *suggest* that such differences *may* be real. The question whether differences are real, and the related questions concerning their specific nature, intensity, or frequency, are properly matters for another and major investigation. Here we have at least raised what seems to us an important issue, and indicated the possibility that Negro children of four to five show some distinctive personality traits—traits quite out of line with the popular conception of the distinctive personality traits of Negro adults. (Goodman 1952; App. D)

Goodman never correlated her racial-preference and self-identity data. It would be more than twenty years before other researchers would see the need to collect both self-identity and group identity data in studying Black identity.

Had researchers of the 1940s, 1950s, and early 1960s followed through on the implications of the "forgotten" studies, they would have uncovered themes of survival, celebration, cultural vitality, endurance, and outright strength in the everyday psychology of Black Americans. As pointed out in Chapter 1, social scientists of these early years, preoccupied with the image of Richard Wright's Bigger Thomas, seldom considered that anything other than degrees of pathology could be used to depict Blacks. Now we can add that for the few who knew otherwise, many were fearful of studies that would result in a public discussion of Black strengths—"fearful" in the sense that such studies might be used by racists and their apologists as "proof" that Blacks were faring well under a benevolent and well-intended system of economic, political, educational, and social segregation. Hindsight can provide marvelous resolution power. Nevertheless, I do not think it would have required great ingenuity on the part of progressive social scientists of that era to have designed studies that differentiated between the intent of racists to dehumanize and underdevelop Blacks and the ability of Blacks to fashion, out of a matrix of family, friends, and community (Barnes 1972), a sense of self and racial identity that was positive, textured, and three-dimensional by anyone's standards.[2] In such studies, Black informants would probably have stressed the interplay of two realities—one white, hostile but powerful, and thus unavoidable, and the other Black, enigmatic, familiar, too often poor but somehow nourishing—along with an outline of the identity each had forged to negotiate transactions between and within each world. Practically all informants would have confirmed that the "material conditions" commonplace in Bigger Thomas's world also framed their own, but few would have found Bigger's perspective on life or the solutions he applied to be typical of Black identity. From time to time, the respondents would have checked to see that the researchers' notes reflected the totality of the Negro experience and that they were not becoming overly enchanted with any one aspect of the story. Consequently, while understandably proud at having secured an identity that would be becoming to any American, they would remind researchers that it was achieved under difficult circumstances and was not to be romanticized when discussing personal, psychological strengths. Of course, such follow-up studies were never conducted. Rather than risk romanticization, researchers left the story of such informants untold, and the diversity inherent to the study of Black identity went undocumented. I hope their voices, images, and stories find resonance in my work.

2. See, especially, Herbert G. Gutman, *The Black family in slavery and freedom, 1750–1925* (New York: Pantheon Books, 1976); Kathryn L. Morgan, *Children of strangers: The stories of a Black family* (Philadelphia: Temple University Press, 1980); Thomas L. Webber, *Deep like the rivers: Education in the slave quarter community, 1831–1965* (New York: Norton, 1978); Joe William Trotter, Jr., *Black Milwaukee: The making of an industrial proletariat, 1915–1945* (Urbana: University of Illinois Press, 1985); and Dennis Dickerson, *Out of the crucible: Black steelworkers in western Pennsylvania, 1875–1980* (Albany: State University of New York Press, 1986).

Summary of Part One

Part One has presented an overview and reinterpretation of the history of the study of Black identity, covering the years 1939–1968, the period during which the Negro self-hatred thesis evolved, and 1968–1980, the period of nigrescence in which Blacks affirmed the evolution of a "new" Black identity.

We began with the work of two husband-and-wife research teams, Ruth and Eugene Horowitz and Mamie and Kenneth Clark. In the mid to late 1930s, Eugene and, especially, Ruth Horowitz articulated the key theoretical framework and methodological concerns that would guide the study of Negro and Black identity. Ruth Horowitz saw the self-concept as consisting of two domains: a general personality, or personal identity, domain (PI), and a domain of social or racial attitudes that constitute one's group identity, or reference group orientation (RGO). Moreover, Ruth Horowitz assumed that although the two domains were in one sense distinct, each was linked to the other. Thus the nature of one's social attitudes was thought to determine aspects of one's personality, and vice versa. In dealing with ethnic or racial self-concept studies, she thought that the attitudes

Blacks held about being Black determined aspects of their personality or their personal identity structure (PI). PI determined RGO, and RGO determined PI; in the context of empirical research, this would mean that measures of PI and RGO would show a positive linear correlation.

This last point is extremely important. When she conducted what is now recognized as the first empirical study of Negro identity, Ruth Horowitz did *not* measure both PI and RGO; she measured only RGO. Her belief that the two domains were highly correlated became her rationale for measuring only one domain. Employing group identity measures first identified by her husband, Ruth assessed only the RGO of white and Negro preschoolers, but she pointed to anectodal evidence gleaned from the children's behavior and speech during collection of the group identity data as proof that the relationship between RGO and PI was being unearthed in what was essentially a univariate experiment. This became the standard model for conducting Negro or Black identity experiments from 1939 to the early 1970s. Only one domain would be measured, but in the discussion section both domains would be discussed "as if" the two domains had been assessed. Consequently, the famous Clark and Clark Negro identity studies of the 1940s employed only RGO measures (doll-preference and color-preference tasks), but, like Ruth Horowitz, the Clarks used anecdotal "evidence" of personality involvement to justify their conclusion that self-esteem factors were driving the choices that children made on the racial-preference tasks. More recently, certain PI devices have become very popular with researchers; thus, often only PI is assessed in studies of Black identity, with RGO dynamics inferred on the basis of the PI findings.

In her seminal RGO experiment of 1939, Ruth Horowitz claimed to have discovered a "wish fulfillment" tendency in Negro preschoolers, involving the "wish" or desire to be members of the white, rather than the Negro, race.

Shortly thereafter, the husband-and-wife team of Mamie and Kenneth Clark published a series of research reports that were highly critical of Ruth Horowitz's study. They noted that Horowitz's sample was so small it precluded drawing any inferences about the general personality dynamics of Negro children. Ruth Horowitz had worked with a sample that included only 7 Negro children; the Clarks tested more than a hundred children. Ruth Horowitz studied too few children to allow for groupings by age or skin color; the size and stratification of the sample employed by the Clarks made it possible for them carefully and successfully to control for these and other potentially mediating variables. The overall tone of the Clarks' early work was that the study and evolution of Negro identity in children was a complex problem and that unless one took into consideration the physical characteristics and individual circumstances of Negro children, poorly designed RGO experiments (such as the one by Ruth Horowitz) could "mislead" researchers into thinking Negro children had an identity problem when, in fact, less alarmist explanations might be more valid. Given that others have tried to link the entire corpus of racial identity studies produced by the Clarks in the 1940s with their demonstration of Negro self-hatred, our close reading of their initial studies surprisingly showed them to be cautioning against such a conclusion.

The early work of the Clarks focused on the ability of preschool and young Black children to self-identify with symbols or figures represented by the color brown; in their later experiments, the emphasis shifted to the racial preferences of Black children. In other words, given that Black children can and do correctly self-identify, what are their racial preferences? As before, the resulting data continued to support a complex picture, but the interpretative lens of the Clarks, who had at one point been extremely sensitive to this complexity, somehow lost its sensitivity as they fell into line with the intellectual trends of the time and began to see nothing but simplistic patterns of pathology in the personal and group identity of the average Negro. While their data actually revealed a number of patterns and trends, including a very clear-cut in-group racial preference among southern Black children of all ages, what impressed the Clarks more were findings that might be construed as evidence of self-hatred. Their racial-preference studies eventually became an extremely important part of the pejorative tradition in the analysis of Black life that dominated the social sciences and the popular press during the 1940s, 1950s, and early 1960s.

Of course, there is reason to believe that had the Clarks continued to champion a complex perspective that would have allowed a discourse in Negro identity to incorporate positive trends, their later work on racial preference might have been set aside, if not discredited, by the Zeitgeist (recall the "forgotten" studies discussed in Chapter 4). In its struggle to destroy legal segregation, the NAACP defense team did not need complexity or texture—it needed clear-cut evidence that Negroes were being damaged by racial segregation. The Clarks were not in a position to argue the inconsistencies between research findings and the texture of Negro life because, unlike such observers of the Negro experience as Zora Neale Hurston, Melville Herskowitz, and W. E. B. DuBois, they were not experts on Negro culture. Over time, they drifted toward a more pathological view

of Negro life. As clinicians, they were more attuned to the existence of Negro psychopathology than the observance of (positive) Negro mental
health. Thus, ironically, though neither was an expert on Negro culture,
the Clarks began to be viewed by society at large as experts on Negro
identity and the "psychology of self-hatred." By the early 1960s, in fact, Negro identity and Negro self-hatred had become one and the same. The self-
hatred thesis, or what the literary figure Richard Wright called the Bigger
Thomas personality, and I call the Bigger Thomas syndrome, went unchallenged until the late 1960s.

The Black Power phase (1968–1975) of the Black Social Movement
(1954–1975) gave birth to any number of revisionist works on the Black
experience. For example, E. Franklin Frazier's pejorative interpretation of
the history of the Negro family was replaced in 1976 by Herbert Gutman's
thesis of Negro family complexity, stability, and endurance; Stanley Elkin's
1954 interpretation of slavery as a categorically dehumanizing episode was
replaced in 1972 by John Blassingame's view of slavery as a complex, textured, and layered period in history during which the average slave, with
no help from the slaveowner, managed to salvage a great degree of humanity and dignity. Far from romanticizing the Black experience, these and
other scholars pointed out that a pejorative perspective on Black life was
not capable of providing the frame of reference with which to interpret
the multidimensional and often positive data they were discovering for the
period covering slavery to the onset of the civil rights phase of the Black
Social Movement. It was only a matter of time before revisionists would
turn their attention to the study of Black identity.

As shown by the need to produce this book, the Negro self-hatred
thesis has proved resistant to reinterpretation. The Black Power phase of
the movement was accompanied by the emergence of Black identity, or
the psychology of nigrescence. Blacks proclaimed that their identity was
being transformed into a positive and strong Black identity. But in moving
to a positive identity, Blacks seemed to be confessing to their former self-
hatred. Research trends also show that, compared to earlier research that
went into the documentation of Negro self-hatred, the Black movement apparently did enhance both the PI and the RGO domains of Black identity.

In Chapter 2, we reexamined the Black identity research, differentiating personal identity (PI) from reference group orientation (RGO) research. Instead of finding positive changes in both PI and RGO
components of Black identity, there were patterns of continuity and
change. The personal identity, or general personality, characteristics of

Blacks, such as level of self-esteem, tested at normal levels *before* and *after* nigrescence (continuity trend); at the same time, nigrescence seemed to change the salience of race and culture in the identity structure of many Blacks (RGO change trend). By inference, at least, we were able to speculate that this pattern of strength at the PI level of Black psychological functioning probably could be projected as far back as the days of the Clark and Horowitz racial identity studies, which in themselves gave some hint of the existence of this strength, even at the RGO level (recall our analysis of the Clark data in Chapter 1).

In other words, our thinking about Negro self-hatred and Black identity change was being challenged. At the heart of this challenge was the need to rethink whether PI and RGO are actually highly correlated. Given that PI and RGO are highly predictive of one another, how could the PI factor for Blacks have been positive at a time when the Clarks and others were recording Black RGO patterns that were out-group oriented? Similarly, how could nigrescence involve change toward an in-group orientation (change in the RGO factor), but little evidence of change in the PI structure of Black identity?

We noted that such findings are problematic to the extent that one assumes a body of literature exists that shows PI and RGO are highly correlated. But in studies of Negro or Black identity, the only reference cited as "evidence" of a correlation between PI and RGO is the work of the late Kurt Lewin (1941, 1948) in which he analyzed self-hatred in Jews. And Lewin simply affirmed the association—he presented neither data nor references to empirical findings that would move such affirmations beyond the point of persuasive rhetoric. In short, we found in Chapters 3 and 4 that much of the discourse on Black psychological functioning, including both the Negro self-hatred thesis and the "new" Black identity phenomenon, is based on univariate studies in which the nature of the relationship between PI and RGO is taken for granted. Thus, between 1939 and 1960, not a single PI × RGO correlational study is cited in the literature, and few such studies are referenced between 1960 and the early 1970s.

Chapter 3 presented perhaps the first major review of Black identity PI × RGO correlational studies. And results showed that in Black identity dynamics, there is no overall pattern of a relationship between PI and RGO. That is, the variability that Blacks demonstrate on general personality, self-esteem, and personal identity tests is not correlated with the variability they evidence on measures of racial preference, group identity, or reference group orientation. Mentally healthy Blacks do not necessarily share the same racial identity and, likewise, having a certain racial identity is no guarantee of mental health.

Chapter 4 offered four factors to help explain why the mental health dynamics of Blacks have never been easily predicted by measures of racial identity:

1. Far too much of the discourse on the mental health characteristics of Blacks across the life span has been premised on group identity information gotten from Black preschool children. Group identity preferences of extremely young children cannot even predict their own future racial preferences, let alone their general personality dynamics and attributes. This was evident in the earliest racial-preference studies. The so-called out-group orientation that Kenneth and Mamie Clark (1947, 1950) recorded with their subsample of three- and four-year-old children "disappeared" in their subsample of six and seven year olds. Even if one could find evidence of a strong relationship between PI and RGO during Black adolescence and adulthood, the racial attitudes and preferences of Black children younger than four or five years of age would give us very little insight into future trends. In short, it is an intellectual absurdity to ground a discourse on Blackness across the life span on the uniformed, naive, and cognitively inconsistent and unstable racial preferences of Black preschoolers.

2. Whether measured by doll preferences in children or various attitude scores in adults, the mentally healthy pattern expected of Blacks and whites across the life span has been a same-race, or monoracial, reference group orientation. Such a standard is generally based on the presumed mentally healthy racial attitudes found in whites, for especially in the case of racial-preference studies, white children of various ages have traditionally exhibited a white preference pattern. Conversely, an attraction to "white" in Black children is thought to be problematic, if not symptomatic of self-hatred. Such a monoracial standard has never taken into consideration that although white children are often socialized to see the world in monoracial terms, Black children are raised to be attracted to, appreciative of, and capable of functioning in both the white and the Black worlds. Monoracialism is a poor predictor of mental health in white as well as Black children, but the bicultural propensities of Black children make it nearly impossible for Black children ever to demonstrate as high a level of monoracialism as has been found in whites. Chapter 4 discussed an experiment in which the researcher compared the aggregate scores of Black and white children for a popular racial-preference test. The white children in

the experiment tended to select white, resulting in a monadic preference. In contrast, the Black children tended to show a split pattern, indicating a preference for both Black and white. In scoring for the "same race," or monoracial, pattern, the device was stacked against the Black child, who tended to be bicultural. The Black child's lower monoracial score was not a function of same-race rejection but resulted instead from an attraction to both choices. We reviewed studies that showed that this biculturalism is a functional and highly positive attribute and should not be mistaken for notions of "split personality" or world-view confusion.

3. If the unaccounted-for biculturalism of Black children can cause interpretive problems for investigators who presume that Black children should display monoracial preferences, the inherent flaw in the monoracial thesis becomes even more acute when it is applied to Black adults. Living in a modern, urban, complex, highly technological, and stratified society, adult Black Americans (as well as most mature Americans) develop reference group orientations that are multifaceted, layered, and flexible. Different situations may call for different roles and priorities, and multiple allegiances. In a "racial identity" experiment for which monoracialism and level of self-esteem are the focus, the resulting low correlation between monoracialism and self-esteem may reflect, in part, the investigator's failure to identify all the other reference groups that feed into a person's self-esteem matrix.

4. Finally, we noted that one could misinterpret the significance of the lack of an overall relationship between PI and RGO in studies of Black identity to mean that social anchorage and a sense of connectedness or belongingness were not common in the group identity and general mental health patterns of Black people and, by inference, formed an unnecessary element in the general human condition. How could the group identity of Black people not feed into their mental health profile?

Our solution was to stress the distinction between experimenter-ascribed and subject-affirmed group identity (RGO). In the experimental setting, RGO is a societal, sociological, and often demographically derived construct ascribed to the subject by the experimenter. The investigator sees that a subject is physically Black, and therefore presumes that Blackness is, or ought to be, highly salient to his or her group identity. In the typical Black identity study, the salience of race is used as a benchmark of mental health. Blacks who make race highly salient (i.e., evidence a high same-race, monoracial score) are said to have a high, or positive, Black group identity; those who do not, a low and negative one. This imposed RGO, based on the experimenter's definition of what is important, can be called ascriptive group identity, or ascriptive RGO.

But race need not be the most salient dimension of a Black person's reference group orientation. Some Blacks make religion, sexual preference, socioeconomic status, simply being an "American," or any number of other reference group orientations more salient than race. In such instances, clearly the subject is operating with a definition of his or her reference group that is radically different from the one ascribed by the experimenter. That is, each Black person probably does have a "group identity," but the one that he or she personally affirms may be different from the one ascribed by the experimenter or society at large (we referred to this personally affirmed group identity as the personal RGO). Confronted with the monoracial, either/or choice of most racial identity tasks, Blacks with personal RGOs that differ from their ascribed "Black" RGO may score "low" on Black identity, causing the experimenter to conclude incorrectly that such Black subjects are examples of Blacks with a negative identity or "no" identity. With this in mind, we noted that a low score on a Black identity task does not, in and of itself, predict the absence of an identity or the operation of low self-esteem.

Keep in mind that even when one has knowledge about a person's personal RGO, it is tricky business to predict that person's PI characteristics, such as level of self-esteem. For example, some Black persons with a Black identity have high self-esteem; others, although they share the high self-esteem groups' sense of belongingness and connectedness to Black people, nonetheless experience low self-esteem. There are also Jews with high and low self-esteem and gays with high and low self-esteem and feminists with high and low self-esteem. A feminist could display a strong sense of connectedness to feminist causes and organizations, but the fact that she was sexually abused as a child may make it nearly impossible for her to experience the same level of self-esteem as a feminist who had a more normal socialization. One can easily imagine similar examples for gay people or Jews. Having a sense of belonging (i.e., having a personal RGO) may make it possible for a person to experience phenomenologically a certain level of self-esteem inflation (in reaction to positive things that happen to one's group) or deflation (in reaction to negative things that happen to one's group). In all likelihood, however, the baseline for each person's PI characteristics (e.g., level of self-esteem) is determined not by an ongoing group identity but by previous macrotemporal socialization experiences. The importance of PI is that it determines the level of mental health and the range of interpersonal skills that one brings to a group affiliation. If a member of an organization has average to above-average interpersonal skills and a healthy personality, this increases the options for participation in the organization, including being a leader in it. Yet, for a member who is suffering from low self-esteem coupled with weak interpersonal skills, such PI characteristics can inhibit the range of participatory options—independent of the fact that this member's level of commitment to the group is as high as that of the more mentally healthy member. It follows from this line of reasoning that if I wanted to become knowledgeable about the PI profile of persons affiliated with a particular group, I would not want to administer RGO devices. I would want to assess the PI domain with PI-related measures. The PI domain of the self-concept is extremely important when one wants to predict the PI characteristics of human behavior; this behavior is poorly predicted by most RGO measures.

If RGO does not predict PI, what does it predict? A more extended commentary follows in Part Two, but for the time being let us note that having RGO information allows us to make predictions about the content of a person's world view, the organizations he or she is likely to belong to, the nature of his or her ideology, and the nature of the image the person has toward a reference group. In a similar fashion, we might be able to predict, on the basis of RGO inputs, which organizations, ideologies, world views, religious beliefs, and the like a person is likely to reject. PI inputs cannot give such insights. Consequently, the difference between Blacks with limited and advanced levels of Black identity development is not in the area of PI but in such correlates of RGO as the nature of racial self-image, the salience of race to everyday life, the choice of organizational membership, the racial or ethnic or cultural composition of formal and informal social networks, the kinds of literature read, and ideology. For example, Black people operating from the perspective of the traditional Negro may differ radically from Blacks guided by the "new" Black identity insofar as cultural values, artistic preferences, political propensities, social preferences, and world view are concerned, yet be undifferentiated across measures of self-esteem, anxiety, personal worth, happiness, contentment, depression, and the like. Thus the significance of reference group orientation (RGO) or ideology or nationalism or group identity does not rest in a capacity to create, change, or enhance elements of personality but in a capacity to bring consensus, unity, or a sense of peoplehood to a group of people who, as individuals, represent a broad range of personalities, self-concepts, levels of militancy, and levels of self-esteem.

Part One has attempted to show that, given the myopic focus of most of the research on Blackness, we have just begun to understand the vast diversity that constitutes the Black experience.

PART TWO

The Psychology
of Nigrescence

From the traditional perspective and from the mainstream research literature on Black identity examined in Part One, I want to shift the focus to a
perspective that, except for counseling psychology and cross-cultural psychology, has largely been neglected by mainstream academic publications:
the theoretical and empirical literature on the psychology of nigrescence.

The study of *nigrescence* (a French word that means the "process of
becoming black") evolved in the late 1960s as observers, especially Black-
American psychologists, tried systematically to map and codify the identity
transformation that accompanied an individual's participation in the Black
power phase (1968–1975) of the Black Social Movement. First and foremost, this literature is important to students and scholars of Black identity
because it offers an inherently more complex perspective from which to
frame a discourse on Black identity. This is true not only at the theoretical
level but also at the level of research, for nigrescence research tends to be
multidimensional when compared to the univariate approach found in the
traditional literature. Second, nigrescence offers a chance to examine, at a
detailed and even intimate level, what happens to a person during identity
change. It is one thing to study psychological phenomena under steady-
state conditions; however, often the potency and full potential of constructs
or variables such as PI and RGO are not appreciated until each is manipu-

lated under controlled circumstances or closely observed during naturalistic conditions of perturbation. What are the dynamics of RGO and PI during change, and is the metamorphosis better mapped by linear or nonlinear trends? More than likely, our knowledge of the nature and complexity of each component of the Black self-concept can be enriched as we observe PI and RGO under steady-state and fluctuating conditions.

Nevertheless, nigrescence theory is in need of revision. As originally formulated, nigrescence theory outlined a process of Black identity change that transformed self-hating Negroes into committed and self-accepting Blacks. That is, when theorists wrote about the identity to be changed, usually as part of the first stage of multi-stage models, they typically took for granted the traditional literature's portrayal of the self-hating Negro. Thus most nigrescence models implied that Black identity change involved "total" change, resulting in the enhancement of personality attributes at the PI level and a stronger and more positive in-group orientation at the RGO level.

Recall that the evidence presented in Part One showed that the PI traits of Black people were at healthy levels *before* and *after* the Black 1960s, however. There was a pattern of PI continuity that ran alongside the evidence of change in RGO that accompanied the Black Social Movement. Should this pattern of change in one dimension and continuity in the other be repeated in a review of the empirical research on nigrescence, a corpus that probably offers the best perspective on Black identity change, we should not be surprised. But such a finding would underscore the need to rethink certain aspects of nigrescence theory.

Because the nigrescence approach adds more texture to the discourse on Black identity in *adults* than is found in the traditional literature, where the subjects have far too often been children (e.g., the doll study), a review of the nigrescence literature can complement and expand the synthesis offered at the end of Part One. For example, more so than mainstream findings, nigrescence research offers a layered and multidimensional picture of the often abused concept of Black self-hatred.

Chapter 5 opens with a historical overview of the evolution of the nigrescence orientation, progresses to a review of empirical studies, and ends with a summation of important findings. This sets the stage for the presentation in Chapter 6 of a revised version of my own nigrescence model, the first revision since 1971.

The development of a Black perspective has been and continues to be part of the struggle Blacks often must wage against social forces that, left unchecked, result in Black miseducation or cultural deracination. In effect, Blackness is a state of mind, not an inherited trait, and its acquisition often requires considerable effort. For example, one is born a Jew, but one becomes Jewish in one's thinking, as defined by a spectrum of Jewish thought; one is born female, but a woman becomes a feminist, as defined by a spectrum of feminist thought. Likewise, a person is born with the physical characteristics of a Black person (ascriptive RGO), but must work toward the development of one of the many Black or Afrocentric reference group orientations (personal RGO).

There is no one way to be Black. Being Black involves a wide spectrum of thoughts and orientations. The discourse on becoming Black and what it means to be Black echoes throughout Black history. Witness the slave narratives and the debates between slaves; the interchanges between Booker T. Washington and W. E. B. Du Bois at the turn of the century; the debates between Du Bois and Marcus Garvey shortly after the great migration of Blacks from the South to the North in the 1920s; the exchanges between Langston Hughes, Richard Wright, and Zora Neale Hurston during the 1940s; the recent debates between Alice Walker and Ishmael Reed; and the competing messages about Blackness that "rap" groups broadcast to Black youth.

|I|■|■|I|I

CHAPTER 5

Black Militancy
and the Psychology
of Nigrescence

Black Identity as an Archetype

The contemporary Black Social Movement lasted from about 1954 to 1975 and had a civil rights and a Black Power phase. The civil rights phase began with the 1954 U.S. Supreme Court decision on school desegregation (*Brown* v. *Board of Education*), peaked in 1963 at the March on Washington, and declined between 1966 and 1968. The Black Power phase (sometimes called the Black Revolution, the Black Separatism phase, the Black Consciousness Movement, or the period of Black militancy) began with the 1965 Watts riots, surged as a consequence of the introduction of the term "Black Power" by Stokely Carmichael during the 1966 march through Mississippi, peaked from 1968 to 1969 in the aftermath of the assassination of Martin Luther King, Jr., and lost its "mass movement" dynamic by 1974 or 1975 (some would say a year or two earlier). Today we take the concept Black identity for granted; in fact, however, Black identity is a contemporary term given credence by events primarily associated with the Black Power phase of the Black Social Movement.

During the Black Power period, and especially from 1966 to 1970, militancy and Blackness became linked; consequently, the earliest research on the new identity sought to develop political, sociological, and psycho-

logical profiles descriptive of an archetypal Black militant. In the introduction to his review of empirical studies on Black Americans, Caplan (1970)
stated:

> What clearly emerges from the recent research findings on Ne-
> groes is a picture of a new ghetto man: a Black militant who is
> committed to the removal of traditional racial restraints by
> open confrontation and, if necessary, by violence; a ghetto man
> who is very different in his actions and sympathies from the
> Negro of the past and from the White ghetto dwellers of an ear-
> lier period in this country's history. He is a ghetto man whose
> characteristics are seldom recognized and understood by most
> White Americans. It is the purpose here to describe him based
> on empirical data, to determine what he is like as a person,
> how large a segment of the Negro community he represents,
> what he wants, and how he intends to get it. (p. 59)

The Black militant profile was usually compared to one depicting the
characteristics of nonmilitant, or traditionally oriented, Blacks. The Black
community itself adopted labels offered by the Nation of Islam and made
popular through the oratory of Malcolm X. Thus the Black militant was said
to have a "Black identity" and the nonmilitant, a "Negro identity." (As an
aside, it is one of those historical paradoxes that during the Garvey movement and the Harlem Renaissance, the term "new Negro" was associated
with advanced consciousness; today, "Negro" implies a deracinated identity.)

Kilson (1973) and Sowell (1973) helped popularize a profile of Black
militants along the lines of what Caplan (1970) called the "riffraff" theory of
militancy, a perspective recently revived in a diatribe against any and all
forms of Black identity offered by Wortham (1981). The essential elements
of this characterization involve the perception that Black militancy and radi-
calism follow from experiences of frustration and social alienation and are
more prevalent among psychopathic personalities, the chronically unemployed, and the underclass. For example, Wortham (1981, 235–272) depicts
the militant as "unjust and irrational," "parasitical," "disillusioned and alienated," "a terrorist," "the Prince of anti-mind, anti-morality and anti-life," a
person with "little ego strength," a person who "has a fondness for risks and
no qualms about doing bodily harm to individuals," and, finally, a "hoodlum
and criminal . . . whose violent behavior is an act of violation." As noted by
Daly (1972), the riffraff/madman theory has a long history in society's at-

tempts to "explain" radical elements, but our concern here is with the attempts some observers have made to apply it to participants in the Black Power movement.

Eventually, empirical studies tracing the distribution of militant attitudes among Afro-Americans tended to disconfirm the riffraff perspective. The largest repository of Black pride and militancy turned out to be the youth of the Black middle class (Corson 1970; Edwards 1970; Marx 1967). And Tomlinson (1970) concluded that militants, for the time period in question, were the "cream of the urban Negro youth in particular and the urban Negro citizen in general" (p. 25). Dizard (1970) found Black consciousness affected all segments of the Black community, except persons at either extreme of the socioeconomic scale; the "very well-to-do" were adrift from Black affairs, and wretched poverty dominated the interests of the underclass. From 1965 through the early 1970s (Hahn 1970), militancy spread rapidly, however, and eventually even the underclass and people of means became involved. To quote one writer, "Afro-Americans of all types, the rich and poor, the light-skinned or ebony-hued, educated or disadvantaged, have been touched by the movement" (Cross 1970).

In effect, the riffraff theory had little explanatory value; one of the first profile entries stated that militants were no more socially or personally deviant than their nonmilitant counterparts (Caplan 1970). Having dismissed the mental illness theme, profile studies progressed toward a more realistic, multilayered image of the militant. For example, Hall, Cross, and Freedle (1972) reviewed the empirical literature and constructed a profile showing that, as compared to integrationists or nonmilitant Blacks, Black militants were more likely to: (1) identify with Black cultural values; (2) show a preference for people with dark skin and African physical features; (3) adhere to a strong system of blame ideology; (4) prefer Black organizations that are run solely by Black people; (5) evidence strong anti-white perceptions; and (6) evidence greater aggression and high risk-taking propensities. Adding to this profile, other scholars reported that militants had a collective identity or sense of peoplehood that enabled Blacks from diverse backgrounds to be linked together (Banks 1970; Dizard 1970; Thomas 1970). This collective shared, in varying degrees, a common cultural historical experience (Dizard 1970), resulting in a common world view or "Black referent" (Foster 1971). Familiarity with the world view was not enough, for personal authentication was seen to derive from collective action (Carmichael and Hamilton 1967; Dizard 1970; Stone 1968). When analyzed as a Gestalt, the identity had a circular and self-reinforcing dynamic in that participation in collective events frequently led to an even greater sense of attachment to the group's collective vision (Gerlach and Hine 1970).

Criticisms of Profile Studies

Besides attempting to clarify the nature of Black militancy, a number of scholars examined the characteristics of persons who participated in the riots that flared in Black communities during the Black Power period (1965–1970), in hopes of isolating the causes of riots. The initial "riot studies," which focused on Watts, produced results that argued that relative deprivation, rising expectations, and reactions to economic stress accounted for the origins of riots. Riot studies based on data from riots occurring *after* Watts stressed phenomenological, cognitive–perceptual, existential, and cultural–personality origins (Caplan 1970; Cross 1970; Dizard 1970; Gerlach and Hine 1970). The deprivation–frustration–reaction-to-stress theories suggested that a certain threshold for stress was triggered by environmental conditions, and that Black people exploded under the burden of oppression. The competing perspective placed greater significance on ego identity and ideological variables.

A third possibility found elements of truth in both the "reaction to oppression" and "search for identity" interpretations. A synthesis of the two suggested that (1) the Watts riots of 1965 were primarily precipitated by deprivation–frustration factors; (2) in a serendipitous fashion, Black Power, Black revolutionary rhetoric, and riot ideologies were created and legitimized during and as a consequence of Watts; (3) as the Black movement penetrated Black life, Black poets, musicians, dramatists, orators, scholars, and other leaders created, developed, and refined ideologies, frames of reference, and perspectives that at first built on, later eclipsed, and eventually replaced the significance of deprivation, frustration, and economic stress for sustaining the movement. Such an interpretation argued that Watts represented a *reaction* to white oppression that in turn gave birth to *new* attitudes, ideologies, and lifestyles that later proved more essential in understanding the ideas and behavior of riot participants in insurrections that took place *after* Watts (Bennett 1969; Gerlach and Hine 1970). This line of reasoning pointed to a major limitation of riot studies, or "profile studies." That is, conclusions drawn on the basis of isolated profiles, typologies, or polarities are inherently insensitive to the evolution of new attitudes across time and space:

All too frequently, analytical articles and commentaries focus on
the Black militant, the Black middle class, or the apathetic Black
person, creating the impression that each state or condition is
unrelated to the other. A closer look suggests that today's Black
theoretician was a well-programmed conservative three years
ago and an impulsive rhetorical revolutionary last year! Obviously, Blackness is a state of mind and, as such, is explained by
dynamic rather than static paradigms. (Cross 1971, 15)

Hall, Freedle, and Cross (1972) underscored the limitations of the profile perspective by noting the conflicting conclusions drawn from empirical
studies on the relationship between Black militancy and hostility toward
whites. Such studies typically assumed that "militancy" was an "either/or"
state; in which case, findings of intense hostility toward whites appeared to
be in conflict with studies of "Black militants" that found the reverse trend.
But Hall, Freedle, and Cross (1972) pointed out that when militancy is
viewed in the context of identity change, "it appears that intense hostility
toward Whites is frequently associated with persons who have just encountered militancy, while internalization of values, ideologies, and attitudes associated with Blackness are paralleled by *decreases* in anti-White feelings"
(p. 2). Militancy, from their perspective, was not an either/or phenomenon,
and many of the riot and profile studies obscured the importance of *process*
in their analysis of militancy: "The language of contemporary psychology,
particularly that dealing with Black Americans, is basically monadic: phenomena are described in terms of entities and the characteristics which a
person possesses instead of processes in which he is engaged" (Clark 1971,
33).

The limitations that these and other scholars noted about profile
studies can be summarized by four points: (1) Profiles of typical Black militants tended to obscure the importance of those processes producing the
new Black person; (2) such studies unintentionally promoted a rather fixed
conceptualization of Black identity/militancy, which obviated the detection
of evanescent dimensions of identity in transition; (3) as important, if not
more so, as the existence of conservative or militant types was the possibility that most militants were former conservatives who had been transformed into "new" Black people; (4) the transformation of Negroes into
Afro-Americans seemed to involve a multistage *process* for which extreme
militancy was an important but nonetheless transitory phase. These criticisms were forged by process-oriented observers of Black identity change

who thought that profile studies reflected a nonprocess perspective. To them, nonprocess studies relied on a "single snapshot" of the (new) Black person, generally taken at the height of militancy. The process writers noted that militancy was less an identity and more a *trait* of identity during metamorphosis. In place of a single snapshot, they would require a series of pictures, if not a motion picture. We should note, however, that process writers were not rejecting typological research strategies. They generally understood that once large numbers of Black people had *internalized* the new Black identity, a nonprocess, or steady-state, profile of the new identity would be extremely important. They did object to the application of research techniques that assumed steady-state conditions when all the evidence seemed to point to a condition of identity in transition.

Models of Psychological Nigrescence

If the ideal goal of the nonprocess studies was articulation of the similarities and differences between old and new Black identities, then process studies sought to isolate the developmental stages a person traverses in moving from an old to a new Black identity. Essays and empirical studies written from a process perspective were presented as microtemporal developmental models. These models sought to describe and explain how an adult identity, the product of *macrotemporal* socialization experiences, could be fundamentally transformed through microtemporal forces linked to an even more comprehensive social dynamic: a social movement. In effect, the focus was on individual adult identity change within the context of a social movement (Kelman and Warwick 1973).

By embracing a developmental orientation, observers of Afro-American life in the 1960s followed a path charted in commentaries on social change in the Third World, especially in Africa. For example, Frantz Fanon, the late revolutionary psychiatrist whose books on social change in North Africa inspired a number of American thinkers, was very much wedded to a process perspective. In *Black Skins, White Masks*, Fanon (1967a) depicted the attempt of Blacks from the Antilles to achieve a European identity devoid of Africanism; his subsequent works (1) described the agony and struggle for a more authentic self-image (Fanon 1967b); (2) analyzed the pitfalls of identities and ideologies grounded in racist-oriented reactionary nationalism (Fanon 1963); and (3) presented an identity and social order supported by humanism and socialism (Fanon 1963). Memmi's (1967) extended essay focused primarily on the behavior of the colonizer and colonized *before* change is instituted; like Fanon, however, he concluded his analysis by noting that the oppressed generally attempt to extricate themselves from the rule of the "Mother country" by totally rejecting the culture and credibility of all Europeans, embracing a nationalist identity embedded in a glorification of the past.

Of course, our primary concern here is not the Third World but the use of the process perspective in the analysis of Black American identity change, and the appearance of what I have termed *nigrescence models* (Cross 1978a). *Nigrescence*, the "process of becoming Black," and models on the psychology of nigrescence depicted the stages of the Negro-to-Black identity transformation experienced by many Black adults in the Black Power period. After the murder of Dr. Martin Luther King, Jr., the Black community became enchanted with Black Power, and the dynamics of the Black Power period were relatively simple in the northern, southern, eastern, and western sections of the United States. Consequently, observers of Black life from every region of the country penned nigrescence models during the late 1960s and early 1970s. Among Blacks themselves, perhaps it is not surprising that the most significant efforts at nigrescence model building were attempted by Blacks whose previous training and work was in process psychology. For example, Charles Thomas received his doctorate in counseling psychology, and he based his nigrescence model on his experiences as a clinical and community psychologist in the Watts community of Los Angeles. Although I eventually completed an academic research doctorate, my experiences as a clinician in Jacksonville, Illinois, and my participant observation of Black life in Evanston and Chicago, provided the foundation for my analysis. Jake Milliones refined his model as a graduate student in clinical psychology at the University of Pittsburgh, and Bailey Jackson's formulations evolved from his work as a trainer and process consultant in Albany, New York. Although they were not clinical psychologists, most of the white scholars who contributed to the nigrescence orientation, such as Muzafer Sherif and Carolyn Sherif, Luther Gerlach, and Herbert Kelman, were familiar with the application of a developmental and process perspective to problems of social change.

Between 1968 and 1976, many scholars produced nigrescence models, among them Gerlach and Hine (1970), Crawford and Naditch (1970), Downton (1973), Sherif and Sherif (1970), Napper (1973), Pinderhughes (1968), Kelman and Warwick (1973), Toldson and Pasteur (1975), Milliones (1973),

Jackson (1976a), Thomas (1971), and Cross (1971). These models, especially the ones by Cross, Milliones, Jackson, and Thomas, have been the object of a number of empirical studies and are reviewed later in this chapter.

Interest in process models of Black identity development in particular, and minority identity in general, has remained very much in evidence, especially in the field of counseling psychology (Morten and Atkinson 1983). Moreover, Bailey Jackson and his colleagues at the University of Massachusetts have recently explored the implications of the nigrescence process for the construction of identity development models for the Asian-American (Kim 1981) and white-American experience (Hardiman 1982). In a similar fashion, Dana Finnegan and Emily McNally (1987) have applied the nigrescence paradigm to an analysis of the stages of the development of a gay/lesbian identity. While the original nigrescence models were designed to explicate psychological metamorphosis that was very period specific (1968–1975), and context bound (i.e., identity change within a social movement), perhaps the major significance of more recent efforts has been to show that nigrescence and minority identity models are proving useful in the analysis of traditional macrotemporal development issues unrelated to social change (a steady-state as opposed to a social-change context).

Stages of the Paradigm

Recently, Thomas Parham, Janet Helms, and I (Cross, Parham, and Helms, in press) summarized the stages that are common to most nigrescence models. Nigrescence models do share certain features, and rather than draw elaborate comparisons, I summarize the stages of my own, unrevised model here (the revised model is discussed in the next chapter).

Stage 1 (the Pre-encounter stage) depicts the identity to be changed. A state of deracination, similar to the notion of the "colonized mind" or Carter Woodson's "miseducated Negro," is said to transcend class lines, making potential converts of poor and middle-class Negroes. Like other observers of nigrescence in the early 1970s, I assumed that Negro self-hatred was an established fact; consequently, my model, and every nigrescence model of the time, implied that the average Negro American was "self-hating and deracinated," and thus very much in need of identity change. Moreover, most of us made little distinction between personal identity (PI) and group identity, or reference group orientation (RGO), but when we did, it was clear that we assumed that the identity to be changed showed damage at both levels. Consequently, my depiction of the identity to be changed was a reca-pitulation of Kenneth Clark's self-hating Negro—thus the title of my model, *The Negro-to-Black Conversion Experience.*

In stage 2 (the Encounter stage) I suggested that in being socialized to take for granted the white perspective on life, especially as it applies to race relations, a person tends to feel comfortable with the old world view and identity, and is thus resistant to radical change. The "encounter" describes a personal experience that temporarily dislodges someone from his or her old world view and identity, thus making the person receptive (vulnerable) to conversion.

Stage 3 (the Immersion–Emersion stage) depicts the intense period of transition when the convert is attempting to destroy the old identity and at the same time experiment with and move toward the new identity. The first phase of this stage (Immersion) depicts behavior synonymous with that of someone who has "just discovered Blackness," as manifested in the con-struction of the "correct" ideology and world view, glorification of African heritage, either/or thinking, Blacker-than-thou attitudes, unrealistic expecta-tions concerning the efficacy of Black Power, a tendency to denigrate white people and white culture, and a preoccupation with proving that, as seen by "others," one is Black *enough*. While the first phase involves immersion into a total Black frame of reference, the second phase (Emersion) represents emergence from the dead-end, racist, oversimplified aspects of Immersion. In effect, the person's emotions level off, and psychological defensiveness is replaced by affective and cognitive openness, allowing the person to be more critical in his or her analysis. Since he or she is no longer so "ego involved," the strengths and weaknesses of Blackness can now be sorted through.

Stages 4 and 5, Internalization and Internalization–Commitment, de-pict the further "mellowing" of the new identity. Compared to the transi-tional stage, the person is described as having shifted from the insecure and anxious moments of early conversion to confidence in personal standards of Blackness; from uncontrolled rage toward white people and a perception of them as a distinct and evil biologic group (whitey-as-devil perceptions) to controlled anger toward *systems* of oppression and injustice and racist insti-tutions; from symbolic rhetoric to quiet, dedicated, long-term commitment; from unrealistic urgency to a sense of destiny; from anxious, insecure, rigid, inferiority feelings to Black pride, self-love, and a deep sense of Black com-munalism.

Empirical Studies of Nigrescence

A literature has evolved from the nigrescence thrust, the bulk of it consisting of empirical studies, including a significant number of unpublished dissertations and master's theses from various fields of pscyhology. This last point should come as no surprise. If they are not products of the Black Social Movement, Black doctoral students of the last ten to fifteen years have often been influenced by the experiences and ideas associated with the movement. The typologies implicit in the stages and dynamics of the process as a whole have proven relevant to postmovement identity discussions; consequently, studies continue to appear. Thus, what began as a very time-specific focus has expanded to include contemporary applications.

Nigrescence studies are but a modest subset of the general literature on Black identity. Both are guided by the same generic perspective in which self-concept (SC) is thought to be equal to the sum of one's personal identity components (PI) and group identity characteristics (RGO), with the added feature in nigrescence theory that different configurations of PI and RGO are associated with each stage of identity development. Keep in mind that general studies frequently employ children as subjects, while nigrescence studies focus on adults. Nevertheless, when the focus of both kinds of studies is adult identity functioning, identical PI instruments are apt to be employed, although general studies tend to be univariate explorations, and nigrescence research tends to be multidimensional and multimethod. General studies neither intentionally address nor include dedicated measures of the stages construct; nigrescence research, an essentially RGO venture, seeks to confirm nigrescence-specific hypotheses through the application of psychometric devices designed to operationalize nigrescence (i.e., RGO) constructs. Thus, at the PI level, results from both kinds of studies can be directly compared, but at the RGO level, the general studies provide, at best, only indirect information about the more elaborate nigrescence perspective.

Depending on the nigrescence model in question, it is generally either implied or explicitly stated that empirical studies will show nigrescence acts as a corrective for psychological damage presumed to be reflected in both the PI and RGO components of the stage 1 (i.e., Pre-encounter, or Negro) identity. In this expectation, nigrescence theory reveals itself to be, in part, an extension of the traditional, or "self-hatred," perspective. In other words, students and scholars of nigrescence enter into their research with the expectation, if not bias, that should nigrescence prove to be of any consequence, both the personal identity (PI) and reference group orientation

(RGO) components of the Black self-concept will show positive enhancement across the stages, this being especially true for comparisons involving persons in stages 1 (Pre-encounter) and 4 (Internalization). The Pre-encounter configuration was originally conceived to involve negative RGO values, such as high anti-Black scores, in combination with neurotic to pathological scores on various PI measures; the obverse is true for internalization. Of course, related hypotheses also have been explored, but the theme of negative-to-positive change has often been the central object of study.

One last point: During the preparation of this manuscript, I began and completed a comprehensive review of the nigrescence literature in collaboration with Thomas Parham and Janet Helms (in press). That effort reviews far more material than is necessary to cover at this time. The PI and RGO section that I had originally written for inclusion in the current work eventually was integrated into the more comprehensive review by Cross, Parham, and Helms (in press). Consequently, there is a certain degree of overlap in the way both works depict the PI and RGO empirical research. With regard to the source of key interpretations and conclusions, however, I have made certain to cite, wherever appropriate, the collaborative review. Finally, for those interested in nigrescence research beyond the implications of PI and RGO findings, the more extensive review should be consulted.

The Effects of Nigrescence on Reference Group Orientation (RGO)

The entire review stresses a comparison for three points in the nigrescence process: Pre-encounter, Negro, or traditional identity stage; the Immersion–Emersion stage[1] (i.e., the vortex of change), and the Internalization stage (the point at which the new identity becomes habituated). Beginning with group identity or reference group orientation (RGO), research to date shows nigrescence affects RGO at four levels: racial self-image, attitudes toward one's ascriptive group, choice of organizational membership, and ideology.

RACIAL SELF-IMAGE

In a series of studies conducted while the Black Social Movement of the 1960s was ongoing, changes in the Black racial self-image were explored

---

1. Some models (Milliones 1973; Thomas 1971) incorporate more than one transition stage.

both from the vantage point of those observing change in others (Cross 1976; Hall, Cross, and Freedle 1972; Hall, Freedle, and Cross 1972) and persons reflecting on change in themselves (Cross 1979; Krate, Leventhal, and Silverstein 1975; Williams 1975). With those who were observing change in others, experimental manipulations revealed that the discourse on observed Black identity change was orchestrated by descriptive categories (Hall, Cross, and Freedle 1972; Hall, Freedle, and Cross 1972) or character-based images or typologies (Cross 1976) incorporated in the stages of nigrescence. For example, Cross (1976) started by having 120 Black college students produce single-paragraph descriptions of either Black stereotypes associated with the Black movement or images of Blacks at different points in the identity change experience (i.e., "process" images). In a subsequent paragraph-comparison experiment, both the stereotypic and process paragraphs were shown to form three image clusters. The Negro, Black militant, and a third cluster called "internalized Blackness" formed the three stereotypic clusters. Persons who have "not discovered Blackness," "just discovered Blackness," or "been Black for some time" accounted for the process images. In a final manipulation, ten judges familiar with the Cross model rated all 120 paragraphs for content across three stages (Pre-encounter, Immersion–Emersion, and Internalization). The results showed the following:

> The themes, attitudes, behavior patterns and emotions . . . used to describe the Pre-encounter, Immersion–Emersion and Internalization episodes of psychological nigrescence are similar to the descriptors Black subjects incorporated in written characterization of stereotypic and non-stereotypic "actors" linked to the "old" (Negro) identity, transition identity (Black militant), and internalization of the new self-image (mellowing of Blackness). The "Negro" and "not discovered his Blackness" descriptions included themes of shame in relation to being a member of the Negro race, limited knowledge of Black History, the desire to be disassociated from the Negro race and striving for social acceptance on terms dictated by white society. The "Black Militant" and "just discovered his Blackness" paragraphs described persons who were cultural chauvinists, high risk takers, preoccupied with the discovery of the "correct ideology" and/or "the right value system," analyzing events or persons from an "either/or" perspective, manifesting "blacker-than-thou" attitudes, and experiencing a newfound sense of intimacy with everything

Black. The paragraphs coded "accepted and internalized Black-ness" and "has been Black for some time" presented the image of a person who was relaxed, confident, capable of self-criti-cism and whose ultra-nationalistic perspective was giving way to a more "inclusive" world view. Obviously, these descriptors complement the ones to be found in the Cross and Thomas Models. (Cross 1976, 110–111)

In a similar vein, Hall, Cross, and Freedle (1972) gleaned a series of sentence-long descriptors from each of the five stages in the Cross nigres-cence model, and these items formed the basis of a Q-sort task. When asked to sequence the items in a fashion that captured their perceptions of how the new Black identity evolved, both Black and white observers produced clusters that duplicated the stages of nigrescence.

In three studies (Cross 1979; Krate, Leventhal, and Silverstein 1974; Williams 1975), the focus shifted from observed to self-perceived change. Krate, Leventhal, and Silverstein (1974) recast the items from the Hall, Cross, and Freedle Q-sort items into first-person statements. They asked 25 male and 25 female low-income Black college students to sort the items in accor-dance with how they viewed themselves (1) "now," (2) four years ago, (3) two years ago, and (4) how they see themselves in the future. Results showed that the subjects perceived themselves as changing or having changed from a past Negro identity to a new Black identity in the present and future, and the pattern revealed was consistent with the nigrescence formulation.

Using different procedures and studying an older population, Williams (1975) reported the same trend; but perhaps the best demonstration of self-perceived change in the RGO domain of Black identity came from a study by Cross (1979). Cross studied 65 Black male and female college students, all of whom were activists in the Black Student Movement. Each subject completed two inventories, including the Stages Questionnaire. The 55-item questionnaire consisted of 10 filler items and items representing the Pre-encounter (stage 1), Immersion–Emersion (stage 3, or transition stage), and Internalization (stage 4) stages of the Cross model. The study was conducted in 1972. Using this date as a point of departure, the response format allowed the respondent to determine whether or not each item was applicable to his or her self-description for different time periods in his or her life history. Each item depicted a personal attribute, belief, fantasy, or behavior pattern written in the first person and the present tense, and whether intentionally or not (the PI and RGO distinction was an implied but not explicit differential in the nigrescence literature at this time), all the items except four (46, 42, 38, and 40), assessed RGO, not PI:

Items from Stages Questionnaire (Cross 1979)

Pre-encounter Items

2. I often say—"Why should I be judged by my race?"

4. I believe that kinky hair doesn't look as nice as straight hair.

12. I don't know much about Black history.

20. An integrated or white organization is better than a Black one.

37. I believe straight hair is good hair.

39. Please, don't call me African or Black.

49. I hold back my feelings about race.

55. The way some of the our people are behaving, we will not be accepted.

17. I think being light or brown is better than being a dark-skinned person.

22. I sometimes feel that Black people are inferior to white people.

46. My goal in life is to make it for myself.

43. I feel it is important for me to speak good English.

8. I just want to be seen as an individual and a human being.

26. If you are going to make it, you have to learn how to take the man's insults and keep trying.

31. I get disgusted by the loudness of some of our people.

Immersion–Emersion Items

3. I'm feeling and acting as though I had blind faith in Blackness.

6. My anger runs deep and I have been having daydreams in which I see myself killing white people.

10. I seem to be placing labels on everybody—he's an Uncle Tom, or she's middle class, or he's counterrevolutionary, or she's bourgeoise.

18. The way I dress, my hair style and other symbols of Black militancy are extremely important to me.

23. I feel very defensive about my level of Blackness.

36. I tend to be rather critical and short tempered with practically all white people as well as with Black folks who are not together.

51. Confrontation, bluntness and an either/or approach describes the way I talk to people about racial issues.

54. I feel social pressure to be Blacker than I am.

16. I act in a rather "Blacker-than-thou" manner.

19. To me nothing that is white is good and everything of value must be Black.

32. I'm so angry you could probably measure my Blackness by the level of hatred I feel toward white people.

42. My thoughts are rather rigid, I tend to think in absolute terms and my ideology has an either/or quality.

25. My emotions are like an exciting "sea of Blackness," and it is such a wonderful feeling it makes me want to shout to the world—"I'm Black and I'm proud."

27. My body is filled with anger, pride and energy—I feel ready to do whatever is necessary for liberation.

30. I'm thinking about Black liberation almost all of the time, and it's difficult for me to concentrate on anything else.

48. I feel as though I'm being covered all over with Blackness and at the same time my mind and body are being washed of all whiteness.

53. I act and feel as if I have lost all fear and would do anything for Black liberation.

Internalization Items

7. It is easy for me to criticize Blackness without feeling like a "traitor" to the cause.

14. I take criticism of the Black movement without getting angry or defensive.

21. I can deal with persons on a Blacker-than-thou ego trip without feeling defensive or shaky myself.

35. I feel like I'm living my Blackness rather than trying to prove it to someone.

38. My ideology is flexible and I tend to be calm.

44. According to the way I act and feel, it would be easy for someone to conclude that my Blackness is based on pro-Black ideas rather than anti-white concepts.

47. My anger and rage is moderate to low, while my level of Blackness is high.

40. I am patient and understanding toward people who do not have my level of awareness.

5. Certainly I wish a revolution were possible, but I feel that the struggle for Black liberation will take years of dedicated work.

11. I am confident, non-defensive and at ease with my own personal sense of Blackness.

28. It is very clear to me that some ideas about Blackness are good while others need to be rejected.

52. My friends tell me I'm Black and easy to talk with.

54. I feel at ease and comfortable with my level of Black awareness.

The repeated-measures technique incorporated in the response format of the Stages Questionnaire made it possible for the researcher to trace and graphically display the trend for each stage-related attribute cluster, the results of which are reproduced in Figure 2. In general, the activists used items from the Pre-encounter (stage 1) attribute cluster to describe themselves before involvement in the Black movement, and attributes from the Internalization (stage 4) subscale framed the present self-description. The trend of the Pre-encounter and Internalization clusters followed an inverse linear path, as the old identity was rejected and subsequently replaced by the new racial self-image. The pattern of the Immersion–Emersion stage (stage 3) clearly indicated that the activists perceived themselves as having experienced a "transitional" state between the collapse of the old world view and the habituation of the new. In effect, the student activists were deracinated Negroes in the past; they traversed an evanescent Black militancy period; and, at the time of the study, they perceived themselves to be in or headed toward a period of "mellowing," incorporation, habituation, or internalization.

That Hall, Cross, and Freedle (1972) were able to show that this self-perceived identity change can be tracked accurately by those observing it, including whites, means, among other things, that certain aspects of the transformation process have a very assessable, perhaps even public, dimension. The early stages of any social movement frequently see an emphasis on demonstrative display of the new identity, and symbolism can take on extraordinary importance. Enty (1979) conducted a survey on a predomi-

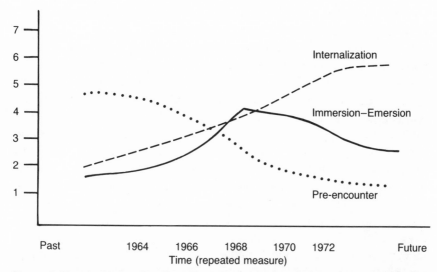

Figure 2. Trend of means for Pre-encounter, Immersion–Emersion, and Internal-ization subscales of Stages Questionnaire, showing applicability of each attribute cluster to self-perceived image of self over time. As reported for all subjects (*N* = 65) in Cross 1979.

nantly Black college campus at the zenith of the Black Power movement, and students with high (but not low) Black identity scores were more likely to style their hair in a "natural" ("Afro") and to wear African clothing and African-inspired jewelry. Shortly after the nigrescence period commenced, Jackson and Kirschner (1973) found that even something as obvious and straightforward as the name by which one self-identified determined one's stage position. Stage 1 Blacks tended to self-designate as "colored," "Negro," or "human being," while persons in the other stages preferred the labels "Black," "Black American," "Afro-American," or even "African." By the mid 1970s, self-designation and personal appearance remained important ele-ments of the new identity; shortly thereafter, however, new studies reported that such factors no longer differentiated persons across the stages, that is, "Black" became a normative label for Blacks (Parham and Helms 1981; Weston 1975, 1977). Following his discovery of this turn of events in the course of conducting the first of two related experiments, Weston (1975) argued that when a social movement takes on general significance across all sectors of a society or group (in this case, the Black society), the "aware-ness" level of even those less-involved group members may be raised. This means that noninvolved members may come to share surface-level aspects of the raised consciousness found in highly involved persons.

Weston (1977) further explored this distinction between surface and more deeply held attitudes about Blackness in his dissertation. He found that low-income Black high school students with low awareness were more apt to model their behavior after a white model; high awareness, reflecting Internalization (stage 4), seemed to induce Black-on-Black modeling behavior. As in his first study, Weston (1975) reported that the differences between people positioned in stages 1 and 4 may not be evident at the surface level. That is, both low- and high-awareness Black high school students identified with the Black rather than the white model when the modeling involved a positive situation. Nevertheless, after a mildly negative dimension was introduced as part of the task, the low-awareness students shifted allegiance to the white model, while the high-awareness students continued to identity with the Black model. Under pressure, so to speak, surface awareness versus more deeply rooted awareness was revealed.

BLACK PERCEPTIONS OF BLACKS

In addition to changing the Black persona and public presentation of Blackness, nigrescence has also been shown to affect deep-structure attitudinal components of the negative and positive images Blacks hold toward Blacks as a group. Milliones (1973), Brown (1979), and Denton (1985) reported that Blacks in stage 1 held negative stereotypes of Black people, not unlike those associated with the attitudes of racist whites. Concomitant with progress through the stages, however, these negative in-group perceptions diminished in a linear fashion, and by the Internalization stage were nearly expunged. Williams (1975) found a similar yet more complicated pattern. As in the previous instance, stage 1 Blacks scored high on an anti-Black measure, but the lowest score was obtained during the transitional stages, not during Internalization. The path traveled was one of being hypercritical at stage 1, romantic and "Blacks can do no wrong" during the transitional stage, and accepting and with a capacity for realistic criticism at the Internalization stage. Using a two-part inventory of "Black affiliation," one part to scale how a respondent saw himself or herself affiliating with other Blacks ("I look forward to being in the company of other Blacks," "I give consistent support to other Blacks"), the other part to measure how a respondent saw other Blacks affiliating with him or her ("Other Blacks are consistently supportive of me"), Denton (1985) essentially replicated Williams's findings. Stage 1 Blacks recorded very low scores, indicating alienation and distance from other Blacks; people in the transitional stage (Immersion–Emersion) had dramatically high scores, reflecting an uncritical, almost religious sense of connection to fellow Blacks; but by the Internalization stage, the scores had dipped and then "leveled," suggesting a sense of belonging, engagement, and mutual support tempered by realistic expectations.

The analysis so far suggests that Pre-encounter profiles reflect a great deal of anti-Black content. However, a reanalysis and reinterpretation of these findings, carried out by Cross, Parham, and Helms (in press) and discussed in a later section, produced results indicating that the Pre-encounter stage may incorporate at least *two* typologies, one fitting the "Negro self-hatred" profile, in which the person feels distant from Black people and has internalized negative stereotypes of Blacks, and a second that, while exhibiting certain Pre-encounter world-view attributes, also shows high Black affiliation tendencies, a low level of internalization of negative Black stereotypes, and a general sense of affection and connection to Blacks. Other than the fact that they place low salience on racial and cultural issues, some Pre-encounter people may hold very positive perceptions and attitudes toward Blacks, in which case nigrescence would not "change" these already positive attitudes; instead, it would raise the salience of race and culture, which translates into the changing of one's priorities. For another group, one that begins at the Pre-encounter stage with low salience and *negative* racial images, the nigrescence experience would work to affect both these attributes. Such findings suggest that, contrary to original nigrescence theory, self-hatred and the Pre-encounter stage are not synonymous. (I further analyze the possibility of bimodal trends at Pre-encounter later in the book.)

BLACK ORGANIZATIONAL MEMBERSHIP

Nigrescence seems to predict organizational membership. In a study by Williams (1975), no one positioned at stage 1 belonged to a "Black oriented" organization, while subjects in the transitional and Internalization stages showed a strong tendency to organize with other Blacks around political and cultural issues. Two studies (Davidson 1974; Weston 1975) exploring the same topic produced results with a slightly different and very insightful twist. Davidson (1974) found that students scoring low on a nigrescence-oriented Black identity scale were no less active in college than others. In contrast, the organizations in which the low-awareness students participated were frequently white oriented or showed little connection to Blackness. Advanced or high Black identity scores predicted participation in activities and membership in organizations for which Blackness was highly salient. Along the same lines, Weston (1975) reported that Blacks positioned across the stages do not differ in their tendency to hold membership in all-Black organizations, but for stage 1 people, the groups joined were often religious or apolitical in nature; at stages 2 and later, this was not true. After reviewing such findings, Cross, Parham and Helms (in press) concluded that nigrescence may not differentiate active from nonactive people, but it may determine the kinds of organizations toward which a person is attracted and in which he or she is active.

IDEOLOGY

In line with the changes in the Black persona and group affiliation tendencies, nigrescence has shown the capacity to transform a person's racial frame of reference, or ideology (Williams 1975). In its earliest expression, during the transitional stage (stage 3), a utopian concern for an all-Black world is framed by anti-white sentiments:

> The critical dimension separating Stage III respondents from
> the other stages was anti-White sentiment. Stage III subjects
> demonstrated significantly more general anti-White sentiments,
> were more angry at Whites for the discrimination experienced
> by Blacks and had more fantasies about killing Whites, than
> subjects from any other Stage. (Williams 1975, 79–80)

During the transitional stage, intense anger directed at whites is frequently the way in which new converts communicate that they are in the "process" of destroying all their connections to the "white world." At the same time, they feel the need to communicate dramatically and publicly that a new "self-image" and ideology are becoming part of their life. The converts may accomplish this through changes in their personal appearance—to adopt African hairstyles and African jewelry and clothing; speech pattern—sometimes Black English and the mannerisms of urban Black America are stressed; at the college level, interest in an African language may take hold; value system—the value system developed by the Afrocentric theorist Maulana Karenga continues to be popular with new converts; and self-designation—it is not uncommon for the person to "add" an African nickname or to change his or her name legally to an African name. The complex, tension-filled, "push–pull" transitional stage pattern of disengagement from the white world and energetic acceptance of an ideology and self-image perceived to be totally Black has been captured in at least three investigations that have explored the large-scale nigrescence-related survey data set maintained at the University of Pittsburgh (Brown 1979; Denton 1985; Taylor 1986). The Pittsburgh studies present an image of people in transition who are rejecting white society and enthusiastically embracing Black society, while advocating an ideology calling for separatism and "a policy of racial polarization in the social, educational, and religious infrastructures of American society" (Denton 1985, 57).

The militancy, audaciousness, and certitude with which persons in the transitional stage present their new self-image and new ideology actually belie a great deal of psychological vulnerability. People in transition have been shown to be very defensive (Napper 1973); the defensiveness may be thinly disguised as an insufferable "Blacker-than-thou" attitude toward other Blacks (i.e., an attitude in which the person claims that his or her Blackness is "purer" and more correct than another's) and arrogance and hostility toward whites. The transitional pattern is one in which anti-white perceptions, coupled with demonstrative displays of Blackness, seem to provide a protective psychological shield behind which the person frantically sorts out the complexities of Blackness. Over time, as the new convert gains self-confidence, his or her ideological stance becomes less facile and more complicated and substantive. We have already noted that Williams (1975) and Denton (1985) found anti-white attitudes as well as Black separatist perceptions peaking during the transitional stage, but their data also showed that with advanced awareness, the anti-white perceptions declined dramatically. Ideological discussions seemed to take on considerable texture, including the reincorporation of elements once associated with "whiteness":

> The mellowing of Black students appears to have been a highly complex phenomenon, one that challenged them to isolate substantive from diaphanous Immersion/Emersion traits and to develop enough personal insight, interlaced with a touch of humility, to be able to recognize and carry over strengths of the old self-image for construction of the new. The interface of the old with the new was demonstrated by the students' response to item 43 on the Stages Scale, an item classified as a Pre-encounter attribute: "I feel it is important for me to speak good English." Students associated this statement with the old identity because it reminded them of their attempts to develop qualities that would increase their chances of being accepted by White society, as well as of the shame they once felt toward "Black English" (read "bad English"). During the Immersion/

Emersion Stage the students sought to affirm their relationship
with the masses and Black culture; consequently, trying to be
White, to act White, or to talk White was anathema to this stage.
But as the mesmeric dimensions of the militancy stage declined, the maturing converts came to understand language as
an important system of communication rather than as a negative or positive symbol of social status; thus explaining the use
of the item to define the self in the present. Wallace . . . has re-
minded us that innovation usually involves the ability to perceive, analyze, synthesize, and act upon pre-existing elements in
a unique manner. Likewise, the new Black self-image is probably composed not of entirely new attributes but of old and new
attributes that are synthesized within a different perspective.
(Cross 1979, 124)

The last point stressed in the above quote—that the new and old become intertwined at the Internalization stage—is underscored by findings
from a number of studies. Having shown that Blacks in the transitional stage
achieved extremely high scores on a measure of Black separatism, Brown
(1979) and Denton (1985) also noted a complex pattern of overlap and
differentiation in the ideology of stage 1 as compared to stage 4 (Internalization) blacks. For example, both groups endorsed independent Black economic activities, but on issues of culture, identity, and education, stage 1
Blacks stressed being American over being Black, while Internalizers emphasized the importance of Black culture, Black education, and Black identity. Both groups seemed opposed to an ideology of (Black) separatism, with
the perspective of the stage 1 Blacks being driven by a commitment to as-
similationism, and, in some instances, varying degrees of anti-Black feelings.
In contrast, the nonseparatist ideology of the Internalizers was drawn on a
pluralistic social canvas in which the distinctive features of the Black experience stood in mild relief. A study by Carter and Helms (1987) also high-
lighted the ideological fusion so apparent at Internalization. In their investigation of values and nigrescence, Carter and Helms found that people at the
Internalization stage had a more Afrocentric value system than was true for
stage 1 Blacks; more dramatic, however, was the degree to which each stage
overlapped on values common to most Americans. Finally, using an ideological measure of system blame versus self-blame, Williams (1975) found stage
1 Blacks prone to blaming Blacks for the problems facing them, while people in the transitional stage had an extraordinarily high orientation toward
system blame. Internalizers fell in between; their ideological posture was

decidedly oriented toward system blame, but it was devoid of knee-jerk (transitional stage) or self-flagellation (stage 1) tendencies, and internalizers seemed capable of both self-criticism and group criticism.

NIGRESCENCE AND SOCIAL CLASS

Most nigrescence studies have been conducted with college populations, and so it is important to point out that Cross, Parham, and Helms (in press) have identified a few studies that document the positive influence of nigrescence on the reference group orientation (RGO) of low-income and poor Blacks. Weston (1975, 1977) found nigrescence dynamics among Black high school males from low-income neighborhoods, and Krate, Leventhal, and Silverstein (1975) successfully identified nigrescence trends among working-class Black college students. Glasgow's (1981) study of male members of the Black underclass living in Watts, California, was conducted during the onset, duration, and aftermath of the Watts riots. His text clearly reveals that a critical number of the young men advanced to Immersion–Emersion (stage 3), with some seemingly headed toward Internalization (stage 4). In a study of a similar group, Terrell, Taylor, and Terrell (1980) found that young incarcerated Black males convicted of serious Black-on-Black crimes were more stage 1 oriented than were those charged with less serious Black-on-Black offenses.

Yet why should one be surprised that nigrescence affects the poor as well as the middle class? What evidence is there that nigrescence is skewed, one way or the other, by class considerations? Several studies report no apparent relationship between social class and nigrescence (Carter and Helms 1984; Parham and Helms 1985). In attempting to explain such a finding, Carter and Helms (1984) commented that the development of a Black identity is more the result of "an individual's interpretation of his or her socialization experiences and personal development than it is a reflection of actual external conditions imposed by social class" (p. 10–11).

Summary of RGO Findings

Empirical research has shown that at the RGO level of the Black self-concept, nigrescence can affect the Black persona and the manner in which Blacks choose publicly to display their Blackness; it can change the internal images and attitudes that Blacks hold toward Blacks as a group; it can predict the kinds of organizations that attract Black membership, and the causes, cultural programs, and social problems that engage their activism; moreover, it can alter and sometimes radically reorient the racial frame of reference and ideology that reticulate Black opinions, values, and priorities.

Given the continued presence, in some circles, of the traditional, or "self-hatred," perspective, some may assume that the evidence reflects a negative-to-positive shift in the valence of RGO variables, as traced across the stages—that is, from a negative persona to a positive persona, from a poor racial image to a positive racial image, from no involvement in Black organizations to high involvement, and so on. While such an interpretation may be understandable in view of traditional theory on Black psychological functioning, it is my opinion that a more careful reading shows far more complex possibilities. In the majority of studies, the shift was not so much from negative to positive, as from low salience to high salience, apolitical to political, Eurocentric to Afrocentric, positive and healthy involvement in organizations that did not stress Blackness to healthy and positive activism in organizations that gave high priority to being Black.

In other words, profound identity change need not involve a negative-to-positive transformation; instead, there may be a profound shift from low salience to high salience and a rearrangement of priorities that accompany change in what is salient. Such an interpretation would require rethinking of the nature of the RGO implications of the Pre-encounter experience, which until recently has almost always been anchored in the self-hatred theory. In the original nigrescence models, mine included, stage 1 persons were generally characterized as having fundamentally negative perceptions of Black people, Black history, and the contemporary Black condition. The overall tone was one of anti-Blackness. We have assumed that at the RGO level, the psychological energy released during the Black 1960s was linked to the transformation of negative attitudes into positive ones. But the empirical findings do not confirm that this negativity existed in the first place! Confirmed, instead, is a picture of latent Black pride, a dormant concern for race and culture, and a general low salience for race. Consequently, in the 1960s, and probably today, the RGO *baseline* for most Pre-encounter types may not have been anti-Blackness but low salience for Blackness. The burst of energy associated with nigrescence may be connected, in part, to the movement from low awareness to high awareness, from low salience to high salience, from dormancy to explicitness. We return to this point at the end of the chapter when our RGO findings are folded into the findings for the effects of nigrescence on PI.

Effects of Nigrescence on Personal Identity (PI)

A modest number of studies have attempted to map the effects of nigrescence on personal identity, or PI. Each study has tended to involve a multidimensional, multimethod approach, resulting in a limited but rich set of results. The overall pattern for PI during nigrescence seems to be one in which converts exhibit a certain "baseline" at the Pre-encounter stage, a great deal of perturbation during transition (Immersion–Emersion), followed by a return to the baseline at Internalization. Unfortunately, none of the studies has been longitudinal; consequently, this pattern of quiescence, volatility, and mellowing remains in need of more exact confirmation. Nevertheless, such results are consistent with established views on nigrescence. These studies produced an unexpected finding, however, which was the discovery of *two*, Pre-encounter prototypes: The first and most dominant portrays Blacks who are psychologically healthy; the second has all the signs of Kenneth Clark's self-hating Negro. Let us begin our discussion with the identification of the basic PI trend across the stages.

NIGRESCENCE AND ROLLER-COASTER PI TRENDS

In retrospective studies by Cross (1976) and by Krate, Leventhal, and Silverstein (1974), persons recalling the details of their nigrescence experience described themselves at Pre-encounter by using cognitive and ideological descriptors that were low or even devoid of strong emotional content. Emotionally laden descriptors, such as rage, euphoria, tenseness, guilt, anger, love, oceanic pride, intense commitment, and lack of fear, dominated their perceptions of what it was like to pass through Immersion–Emersion. Mellow, less tense, more relaxed and comfortable, and at ease with the self anchored their self-descriptions for Internalization. Williams's (1975) multifaceted study also incorporated limited introspective data that complements the above findings.

Studies of the images, descriptive categories, and stereotypes that Black college students associate with nigrescence also fit this pattern: a steady state at Pre-encounter, followed by a burst of emotions during transition, and the fading of emotionality into a new steady state at Internalization (Cross 1976; Hall, Freedle, and Cross 1972). Brown's (1976) study of people in transition showed them to be impulsive and emotionally unstable; Williams (1975) reported similar findings. Studies of nigrescence and self-esteem (Denton 1985; Parham and Helms 1985; Williams, 1975) again provide a picture of steady-state levels at Pre-encounter, fluctuation and perturbation during transition, and leveling at Internalization. Further confirmation of this pattern of control and rationality at stage 1, cognitive dissonance and emotionality at transition, and dissonance resolution and a return to rationality at advanced stages comes from a recent study of nigrescence and cognitive styles by Parham and Helms (in press). They found that a rational mode characterized the cognitive styles of persons at either end state of nigrescence (i.e., Pre-encounter and Internalization); for Immersion–Emersion, perhaps symbolic of the point of transition, neither the logical–rational, intuitive, or conformity mode dominated the cognitive style.

NIGRESCENCE AND PI CONTINUITY OR PI CHANGE

That PI traits should follow a roller-coaster pattern across the stages is a prediction to be found in every nigrescence model. Also predicted is an enhancement of PI. That is, PI is depicted as negative, neurotic, or pathological at stage 1, for which, it is presumed, nigrescence can provide relief. Based on the PI findings from the general literature, which showed that Black PI levels were adequate *before* and *after* the nigrescence cycle of the Black 1960s, we can see that, at least in an "indirect" way, this negative description of the person in stage 1 of nigrescence theory has already come under challenge by findings from the general literature.

As an important aside, we should keep in mind that the evidence from the general literature of "no change" or a PI continuity trend offers a more important challenge to nigrescence theory than has often been considered. Earlier in this chapter, as part of our introduction to empirical studies on nigrescence, I pointed out that while the RGO measures often used in the general literature (typically univariate measures of RGO) are not comparable to those used in empirical studies of nigrescence (typically multidimensional measures of the stages construct), both kinds of studies have employed identical methods and procedures to operationalize the PI variable (more often than not, standardized measures of personality, self-esteem, anxiety, introversion–extroversion, level of happiness, self-actualization, and the like). Consequently, the findings from both kinds of studies are not as indirect as one might imagine, since both the general and nigrescence-specific empirical studies have examined nearly identical PI constructs by administering similar, if not identical, PI instruments, on samples of subjects drawn from the same general population. Furthermore, many of the two kinds of studies were conducted during the same time period (1968–1975). Thus the scores of PI studies from the general literature that show Blacks entered and existed in the nigrescence period of the 1960s with equally adequate levels of PI can be interpreted as a very significant, "indirect" challenge to current nigrescence theory, especially as it pertains to the dynamics of the Pre-encounter stage.

What of the more "direct" evidence that comes from empirical studies of nigrescence? Of course, the best and most direct way to trace the effects of nigrescence on PI would be through longitudinal studies; to my knowledge, however, nigrescence-oriented longitudinal studies have not been conducted. The closest thing we have to longitudinal evidence are six laboratory nigrescence studies (Carter 1974; Griffin 1975; Jefferson 1981; Livingston 1971; Lunceford 1973; Suggs 1980) involving attempts by clinicians and trainers to replicate the nigrescence experience as a T-group experience, a human relations experience, or a Black culture experiment in which subjects are exposed to nigrescence or Black studies materials and, after a period of time, are tested to see whether such exposure changes components of their self-concepts. These "nigrescence laboratory experiments" are very similar to the research on Black studies and self-concept reviewed in Chapter 4, the findings for which showed that exposure to Black studies affects RGO, but not PI (still another challenge to nigrescence theory).

When the findings from these six studies are looked at collectively, the results indicate that to the extent a nigrescence experience is able to induce change in the self-concept of an individual, it is typically registered at the level of RGO or group identity, and seldom at the PI or self-esteem level.

Since another review (Cross, Parham, and Helms, in press) provides a close reading of all six studies in question, we can devote more space to a detailed exploration of what is perhaps the best example to date of a nigrescence human relations experiment, or T-group experience. I am referring to a study by Carter (1974), whose dissertation bridged an information-processing or cognitive model of Black studies with a deliberate attempt to manipulate and change Black identity in accordance to the stages of nigrescence. In Carter's experiment, 30 male and female Black undergraduates at Purdue University were randomly assigned to either an experimental, attention/placebo, or control group. In the experimental treatment, participants were exposed to a curriculum of Black musical, literary, and historical information, in conjunction with Black identity-oriented group counseling discussions, the thrust of which was designed to take the participants through the stages of nigrescence. For example, sessions 1 and 2 focused on the first stage, the third session on stage 2, and so forth. Subjects assigned to the attention/placebo group attended meetings at which they listened to music as a group and then experienced nondirective discussion sessions, or "rap" sessions. The experiment lasted ten weeks, with the experimental and attention/placebo groups each meeting once a week for three hours. The control subjects received no treatment and did not meet together.

To measure the effect of the treatment, Carter developed her own Black Self-Concept Scale (BSCS), which is only nominally specific to Blacks. Utilizing the 300 words from the Gough Adjective Checklist, Carter selected 20 adjectives that she, in concurrence with a panel of judges, deemed "Black oriented." In reality, all the words are race neutral and could be used to characterize anyone's personality (i.e., PI traits). Not surprisingly, the results of her scale suggested that the treatment had no effect on "Black self-concept." Since the scale actually measured only the PI dimension, not the RGO factor that Carter had intended, one could argue that the BSCS was at least useful in showing that the experiment had no effect on PI. But the significance of Carter's effort lies, not with her misguided self-concept scale, but the analysis of the daily diaries she had each student keep:

> As mentioned previously, the participants kept a daily diary which was turned in once a week. Random samples of entries were taken for examination. Thus, one entry for each student was selected per week. This weekly entry was selected according to the random number procedure as suggested by Downie and Heath (1970). Since the study ran for ten weeks, each student had 10 entries that were analyzed. Three judges were used to classify all entries. (Carter 1974, 81–82)

Carter instructed the three judges to sort each entry into categories that turn out to be remarkably similar to the PI and RGO constructs being stressed throughout this text. Her PI-related category defined those self-referents that contained no racial or Black cultural content, while her RGO-related category defined those self-referents that clearly did contain Black racial or cultural content. Her scheme made it possible to differentiate negative and positive PI clusters and also a cluster for ambiguous PI material (material that was clearly PI-related but was ambiguous in its positive or negative thrust). This scheme was repeated for the RGO entries:

1. = PI + (positive personal identity self-referent)

2. = RGO + (positive reference group self-referent)

3. = PI − (negative personal identity self-referent)

4. = RGO − (negative reference group self-referent)

5. =API (ambiguous/ambivalent personal identity self-referent)

6. =ARGO (ambiguous/ambivalent reference group self-referent)

In preparing her data for analysis, Carter decided to collapse categories 5 and 6 (the ambiguous PI and RGO self-referent, or categories API and ARGO). Although Carter was working with a small sample, her well-thought-out design resulted in the production of 300 protocols (10 subjects produced 3 entries per week for 10 weeks = 300 entries) and 900 classifications (300 entries × three judges = 900 classifications), which Carter submitted to chi-square analysis. The frequencies Carter observed are reproduced in Table 10. This table incorporates my PI and RGO categories; otherwise, it is very similar to the one Carter employed.

Given that PI and RGO are not necessarily related, then the success of this nigrescence or RGO intervention, which according to Carter's description, had little PI content, should have primarily affected the RGO domain (RGO+ and RGO− categories). This is essentially what Carter found. The overall chi-square was significant, with the difference between groups showing up only on the RGO+ category, and unexpectedly, the collapsed ambiguous category. No other significant differences were recorded. Looking at Table 10, we see that the treatment had no discernible effect on self-critical tendencies, as the negative personal identity (PI−) and negative reference group (RGO−) entries were practically the same for all three groups. But the treatment helped the experimental subjects attain greater clarity and focus in their identities; they presented only 166 ambiguous entries in comparison to the 211 and 216 recorded for the attention/placebo and control groups respectively. On the positive side of the ledger, the treatment did not differentiate the groups in terms of their positive personal identity (PI+) self-referents, each group producing about the same number. In fact,

Table 10
Observed Frequencies of PI and RGO Diary Entries

	RGO −	PI −	A	PI +	RGO +	N
Experimental	7	27	166	34	66	300
Attention/placebo	7	32	211	32	18	300
Control	6	25	216	28	24	300
Totals	20	84	593	94	108	900

Source: Carter 1974.

when the two personal identity categories (PI– and PI+) for all three groups are compared side by side, we see that the treatment had no significant effect on the way the subjects in the experimental group evaluated their personal identities. In effect, the PI dimension of their self-concept seemed unaffected by the treatment. Independent of the failure to effect PI change, the treatment did result in enhanced group identity, as the experimentals recorded 66 positive reference group entries (RGO+), compared to only 24 for the control group and 18 for the attention/placebo group.

As Carter's findings replicate what essentially is the pattern of results for all six nigrescence T-group, or human relations, studies, we can conclude that direct studies of the effects of nigrescence on the PI component of the Black self-concept shows nigrescence has very little influence on the nature of a convert's PI profile, other than to perturb it during the transitional stage. The findings from this small number of studies complement what has been reported in scores of PI studies taken from the general literature, which were described and analyzed in Part One. Taken together, the "indirect" evidence from the general literature and the "direct" evidence from nigrescence research present a compelling pattern of PI continuity, a pattern reflective of adequate psychological functioning before and after the onset of significant identity change at the RGO level of the Black self-concept. Such results call for rethinking the nature and dynamics of stage 1 of nigrescence stage theory in particular, and key aspects about the dynamics of nigrescence theory in general.

If nigrescence does not permanently change PI, does PI contribute little to the dynamics of nigrescence? More specifically, and historically speaking, other than the temporary perturbations connected with the transitional stage, did PI contribute little to the dynamics of the nigrescence movement of the 1960s? For those who believe that the psychological energy unleashed by the Black 1960s was linked to the conversion of low levels of self-esteem into high or more adequate levels, research findings fail to support such thinking. We have been operating under the assumption that in conjunction with group identity or RGO change, the power of the Black Social Movement resulted from the psychological energy released during the conversion of negative PI energy into mentally healthy trends.

But there is another possibility. The movement may have gained most of its force and effectiveness through the forging of a new political and cultural consensus among people who evidenced positive mental health *before* its onset. In other words, preexisting positive mental trends may in part explain the efficaciousness of the movement's participants, just as it does the strength of the more recent nigrescence movement known as Afrocentrism. During the 1960s, nigrescence often changed the priorities of Black adults who once successfully ran all-Black organizations that stressed a more conservative and less cultural nationalist position. Transformed by nigrescence, these already tested adult leaders and organizers had their priorities changed; subsequently, they either joined or helped form new all-Black organizations. Their emerging Black interests were fused with their extant general personality (PI) strengths, and together this made for an explosive combination—one that explains most of the positive energy associated with the dynamics of the movement. Similarly, the movement attracted and (through nigrescence) converted the best and the brightest of Black youth (Dizard 1970; Edwards 1970; Tomlinson 1970), who in turn brought still more preexisting psychological strength to the movement. Thus, while there may well have been some self-hating Blacks who added to the dynamics of the Black movement, in more instances than not, and as the research data clearly imply, the overall character of the movement reflected the involvement of countless thousands of fairly average, mentally stable Black people whose nigrescence experience transformed their racial and cultural priorities, not their personalities.

NIGRESCENCE CORRELATIONAL STUDIES AND SELF-HATRED

Having completed our analysis of positive mental health trends and nigrescence, let us finally turn to a discussion of nigrescence and self-hatred. Three nigrescence-related PI and RGO correlational studies offer insight into Black self-hatred, especially as it applies to the Pre-encounter stage. As a transition into this analysis, note that the concept of Black self-hatred has held center stage in the discourse on Black psychological functioning since the early 1940s, and if the current work has been successful at anything, it has been to show that this preoccupation with self-hatred has time and again kept researchers from discovering Black strengths. I am in no way suggesting that Black self-hatred is a myth, but something in addition to color preference in children or Eurocentric attitudes in adults must be its markers because many Black children who are not self-hating prefer the color white, and many Black adults, positioned at the Pre-encounter stage, evidence a strong PI profile despite their otherwise Eurocentric, or "outgroup," frame of reference. The same holds true for Blacks who prefer Black and are "in-group" oriented. The lack of a relationship between PI and

RGO in Black identity means not only that a white preference does not predict pathology but that a Black preference or being Afrocentric may not predict mental health.

Just as our analysis is driving us toward the conclusion that Black mental health is a multidimensional concept, the comprehension of which is beyond univariate studies in general and racial-preference studies in particular, the same is likely true of the nature of Black self-hatred. It, too, is probably a complex, layered, multidimensional construct, more subject to revelation in studies employing a cluster of measures than single-factor explorations. Three nigrescence studies give credence to this point of view.

In 1985, Thomas A. Parham, a leading nigrescence theorist, and Janet E. Helms, one the major proponents of nigrescence research in the field of counseling psychology and cross-cultural psychology, published the results of a study to determine whether PI strengths or weaknesses configure in any particular fashion across the stages of nigrescence. Parham and Helms (1985) administered the Racial Identity Attitudes Scale (an RGO measure sensitive to the stages of nigrescence) and various paper-and-pencil PI measures to a group of male and female college students. Their method of analysis made it possible to map trends across the stages, as well as to isolate possible differential patterns operating at any particular stage. Their results showed that racial attitudes and PI were significantly related, but most of the variability could be traced to Pre-encounter (stage 1 identity). That is, what at first appeared as an overall relationship was shown to apply only to the Pre-encounter stage. For instance, Internalization (stage 4) of racial attitudes did not show a relationship to PI; advanced identity was associated with neither PI advantages nor disadvantages. But at stage 1 a relationship was discovered, as people with Pre-encounter attitudes were more likely to exhibit mental health deficits. A somewhat overlooked finding, and one we return to shortly, was that the negative propensities linked to the Pre-encounter identity accounted for only a small percentage of the variance. Among other things, this raised the possibility that while a fraction of the Pre-encounter dynamics was associated with self-hatred, apparently a great deal more could be explained by themes other than self-hatred. That is, perhaps some Pre-encounter people were self-hating, but far more were not.

A few years after their findings were published, Parham, Helms, and I began working on what we anticipated would be the most comprehensive review article for the theory and research on nigrescence. I was well into Part One of the current manuscript, and I communicated my puzzlement over their finding of a configuration between PI and RGO variables at the Pre-encounter stage that seemed to form a self-hatred profile. I told them about the forty-five PI and RGO correlational studies that provided almost categoric evidence that PI and RGO in studies of Black identity were not generally related. I pointed out that an examination of the small number of studies that hinted at the possibility that, under certain circumstances, PI and RGO may be connected, especially in the sense of forming an adult Black self-hatred syndrome, ultimately proved frustrating because subsequent analysis revealed no distinct pattern from study to study. I further commented that technically speaking, the history of the study of Black identity has produced very little empirical evidence that reveals, with any degree of precision, when personal identity problems or pathologies are in fact attributable to conflicts in the person's reference group orientation. From my vantage point, their finding was an enigma.

It turned out that neither Parham nor Helms was caught off guard by the revelations about the PI and RGO findings from the general literature because each of them had independently come to the conclusion that the original depiction of Pre-encounter was *too* negative. Nevertheless, their clinical experience had taught them that a certain percentage of people at the Pre-encounter stage are, in fact, self-hating.

Eventually we came to the conclusion that the enigma of self-hatred is akin to the Russian *mariska*[2] dolls (each of which contains a smaller replica of itself) in which the self-hatred cluster is a small subset of a more encompassing stage 1 pattern that is not indicative of self-hatred. We speculated that, like the smallest mariska doll, self-hatred may "hide" from empiricists in the aggregation of data for all stage 1 types, but be vivid as hell for clinicians. And, as fate would have it, clinicians are likely to be the professionals toward whom self-hating Negroes will turn for help and therapy. The clinicians, in turn, will be perplexed when empiricists inform them that placement in stage 1 is not a powerful predictor of self-hatred. That is, most self-hating Negroes may be Pre-encounter oriented, but most Pre-encounter Negroes may not be self-hating. Similarly, most self-hating Black children may have a preference for white, but most Black children who prefer white may not be self-hating. Thus, being Pre-encounter or preferring white may

---

2. The *mariska* doll set is a toy from Russia that at first appears to be a single doll; when opened, however, a smaller doll is revealed inside the first. When the second doll is opened, still another, even smaller doll is uncovered. This process is repeated until one unearths a doll that is a small fraction of the size of the first doll.

be factors that are part of the self-hatred constellation but, by themselves, these factors may be very poor predictors of self-hatred. As we demonstrated at the end of Part One, an out-group orientation and a preference for white can be associated with any number of interpretations and outcomes besides self-hatred. This suggests that self-hatred is a multidimensional rather than a unidimensional construct. A multidimensional, multimethod study may better unveil the smallest "mariska," assuming the researcher is aware that the self-hatred complex is hiding within aggregate data.

With the metaphor of the mariska dolls in mind, we conducted a very close reading of multidimensional, multimethod PI and RGO correlational studies that focused on nigrescence, including the Parham and Helms (1985) study and two other studies (Denton 1985; Williams 1975). The rather involved and lengthy reanalysis of these studies can be found in our review of the nigrescence literature (Cross, Parham, and Helms, in press).

What we found, especially in the reanalysis of the study by Denton (1985), is that in all likelihood the Pre-encounter stage incorporates two prototypes. Persons representing the more dominant type tend to have positive PI attributes and feel close to Black people, but they tend to place low salience on being Black and may even have a decidedly Eurocentric perspective. In a second typology, a cluster of three RGO factors seemed to predict self-hatred at the PI level. Self-hatred, as operationalized by low self-esteem and inadequate self-actualization (Denton 1985), was found in the RGO level of the following Blacks:

1. Those positioned at stage 1 with an identity that reflected an assimilationist, Eurocentric, and white orientation (*stage 1 or out-group, orientation*)

2. Those suffering from a sense of alienation from Black people and the Black community; feeling cut-off and basically unsupported by other Blacks (*alienation*)

3. Those likely to perceive Blacks in terms of the same stereotypes associated with white racists (*anti-Black*)

By itself, the first factor, having an out-group orientation or showing a white preference, is a rather weak predictor of self-hatred because many stage 1 Blacks have high self-esteem, relish Black affiliations, and do not view Blacks through the prism of racist stereotypes. It is the stage 1 profile in combination with a sense of alienation from other Blacks and the internalization of negative images that define self-hatred in the Black community.

Factors 2 and 3 thus add strong elements of negativity to the person's frame of reference; being in stage 1 apparently does not automatically reflect this negativity. This suggests a distinction to be made between being pro-white or having strong Eurocentric preferences or placing low salience toward being Black and being *anti-Black*. We are so accustomed to conceptualizing Black identity in either/or terms that it is difficult to imagine how someone who is pro-white can avoid being anti-Black.

Perhaps the answer can be found in a little-known study completed in the early 1970s. Lois Powell Johnson (1972) set out to construct a "cultural identity questionnaire" based on the notion that pro-white and anti-Black were highly correlated. Johnson developed a 51-item questionnaire, 23 items forming a pro-white subscale and 28 comprising an anti-Black scale. In order to test and enhance the reliability and construct validity of her scale, Johnson administered it, along with a battery of measures, to Black high school and college students. She found that high scores on the variables of anomie, intolerance of ambiguity, alienation, stoicism, and rigidity were positively related to high scores on the anti-Black subscale. Only stoicism and tolerance were correlated with high pro-whiteness. More important, Johnson placed the two subscales in a nomological network to evaluate their construct validity, and she found the pro-white scale had limited predictive power. At the conclusion of her study, Johnson recommended that the pro-white dimension no longer be considered a viable measure of Black self-hatred. From the empirical results reviewed here, perhaps we can conclude that Johnson's long-overlooked study should be given a closer look.

To sum up: The concept of Black self-hatred is no less complex than any other aspect of Black psychological functioning. It cannot be inferred from simple(minded) racial-preference tests, nor is it typical of Blacks in the first stage of nigrescence. Although seldom revealed in the general literature—other than as vague interactions or as the "projections" of investigators—a handful of nigrescence studies have uncovered evidence that an undetermined but probably small percentage of stage 1 (out-group oriented) types exhibit self-hatred tendencies. More specifically, when it is characterized by a Eurocentric perspective, a tendency to feel estranged, distant, alienated, unsupported by, and unaffiliated with other Blacks, plus a tendency to hold negative stereotypes and negative racial images of Blacks, the stage 1, out-group-oriented identity has been linked to depression, low self-esteem, inadequate self-actualization, aggressive as opposed to nurturing social attitudes, a propensity in asocial behavior to commit violent crimes, hostility, tension, hypersensitivity, anxiety, defeatism (Brown 1979; Cross, Parham, and Helms, in press; Denton 1985; Parham and Helms 1985; Taylor 1986; Terrell, Taylor, and Terrell 1980; Williams 1975). As shown by Parham and Helms (1985), and nearly replicated in a more recent study from the general literature (Burnett 1987), the PI and RGO constellation known as self-hatred accounts for very little variance. Consequently, although oppression and racism have resulted in stage 1 Blacks being socialized to see the world with some variant of a Eurocentric perspective, it bears repeating that most stage 1 Blacks "have not internalized racist thinking about Blacks, they nurture and relish the support of Black friends and associates, and they feel good about themselves, personally" (Cross, Parham, and Helms, in press).

In forging a revisionist perspective on the history and study of Black identity, we must keep in mind that any plausible theory of "minority" identity development should be capable of distinguishing between the psychological and philosophical consequences of oppression and the psychological and philosophical triumphs of an oppressed group. Moreover, we must understand that the exploitation of a minority group does not presuppose the dehumanization of a minority group. In fact, from the days of Black slavery through the beginnings of the so-called Black underclass in the early 1970s (Glasgow 1981), revisionist observers of Black life have demonstrated, without resorting to romanticism or distortion, that Blacks have often been able to establish a quality of life at the family (Gutman 1976), community (Dickerson 1986; Trotter 1985), institutional (Anderson 1988; Woodson 1919), social network and organizational (Hine 1989), and artistic and cultural (Dover 1960; Gates 1988; Gayle 1971; Hansberry 1958; Southern 1971) levels seldom anticipated, and never intended, by those who oppressed and exploited Blacks. If the current work has achieved its objective, we can now add that at the level of the psychology of the individual, the multilayered strengths of Black communities have afforded a successful, positive socialization of children who, as adults, have transmitted these strengths to the next generation over many generations. Only in the most recent times, when poor and working-class Blacks have become, in economic terms, superfluous to society, has the modest level of material resources needed to continue this positive tradition been withdrawn, giving rise to the alleged nihilism of the underclass. As an aside, my prediction is that when the research is finally all in, the "negative psychology" of the underclass will be shown to be an exaggeration; the underclass will be revealed to be less a psychological problem than a predicament bought on by systemic and structural changes beyond the pale of any "will power" the members of the underclass are able to muster. On this point, see Ishmael Reed's commentary in the *Nation*, November 30, 1989.

Yet, if an oppressor can control the reference group orientation and political orientation of a minority, it really does not matter that the exploited group has individual members who present extremely attractive profiles on various measures of personal identity (PI). In the early 1950s, many in the Black community turned their backs on Paul Robeson and W. E. B. Du Bois, not out of a sense of personal self-hatred, but because their white-oriented world view (i.e., a fear of communism or of being labeled "un-American") dictated that certain Blacks be viewed as *problems* and others, such as George Washington Carver and Booker T. Washington, be seen as *acceptable*. That today such figures as Du Bois, Robeson, Marcus Garvey, Malcolm X, Angela Davis, Toni Morrison, Rosa Parks, *and* Carver and Washington are held in esteem is hardly symptomatic of personality change but most certainly reflects a dramatic reorganization of the reference group to which the world view of many Blacks is anchored. The essential difference among Blacks, insofar as level of Blackness is concerned, is often less psychological (PI related) than cultural, ideological, and philosophical (RGO related).

All of which is to say that the price of a stage 1 identity—having an "out-group perspective"—is not necessarily poor mental health but the development of a world view and value system that can inhibit one's knowledge about and one's capacity to be an advocate for, the political and cultural interests that flow from the nonassimilated, more "ethnic" Black frame of reference. An out-group perspective in Blacks reflects the extent to which the world view of the dominant group ("Americanism") has been internalized by a minority group member. It is not necessarily self-rejection. In this light, racial identity studies employing RGO outcomes are more apt to uncover political–cultural propensities than psychological traits. With the rising influence of Blacks and other minority-group members who are assimilated and ultra-conservative but otherwise "normal" in their behavior, it is important that we make ourselves keenly aware of PI and RGO distinctions. One value in differentiating between PI and RGO is that change in RGO, whether toward assimilation or increased ethnicity, can be comprehended without resorting to pejorative psychological models that inevitably fail to predict the healthy behavior of the assimilated or to romantic "ethnicity" models that imply that through an increase in the level of one's Blackness, all one's problems can be solved. Nigrescence may change one's focus on life, but it seldom transforms *problems* of personality.

CHAPTER 6

Rethinking Nigrescence

When I first wrote about nigrescence in the early 1970s, I referred to the identity change process as a "Negro-to-Black conversion experience." The same kind of process could probably have been seen in Black behavior during the Harlem Renaissance and the Garvey movement of the 1920s. Ironically, nigrescence then was codified as the emergence of the new Negro:

> In the last decade something beyond the guard of statistics has happened in the life of the American Negro and the three norns who have traditionally presided over the Negro problem have a challenge in their laps. The Sociologist, the Philanthropist, the Race-leader are not unaware of the New Negro, but they are at a loss to account for him. He simply cannot be swathed in their formulae. For the younger generation is vibrant with a new psychology; the new spirit is awake in the masses, and under the very eyes of the professional observers is transforming what has been a perennial problem into the progressive phases of contemporary Negro life. (Locke 1925)

The term Negro is dated today; the self-referents most Blacks employ are Black, Black American, and African-American. In contemporary circles, one is more likely to hear Blacks make a distinction between having a Eurocentric or an Afrocentric identity. But whether we talk about the new Negro in the 1920s, the Negro-to-Black metamorphosis in the 1970s, or the search for Afrocentricity in the 1990s, the five stages of Black identity development remain the same: *Pre-encounter* (stage 1) depicts the identity to be changed; *Encounter* (stage 2) isolates the point at which the person feels compelled to change; *Immersion–Emersion* (stage 3) describes the vortex of identity change; and *Internalization* and *Internalization–Commitment* (stages 4 and 5) describe the habituation and internalization of the new identity.

Stage 1: Pre-encounter

Nigrescence is a *resocializing* experience; it seeks to transform a preexisting identity (a non-Afrocentric identity) into one that is Afrocentric. The focus of the Pre-encounter stage is this preexisting identity, the identity to be changed. Of course, it is possible for a Black person to be socialized from early childhood through adolescence to have a Black identity. At adulthood, such a person is not likely to be in need of nigrescence, although Parham (1989) has extended nigrescence theory to include a concept of *recycling* (i.e., periodic episodes of nigrescence across the life span). More to the point, while nigrescence is not a process for mapping the socialization of children, it is a model that explains how *assimilated* Black adults, as well as *deracinated, deculturalized* or *miseducated* Black adults are transformed by a series of circumstances and events into persons who are more Black or Afrocentrically aligned.

PRE-ENCOUNTER ATTITUDES AND CHARACTERISTICS

Low-Salience Attitudes. Persons in the Pre-encounter stage hold attitudes toward race that range from low salience to race neutrality to anti-Black. Persons who hold low-salience views do not deny being Black, but this "physical" fact is thought to play an insignificant role in their everyday lives. Being Black and having knowledge about the Black experience have little to do with their perceived sense of happiness and well-being, and Blackness contributes little to their life. In a sense, those at the Pre-encounter stage place value in things other than their Blackness—their religion, their lifestyle, their social status, their profession, or something else. Thus they have values and do experience a meaningful existence; it is just that little emphasis is given to Blackness. As long as their Pre-encounter attitudes bring them a sense of fulfillment, a meaningful existence, and an internal sense of stability, order, and harmony, such persons will probably not need any identity change, let alone a movement toward Afrocentricity.

Some low-salience types simply have not given much thought to race issues; they seem to be dumbfounded and naive during racial discussions. They often see personal progress as a matter of free will, initiative, rugged individualism, and a personal motivation to achieve. Others have taken a more conscious route toward neutrality and see themselves as having reached a higher plane (i.e., abstract humanism), beneath which lies what is to them the vulgar world of race and ethnicity. Pressed to give a self-referent, they may respond that they are "human beings who happen to be Black."

Social-stigma Attitudes. A variant of the low-salience perspective can be found in the Black person who, while sharing the low-salience orientation, also sees race as a problem or a stigma. Thus, by default, some significance is attributed to race, not as a proactive force or cultural issue, but as a social stigma that must be negotiated from time to time. The only "meaning" accorded to race is its tie to issues of *social discrimination*; from this perspective, race is a hassle, a problem, an imposition. Such people may indeed have an interest in Black causes, not as a way of supporting Black culture and exploring Black history, but to join with those who are trying to destroy the social stigma associated with Blackness. The need to defend oneself against Blackness-as-stigma can be found in Pre-encounter persons who otherwise have little knowledge of Black history and culture. Consequently, when you ask such people to define their Black identity, they invariably respond by telling you what it is like to be oppressed.

Anti-Black Attitudes. The extreme racial attitude pattern to be found in the Pre-encounter stage is anti-Blackness. There are some Blacks for whom being Black is very important, not as a positive force, but as a *negative reference group*. Blackness and Black people define their internal model of what they dislike. They look on Black people with a perspective that comes very close to that of white racists. Anti-Blacks loath other Blacks; they feel alienated from them and do not see Blacks or the Black community as potential or actual sources of personal support. The anti-Black vision of Blackness is dominated by racist stereotypes or, on the other side of the coin, anti-Blacks may hold positive stereotypes of white people and white culture. In viewing Black people as their own worst enemy, Black anti-Blacks often explain the "race problem" through the prism of some variant of "blame the victim." In positions of leadership, Black anti-Blacks can be very effective in weaving an ideology that bashes Black leaders, Black institutions, Black studies, the Black family, and Black culture.

One is tempted to cluster various *self-destructive behaviors* in the context of anti-Blackness. Certainly, anti-Black attitudes, combined with an overall sense of hopelessness, can lead to drug addiction and other "escapist" solutions. The easy availability of drugs in Black communities, however, entraps some of the brightest and most stable Black youngsters, even as it is likely to attract the most vulnerable. Furthermore, keep in mind that successful Black athletes and highly paid Black performers and entertainers are susceptible to drug abuse, not through feelings of self-hatred and anti-Black attitudes, but from an exaggerated sense of personal efficacy and high self-esteem. These engender a distorted belief that, unlike mere mortals, superstars can experiment with drugs and still be "strong enough" to resist addiction. Of course, once the addiction takes hold, the origin of the habit—whether it is hopelessness or high self-esteem—matters not at all. Priority is placed on whatever sustains and satisfies the addiction. Such persons contribute little to the Black community and, in this sense, fall in the Pre-encounter category.

Pre-encounter thus covers a broad range of attitudes. And these major attitudinal markers of Pre-encounter may be fused with other Pre-encounter characteristics: miseducation, a Eurocentric cultural frame of reference, spotlight or "race-image" anxiety, a race-conflict resolution model that stresses assimilation–integration objectives, and a value system that gives preference to other than Afrocentric priorities.

Miseducation.   In being formally educated to embrace a Western cultural–historical perspective, Pre-encounter Blacks cannot help but experience varying degrees of miseducation about the significance of the Black experience. In fact, Pre-encounter Blacks are frequently "average" products of a formal education system that is extremely monoracial and monocultural (i.e., white and Western dominated) in its emphasis. One reason the need for nigrescence is such a ubiquitous theme in the discourse on Black identity is that it is very difficult for *any* Black American to progress through the public schools without being miseducated about the role of Africa in Western civilization and world culture in general, and the role of Blacks in the evolution of American culture and history in particular. This miseducation does not automatically lead to self-hatred, but it most certainly can distort intra-Black discourse on Black cultural–historical issues and/or Black challenges and problems. Thus, Pre-encounter Blacks do not oppose Black Studies programs because of some "unconscious anti-Black or self-hatred complex"; instead, their cultural bias blinds them to the fact that there are histories besides "American history," that there are cultural experiences besides "Western civilization." The most damning aspect of miseducation is not necessarily poor mental health but the development of a world view and cultural–historical perspective that can inhibit knowledge about, and thus the capacity to be an advocate for, the cultural, political, economic, and historical interests of Black people.

Black anti-Blacks suffer from an extreme miseducation that in fact can result in self-hatred. They tend to have a very distorted interpretation of Black history and thus a very distorted image of the historical, cultural, economic, and political *potential* of Black people. They believe that Black people came from a strange, uncivilized, "dark" continent and that slavery was a civilizing experience. From their vantage point, there is nothing to be gained from a study of the slavery period because "real" Black history begins at the end of the American Civil War. Among poor Blacks, anti-Blacks actually develop the belief that Blacks somehow deserve the misery that comes with poverty, with Blacks being viewed as incapable of anything else. Extreme miseducation can result in a great deal of skepticism about the abilities and capacities of Black leaders, Black businesses, and Black professionals, and an equal degree of romanticism and near mysticism concerning the capacities and talents of whites. That is, if Blacks are thought to be intellectually inferior and technologically backward, whites are seen as intellectually superior and technically advanced.

A Eurocentric Cultural Perspective. As a further extension of the miseducation concept, we note that Pre-encounter persons frequently have been socialized to favor a Eurocentric cultural perspective. With this perspective, notions of beauty and art are derived from a white and decidedly Western aesthetic, as reflected in the content, themes, vehicles of emphasis, colorations, and modes of expressions in cultural and academic preferences. Afrocentricists frequently interpret a Pre-encounter person's preference for Western art as an expression of self-hatred, but this is an error. In rare instances, some Pre-encounter Blacks have been raised in a manner that leaves them nearly ignorant of the existence of cultural perspectives other than the Eurocentric. But most Pre-encounter persons have been socialized to be bicultural; that is, they know about and sometimes appreciate both Black and white artistic expressions. Nonetheless, the low-salience person in particular is apt to give higher status to Western art. For example, Pre-encounter parents tend to socialize their children to place greater emphasis on "high culture" or "classical art forms" (ballet, classical music, modern dance, etc.), than on taking classes in jazz, African dance, and Black literature, which are seldom considered. Although the parents may personally enjoy Black music and art, they may depict Black art as "ethnic," "lowly," "less important;" as something to be lost along the way toward acceptance and assimilation into the mainstream. Thus it is not always true that Pre-encounter/low-salience Negroes lack knowledge or experience with Black art. What separates them from people in more advanced states of Blackness are the *attitudes* they hold toward Black art forms and the preferences they have for Western versus Black art.

It is important to stress that there is nothing offensive or surprising in the fact that Blacks socialized in a Western society such as the United States, England, or France learn to appreciate and become intensely involved in Western art forms. As is well known, some of today's greatest performers and advocates of Western music and culture are Black people and other people of color. In September 1988, I was present at the National Conference of the New York Philharmonic Music Assistance Fund Program, which was attended by practically every active and retired Black musician employed with an American classical orchestra. In preparation for the conference, a number of musicians were interviewed about their career development, and my presentation at one of the sessions involved a summary of the key issues and themes reflected in their transcribed interviews. Time and again it was clear that the musicians had developed a dual aesthetic, and what is more important for the point being made here, their appreciation of European art in no way diminished their liking for African-American music. It is when the appreciation of one art form is used as a rationale to reject or neglect another that we have a problem, and that is often what happens at the level of Pre-encounter, where identification with European music and culture may be employed as a measure of cultural "correctness."

Black anti-Blacks wrongly put white art and Black art on the same continuum, with white art defining what is positive, rational, and highly developed, and Black art connoting that which is exotic, emotional, and primitive. Thus classical music, ballet, and theater define "good art"; jazz, the blues, African dance, and so forth are seen as interesting but less well developed, if not as primitive and inferior imitations of white artistic expression. In its more vulgar expression, Black anti-Blacks may even prefer light skin, "blow-dry" hair, and European facial features.

Finally, it would be a mistake to think that these attitudes are solely a problem of the Black middle class. Even in the inner city or ghetto, where purer forms of Black expression can readily be found, one can find inner-city residents referring to the blues or jazz as low, bad, or sexy. Sometimes such descriptions capture the Black urban residents' notion of what is earthy and soulful, but at other times such terms connote a pejorative perspective toward Black art, Black life, and Black culture. That "good art" is Western art is an attitudes that can be found in Pre-encounter persons in any socio-economic class.

Spotlight, or Race Image, Anxiety. Most Black people, with the exception of those who are anti-Black in perspective, manage to keep from internalizing extremely negative stereotypes that racist whites have of Black people. But although Pre-encounter Blacks do not believe in these stereotypes, they are often overly sensitive to the fact that many white people *do* believe in them. This can lead to a hypersensitivity toward racial issues in which one is constantly on the lookout for any negative portrayal of Blacks. As a positive adaptation, this sensitivity can help the person flush out instances of social discrimination and racism. But, ironically, this sensitivity to discrimination and stereotyping can also lead to an anxiety over things being "too Black." Even though a Pre-encounter person is married to a Black person and lives in a Black community, there are times when that Pre-encounter person may feel the situation is "not integrated enough." Matters are thought to get out of hand when Blacks are too loud or act in a disorderly fashion or, in the context of the 1988 presidential election, are too "Willie Horton"-like. I call anxiety about being too Black *spotlight anxiety*. It is often felt only when the person is in the company of whites, or when the situation is somehow construed as placing one in the "spotlight." It is a concern that is not usually revealed in informal, all-Black circumstances. In this sense, it is almost as though the person accepts as natural those all-Black situations that are "informal," but becomes nervous about formalized or organized, and "public," all-Black efforts. When whites are around, the person with spotlight anxiety may check to determine whether he or she, or some other Black who is present, is acting *too* Black and thus failing to project the best race image. A great deal of pain and sorrow can be associated with such behavior, and there are instances of "Amos 'n' Andy" humor when Pre-encounter Blacks twist their language and actions to fit a contrived notion of appropriate Black behavior.

Blacks who are anti-Black are beyond any anxiety about the race's image; for them, the negative stereotypes white people hold in reference to Blacks are taken as truth. They feel enslaved in a body and community they hate. They feel nothing but a sense of imposition, alienation, and inferiority; their sense of Blackness is clearly that of a *mark of oppression*.

Assimilation—Integration.   In being socialized to see the system as adequate, in suffering various degrees of miseducation about the origin of Black problems, and in having a basic faith in the system, Pre-encounter Blacks are predisposed to accept a blame-the-victim analysis of Black problems and a race-conflict-resolution perspective that stresses assimilation—integration themes. With this perspective, it is felt that if Blacks can "overcome" their "self-made" problems and become part of the system, as is perceived to have happened to previously disadvantaged (white ethnic) groups, the race problem could be resolved. The message is generally framed with great sophistication when articulated by well-educated Pre-encounter Blacks, or it can be stated crudely by others. White racism is viewed as a surface-level problem, one that exists alongside the basic strengths and race-neutral opportunity structures and culture of the society. Once one has managed to work through discriminatory obstacles, so this thinking goes, the onus is on Blacks to prepare themselves in a fashion that will lead to their acceptance by whites. The emphasis is on *one-way* change; Blacks will learn to fit in, while whites are asked simply to stop discriminating. No real demands are placed on white attitudes, white culture, and white institutions because the problem of racism is at the surface level of white institutions and society. Consequently, unlike pluralistic notions of integration or concepts of multiculturalism, this kind of Pre-encounter Black is often wedded to an assimilationist vision of race-conflict resolution and social mobility. In fact, there may be instances where such Pre-encounter Blacks oppose pluralistic and multicultural education as unnecessary, wasteful, or somehow "inferior."

Value Structure and Value Orientation.   In my original nigrescence model, I stressed that Pre-encounter Blacks have radically different value structures (individualism vs. communalism) and orientations (low salience on Blackness vs. high salience for things Black) from Blacks in the advanced stages. But, I now believe that while holding radically different value orientations, Pre-encounter persons do not necessarily differ in their value structures from persons in advanced stages of Black identity development. People in Pre-encounter often have affiliations with secular, political, and religious organizations, and have been known to demonstrate tremendous commitment and even militant dedication to certain issues, beliefs, and causes that go beyond merely "thinking about one's self." These are attributes I originally associated with stage 4 or 5. In other words, the difference between persons at either extreme of the process, insofar as values are concerned, may not be at the level of value structure. Instead, it may be at the level of value orientation. Pre-encounter persons place priority on organizations and causes that have low race salience and/or little nationalistic import, while Blacks who are deeper into nigrescence stress high race salience activities and organizations. At the value-structure level of analysis, however, Pre-encounter Blacks may be no less communalistic or individualistic than Blacks at other stages.

SUMMARY

Whether low salience or anti-Black, the spectrum of Pre-encounter attitudes and world views transcends social-class boundaries. Class status may affect how Pre-encounter attitudes are expressed, but the generic messages, priorities, and preferences embedded in middle- and lower-class Black expressions are generally equivalent. Thus, low salience can be found in a middle-class Black professional for whom Blackness has little meaning or can be seen in an inner-city resident whose primary vehicle for meaning and purpose in life is the Christian church. At the more negative extreme of Pre-encounter, Blacks who are anti-Black can include a middle-class Black youth who has joined the ranks of a white-dominated, "punk" street group or an inner-city youth who, as a member of a Black street gang, pushes dope on other Black kids. Pre-encounter people can be rich or poor, light skinned or ebony hued, live in Vermont or Harlem, and attend overwhelmingly white schools or all-Black institutions.

In the past, oppression and miseducation have been the main factors determining the social production of Pre-encounter attitudes. Today, such attitudes are evolving as a result of the *success* of the Black 1960s. Black success, as well as white oppression, can produce Pre-encounter attitudes. Over the past twenty years, some Blacks have experienced what, by any standard, would be called success within the American system. They are rich, they live in exclusive communities, they manage and sometimes head major corporations, and their children attend the finest educational institutions money can buy. They are major contributors to organizations that advocate Western culture. In the overall scheme of things, they are practically invisible to the Black world. Thus their success, not their experience with oppression, has led them to embrace Pre-encounter attitudes. Of course, not all successful middle-class and wealthy Blacks can be categorized in this fashion. And the point I am making here is not a negative stereotyping of the wealthy and the middle class, but a reminder to the reader that what can lead to the production of Pre-encounter attitudes in Black people covers a multitude of situations and circumstances. As is true in all the stages, Pre-encounter is an attitude or perspective, not an inherited or divinely ordained trait. People who share the same Pre-encounter-oriented racial and cultural frame of reference do so through a variety of social experiences and circumstances, including instances of success and oppression.

It would be a mistake to assume that Pre-encounter is a form of mental illness. Blacks who are anti-Black may very well evidence poor mental health, but the great majority of Pre-encounter Blacks are probably as mentally healthy as Blacks in the more advanced stages of nigrescence. The key factors that separate Pre-encounter Blacks from those who are Afrocentric are value orientation, historical perspective, and world view. The complexity of the American economy means that there are all sorts of ecological niches within which Blacks are socialized, and each niche may support the growth of very particularistic world views, many of which are not framed by a racial or Afrocentric perspective. Pre-encounter Black are part of the diversity of the Black experience and must be understood as such.

Nevertheless, whenever life's circumstances result in the social production of a Black person for whom "race" has limited personal salience or, in the case of the Black who is anti-Black, extremely negative personal salience, the scene is set for a possible identity conversion experience.

Stage 2: Encounter

The Pre-encounter identity is usually the person's first identity, that is, the identity shaped by his or her early development. This socialization involves years of experiences with one's immediate family, extended family, neighborhood and community, and schools; it covers the years of childhood, adolescence, and early adulthood. It is a tried and fully tested identity that serves the person day in and day out. It helps him or her feel centered, meaningful, and in control by making life predictable. Although we can tolerate and can even come to enjoy a certain amount of change and variety in our external environment, it is almost impossible to imagine a world in which, at the beginning of every day, we had to reconstruct our identity. The predictability and stability functions of one's identity serve as filters against rapid and dramatic identity change. A person's identity filters incoming experiences so that the information "fits" into his or her current understanding of self and the world in which he or she lives. Any fully developed identity, let alone a Pre-encounter identity, is difficult to change. Stage 2 of the nigrescence process tries to pinpoint those circumstances and events that are likely to induce identity metamorphosis in an individual.

Since a person's ongoing identity will defend itself against identity change, the person usually has to experience some sort of *encounter* that has the effect of catching him or her "off guard." The encounter must work around, slip through, or even shatter the relevance of the person's current identity and world view, and at the same time provide some hint of the direction in which to point the person to be resocialized or transformed.

Sometimes the encounter can be a single dramatic event. In the late 1960s, the death of Dr. Martin L. King, Jr., sent thousands of Pre-encounter Negroes on a search for a deeper understanding of the Black Power movement. In like manner, being personally assaulted or witnessing a friend being assaulted by the police, watching a televised report of a racial incident, or meeting with a friend or a loved one who is further advanced into Blackness may "turn a person on" to his or her own Blackness. Middle-class Blacks who have somehow managed to avoid or escape racial incidents at earlier points in their lives often begin nigrescence after a startling racial episode in college or at their place of employment. Having worked so hard at being the "right kind of Negro," racist encounters can shatter a Pre-encounter person's conception of himself or herself and his or her understanding of the state of Black America.

> I have a white education, a white accent, I conform to white
> middle-class standards in virtually every choice, from preferring
> Brooks Brothers oxford cloth to religiously clutching my gold
> cards as the tickets to the good life. I'm not really complaining
> about that. The world, even the white world, has been, if not
> good, then acceptable to me. But as I get older, I feel the world
> closing in. I feel that I failed to notice something, or that I've
> been deceived. (Walton 1989)

For lower-class Pre-encounter Blacks, encounters with the law and imprisonment can be a turning point. While on the street, doing his or her "thing," the Pre-encounter Black may be oblivious to discussions about Blackness, but incarceration may so traumatize that person that he or she becomes receptive to different interpretations of the meaning of life. Malcolm X is only the most famous of a long list of Black men and women whose search for Blackness followed on the heels of their imprisonment.

In many instances, it is not a single event that constitutes a person's encounter but a series of small, eye-opening episodes, each of which chips away at the person's ongoing world view. These small encounters have a cumulative effect; at a certain point, the straw comes that "breaks the camel's back," and the person feels the push toward nigrescence.

Looked at more closely, we see that the Encounter entails two steps: experiencing an encounter and personalizing it. By this two-step analysis, I mean to split a hair. That is, I want to make a distinction between being in the path or being the object of an encounter event and actually personalizing it by being "turned around by it." For example, in April 1968, not every Black person who heard about the death of Dr. Martin Luther King, Jr., was transformed into a Black Power advocate. Some people "experienced" the event, but it did not lead to change. Others, experiencing the same event (i.e., hearing of King's death), were personally traumatized by it, and it called into question their continued embracement of an integrationist ethos. For these people, the void created in doubting their world view was simultaneously filled by the increasing credibility of something called Blackness. Using a different example, two Blacks working in different but similar white-dominated corporations may each encounter a racist situation. One may respond with the attitude that one must learn to "roll with the punches," while the other may describe the event as "having helped me see, for the very first time, that racism is still an important obstacle in life." An encounter must have a personal impact on the individual, and in a powerful way. In the course of a year, let alone a lifetime, just about every Black person is exposed to information or some sort of racist situation that has the potential to be an encounter, but unless the person, for whatever reason, personalizes that encounter, his or her ongoing world view or attitude about race may go unchanged. One last point: The Encounter need *not* be negative. A racist event may revolve around exposure to powerful cultural–historical information about the Black experience, information previously unknown to the person involved. Giving credence (i.e., personalizing) to this information may challenge someone radically to rethink his or conception of Black history and Black culture. Even in such instances, however, a negative side to the Encounter is often introduced, for it is almost inevitable that the person will become enraged at the thought of having been previously mis-educated by white racist institutions.

While an encounter may eventually steer a person toward nigrescence, the person's initial reaction may be one of confusion, alarm, anomie, or even depression. It can be a very painful experience to discover that one's frame of reference, world view, or value system is "wrong," "dysfunctional," or, more to the point, "not Black or Afrocentric enough." Such reactions are generally temporary. Somehow the person picks himself or herself up and begins cautiously and perhaps even fearfully to test the validity of the new perceptions. On the outside, such a person is generally very quiet; internally, a storm is brewing. He or she will seek out new information or attend meetings in order to assess whether or not to submit to change.

Each individual ponders very personal questions. The Black intellectual wonders: "Have I been unaware of the Black experience, or was I programmed to see little value in its study?" A ghetto youth asks: "Am I simply trying to get over on a day-to-day basis, or am I denying the fact that my hustle involves exploiting and even endangering my own people?" A Black college student reflects: "Am I being prepared for the future, or am I being miseducated for someone else's purposes?" Tentative answers are obvious, and the person quickly compares the implications of his or her new insights with the manner in which he or she has been living (Pre-encounter stance). Previously hostile or, at best, neutral toward Blackness and things Afrocentric, the Encounter jolts the person into at least considering a different interpretation of the Black condition.

The Encounter engenders a great range of emotions; guilt, anger, and general anxiety may become energizing factors. A middle-class person may feel guilty for having denied the significance of race; a lower-class person may feel guilt and shame for having degraded Blackness through street hustle and exploitation. Simultaneously, such persons may feel angry at those perceived as having "caused" their predicament—white people and all the white world. And, each person feels anxious at the discovery that there is another level of Blackness to which he or she should aspire. Inner-directed guilt, rage at white people, and an anxiety about becoming the right kind of Black person combine to form a psychic energy that flings the person into a frantic, determined, obsessive, extremely motivated search for Black identity. The Pre-encounter person is dying; the Black American, or "Afrocentric" person, is beginning to emerge.

Stage 3: Immersion–Emersion

The Immersion–Emersion stage of nigrescence addresses the most sensational aspect of Black identity development, for it represents the vortex of psychological nigrescence. There is nothing subtle about this stage, and with good reason. During this period of transition, the person begins to demolish the old perspective and simultaneously tries to construct what will become his or her new frame of reference. In moving from the Encounter to the Immersion–Emersion stage, the person has not yet changed but has made the decision to commit himself or herself to change. Consequently, on entering the Immersion–Emersion stage, the person is more familiar with the identity to be destroyed than the one to be embraced. Since the person no longer wants to be governed by the familiar (i.e, the self to be destroyed), the boundaries and the essence of the old self are truncated, collapsed, and codified in very pejorative terms, images, and emotions. Any and all values and complexities associated with the "old" self are denied and made to appear useless. But the person is unfamiliar with the "new" self, with the person he or she hopes to become. In effect, the new convert lacks knowledge about the complexity and texture of the new identity and is forced to erect simplistic, glorified, highly romantic speculative images of what he or she *assumes* the new self will be like. This "in-between" state can cause someone to be very anxious about whether he or she is becoming the "right kind" of Black person. He or she is in need of immediate and clear-cut markers that confirm progression in the "right direction."

This state of being "in-between" explains why new converts are so attracted to symbols of the new identity (dress codes, hairstyles, flags, national colors, etc.), code phrases, party lines, ten-point programs, rigid ideologies, and either/or frames of analyses. It is a paradox of social change that the most dramatic displays of the new Black image are often exhibited by those least at ease with their new identity (Cross, Parham, and Helms, in press). Involved with destroying what one currently *is* and simultaneously and instantaneously grasping the essence of what one wants to *become*, a new convert can be vicious in attacks on what seems part of the old self in others (Blacker-than-thou syndrome) and bizarre when affirming the new. Framing the entire transition is a very dichotomized view of the world in which all that is white becomes evil, oppressive, inferior, and inhuman, and all things Black are declared superior, even in a biogenetic sense. If the *absence* of melanin is at the heart of white racist beliefs about white superiority and Black inferiority, during nigrescence the *presence* of melanin becomes a marker for Black superiority and white inferiority. This demonizing of white people and white culture is often a major preoccupation of new converts. With this overview of stage 3 in mind, let us now follow the person through each step of the transitional period.

IMMERSION

During the first phase of Immersion–Emersion, the person *immerses* himself or herself in the world of Blackness. He or she attends political or cultural meetings that focus on Black issues, joins new organizations and drops membership in Pre-encounter-oriented groups, goes to Black rap sessions, and attends seminars and art shows that focus on Blackness or Afrocentricity. Everything of value must be Black or relevant to Africa; the person is swept along by "a sea of Blackness." The experience is an immersion into Blackness and a liberation from whiteness. Phenomenologically, the person perceives himself or herself as being uprooted from the old self and drawn into a qualitatively different experience. This immersion is a strong, powerful, dominating sensation that is constantly energized by rage (at white people and culture), guilt (at having once been tricked into thinking Negro ideas), and a developing sense of pride (in one's Black self, in Black people, and in Black culture). Superhuman and supernatural expectations attend anything Black. One's very being is "beautiful." That the person exists and is Black is inherently wonderful. The person may spend a great deal of time developing an African or Black "urban" hairstyle, and such concerns carry over to style of dress. Converts give themselves African names or simply drop their "American" names, as did Malcolm X; children are named after African heroes. An intense interest in "Mother Africa" becomes evident, which is especially true of people associated with the more contemporary variant of nigrescence, the Afrocentric movement. The label "Negro" is dropped as a self-referent, and preference is given to Black, Black American, or African.

Black literature is consumed passionately. In some instances, people who never before showed an interest in reading teach themselves to read and write. Their new orientation causes them to process all kinds of information focusing on the Black and African experience (film, press, radio). In a related development, a person or group may decide that there is a need for a new periodical, journal, newsletter, or television program; the person or group may try to produce a new information outlet that does justice to the emerging Black/Afrocentric perspective. Like the Negritude movement in Africa, the American-based Afrocentric movement has resulted in an explosion of articles, books, newsletters, journals, and any number of new organizations.

The new convert's attention may be drawn to other than political issues. During the Immersion–Emersion stage, some may experience a creative burst in which they feel "driven" to write poetry, essays, plays, rap songs, novels, or literary "confessionals." A few may turn to the plastic arts or to painting. People who never before sought or experienced any creative activity discover that they are able to express themselves in a totally new mode. Established artists speak of a radical shift in the direction of their art; this happened to LeRoi Jones (Imamu Amiri Baraka), Gwendolyn Brooks, and Don L. Lee (Haki Mutabiti). In explaining the change, these artists state that although they were born Black, their overall socialization and artistic training caused them to look for inspiration and content *outside* the Black experience. For example, some wanted to be "pure" and "free," creating art for art's sake; others admitted that their artistic sensibility was once decidedly Eurocentric. With the realization of his or her Blackness, the professional artist awakens to a vast new world of rich colors, powerful dramas, irony, rage, oppression, survival, and impossible dreams! It is all there within reach; the artist (or scholar) has simply to look in the mirror. (Those familiar with the Black 1960s will recall that the Black Arts Movement was one of the most powerful reflectors of Black identity change.)

Of course, the inspirational aspects of nigrescence go beyond the world of Black art. Countless scholars from the 1960s have testified that the focus of their scholarly activities was often radically transformed by what they learned and experienced from the Black Social Movement. Such efforts continue in the shaping and refinement of the Afrocentric movement, which is struggling to articulate a new frame of reference from which to approach the study of Black life in Africa and America.

During the *Immersion* phase of stage 3, the discourse between Black artists and scholars is generally guided by an aesthetic or analytic frame that incorporates values, methodologies, and interpretive schemes thought to be the exact opposite of those found in white art and scholarship. This belief is not so much explicated as declared. In speeches and articles offered by new converts, an inordinate amount of attention may be given to what the new Blackness is *not*, while what it *is* may simply be affirmed and given little analysis. When the convert has moved beyond the emotionality of early conversion, substantive and even radical concepts about Black (African) and white (European) history, culture, politics, and so on, may be discovered, researched, confirmed, and refined, but early attempts are too often laden with vulgar nationalist, if not blatantly racist, concepts.

For new converts, confrontation, bluntness, directness, and an either/ or mentality may be the primary mode of communication with other people, Black or white. This communication style is associated with the much discussed "Blacker-than-thou" syndrome. As a prelude to passing judgment on whether or not a person has the "appropriate" level of Blackness, Black people are classified into neat categories such as "Uncle Tom," "militant," "non-Afrocentric vs. Afrocentric," "together," "soulful," "middle class," and "intellectual snob." Labeling and passing judgment on others help clarify a person's own identity, but this name-calling, with its attendant ideological fractionation, can produce disastrous results, as can be seen in the California Black Panther versus "US" murders of the 1960s or the well-documented split between Malcolm X and the Nation of Islam. A contemporary variant of Blacker-than-thou comes from the Afrocentric movement, in which some converts see themselves as "more Afrocentric" than others. They often describe Blacks who disagree with their perspective as insane, crazy, mentally ill, confused, unreliable, dangerous, and incapable of making a positive contribution to Black life. Such converts may mean well—as they may merely seek to promote a greater consensus in the Black world—but their zeal for ideological "correctness" can lead to coercive and even fascist tactics.

The name-calling and Blacker-than-thou propensities are all part of the new convert's anxiety that his or her Blackness is "pure and acceptable." We can refer to this anxiety as *Weusi* anxiety. *Weusi* is Swahili for "Black," and *Weusi* anxiety is the anxiety that the new convert experiences when he or she worries about being or becoming Black enough. If the person is left to his or her own devices to work out all aspects of the identity crisis, such *Weusi* anxiety could lead to considerable personal chaos. Generally, however, converts seek and find the social support of others by joining organizations and groups. The groups provide a counterculture to the one being replaced (the "Negro" identity) by entangling the person in membership requirements, symbolic dress codes, rites, rituals, obligations, and reward systems that nurture and reinforce the emerging "new" (Black, or Afrocentric) identity. This can lead to a great deal of conformity on the part of the new recruit. In fact, a paradox of conversion is that while rebelling against the larger society, the new convert may willingly conform to the demands of certain Black organizations. Again, we should keep in mind that the person's new identity is still emerging and has not been internalized; consequently, the person is anxious to demonstrate, in some fashion, that he or she is developing into the "right kind" of Black person. As noted elsewhere (Cross, Parham, and Helms, in press), demonstrating and proving one's level of Blackness or Afrocentricity requires an audience before which to *perform* and a set of group-sanctioned standards toward which to *conform*.

Much that goes into the demonstration of one's level of Blackness takes place within the confines and privacy of Black organizations and is part of the overall theme of the Immersion–Emersion stage. It involves the need to turn inward and simultaneously to withdraw from everything perceived as representing the white world. Yet, ironically, there also develops a need to confront the "man" as a means of dramatizing, concretizing, or proving one's Blackness. The confrontation, especially for Black leaders, is a manhood (or womanhood) ritual—a baptismal or purification rite. Carried to an extreme, the impulse is to confront white people in authority, frequently the police, on a life-or-death basis. When this impulse is coupled with revolutionary rhetoric or a revolutionary program, a paramilitary organization such as the Black Panthers can spring forth. For such people, no control or oppressive technique—including the threat of death—is feared. Frantz Fanon's thesis of "complete freedom through revolutionary violence" comes into the picture at this point, only the circumstances in the United States force the oppressor's death to be fantasized rather than carried out. Consequently, Brothers and Sisters *dream* about, or give a heavy rap about, the need for physical combat, but daydreams and rhetoric are as far as it goes. When warlike fantasies are, in fact, turned into participation in a paramilitary group, such as the Black Panthers, dreams of combat are sometimes actualized in planned attacks on the police. Far more often, however, Black paramilitary groups take on a provocative, ambivalent, "I dare you, whitey" stance.

(As an aside, let me say that I am of the belief that in the 1960s the desire to develop a Black revolutionary army was much stronger than has often been estimated; had there been an unsecured swampland or a rural area to which a Black army could have withdrawn for purposes of recruitment, expansion, training, and development, such attempts would probably have taken place. As it happened, the Black military impulse was able to evidence itself only in well-intended but comedic and too often tragic organizations such as the Black Panther party or the Republic of New Africa.)

Most converts do not get involved with paramilitary activities. The episodes of hatred they may feel toward whites during the Immersion–Emersion stage are worked through as daydreams or fantasies, such as the urge to rip off the first white person one passes on a particular day! During Immersion–Emersion, "Kill whitey!" fantasies seem to be experienced by Blacks regardless of age, sex, or class background. Persons who fixate at this point in their development are said to have a pseudo-Black identity because it is based on the hatred and negation of white people, rather than the affirmation of a pro-Black perspective that includes commitment to the destruction of *racism*, not the random killing of whites.

Finally, during this transitional period, the person experiences a surge in altruism. A constant theme of selflessness, dedication, and commitment to the Black group is evident; the person feels overwhelming love and attachment to all that is Black. The person's main focus in life becomes a feeling of "togetherness and oneness with the people." It is almost a religious feeling, and clusters of new converts can create an atmosphere in which Blackness or Africanity has a spiritual quality.

EMERSION

People are not actually out of control during Immersion, but they often look back on the period as something akin to a happening, as if Blackness were an outside force or spirit that was permeating, if not invading, their being. The second part of the stage is *Emersion*, an emergence from the emotionality and dead-end, either/or, racist, and oversimplified ideologies of the immersion experience. The person regains control of his or her emotions and intellect. In fact, he or she probably cannot continue to handle the intense emotional phase and is predisposed to find a way to level off.

Frequently, this leveling-off period is facilitated by a combination of personal growth and the recognition that certain role models or heroes operate from a more advanced state of identity development. The first hint of this advanced state may be discovered during face-to-face interactions with role models who bring a sophisticated quality to their Blackness, or when reading about the life of someone like Malcolm X, who describes moving beyond a rigid sense of Blackness as a consequence of his experiences in Mecca. How to get beyond the Immersion stage is likely to be different for different people, but once it occurs, it results in the discovery that one's first impressions of Blackness were romantic and symbolic, not substantive, textured, and complex. In fact, a person undergoing Emersion may pull away from membership in organizations whose activities seem designed to "help one feel immersed in Blackness" and toward association with groups or persons who are demonstrating a "more serious" understanding of, and commitment to, Black issues. When the grip of the Immersion phase loosens, and the convert begins to see Immersion as a transitional period and not an end state, and that continued growth lies ahead, he or she is ready to move toward an internalization of the new identity.

NEGATIVE CONSEQUENCES OF THE TRANSITIONAL STAGE

The previous paragraph depicts a person headed toward continued identity development. We should understand, however, that the volatility of this transitional stage can well result in regression, fixation, or stagnation. The Immersion–Emersion stage can inspire or can frustrate an individual. Consequently, the degree of a person's continued involvement in Black affairs may prove significant or negligible. During the transitional stage, a person embraces idealistic, if not superhuman, expectations about anything Black. Minimal reinforcement (i.e, when you are attracted to something, it does not take a great deal of reinforcement to sustain that interest) may carry a person into advanced identity development (evolution to the next stage). Nevertheless, prolonged or traumatic frustration and contestment of expectancies may break a person's spirit and his or her desire to change, in which case regression becomes a real possibility. For some people, intense and negative encounters with white racists lead to their becoming fixated at stage 3. Still other people may give all the appearances of having grown beyond the boundaries of the Immersion–Emersion stage; their behavior and attitudes may suggest a great deal of internalization of the new identity, but for reasons that are not yet clear, they cease their involvement in the Black struggle. In effect, they "drop out." Let us examine more closely these three negative possibilities.

Regression.   It bears repeating that the Immersion–Emersion stage is a period of transition during which the old identity is at war with an emerging, new identity. Someone whose overall experience is negative and thus nonreinforcing of growth toward the new identity may become disappointed and choose to *reject* Blackness. In so doing, the pressure to change will subside, and the pull of the old identity will reconstitute itself, resulting in a regression toward the Pre-encounter self-concept. Not only may the person embrace the old, he or she may do so with considerable enthusiasm, becoming almost *reactionary* in disappointment with and opposition to the "Blackness" thing.

Continuation/Fixation at Stage 3.   Individuals who experience painful perceptions and confrontations will be overwhelmed with hate for white people and fixate at stage 3. Even if they progress beyond the emotionalism of the stage, they may lock on to some variant of the "whitey as devil" philosophy. Distracting rage and hatred may be more of a problem among Black people "on the front lines" of the most brutal and blatant forms of racism and poverty (e.g., life in the inner city or in remote sectors of the rural South). College students, the Black middle class, Black scholars, and securely employed working-class Blacks, who can move in and out of oppressive Black situations or have greater access to insights that point to progressive attitudes, tend to escape the debilitating effects of reactionary hatred. America's recent swing to the radical right has provided fertile psychological soil for reactionary Black identities, ideologies, and organizations. More recently, Blacks of this persuasion have become exasperated with white America's willingness to allow the never-ending growth of the Black underclass; for them, white attitudes of neglect reflect an implicit, if not an explicit, policy of *genocide*. Of course, Black reactionaries deny the historical and contemporary contributions of white progressives and white radicals, choosing to see any and all "Black" issues through a monoracial lens.

Dropping Out. Another response to the Immersion–Emersion experience is "dropping out" of any involvement with Black issues. The dropout does not regress to Pre-encounter attitudes; in fact, he or she may exhibit signs of having internalized the new Black identity (internalization is discussed next). There seem to be two kinds of dropouts. Some people seem exhausted by it all, perhaps seeing the "race problem" as insurmountable and without solution. Such persons may reengage the race question at a later date, but for the time being they withdraw from the discourse on "race." Extreme cases may become depressed and may suffer from anomie. Or perhaps they entered nigrescence with a vulnerable and unstable general personality (PI), and when metamorphosis proved too problematic and stressful, they experienced a mental breakdown. The second kind of dropout includes psychologically healthy persons who drop out because they have achieved a "feel good" attitude about their personal, private, internal sense of Blackness and move on to what they perceive as more important issues in life. They often refer to their nigrescence experience as their "ethnicity phase." This is very much a trend among Black college students; they conform to a Black ethos while in college and then disappear from Black life thereafter.

Stage 4: Internalization

In working through the challenges and problems of the transitional period, the new identity is internalized, evidencing itself in naturalistic ways in the everyday psychology of the person. For the "settled" convert, the new identity gives high salience to Blackness, with the degree of salience determined by ideological considerations. At one extreme are nationalists, whose concern for race leaves little room for other considerations; for others, Blackness becomes one of several (biculturalism) or many saliences (multiculturalism). From a psychodynamic point of view, the internalized identity seems to perform three dynamic functions in a person's everyday life: (1) to defend and protect the person from psychological insults that stem from having to live in a racist society; (2) to provide a sense of belonging and social anchorage and; (3) to provide a foundation or point of departure for carrying out transactions with people, cultures, and situations beyond the world of Blackness.

Internalization is not likely to signal the end of a person's concern for nigrescence. As one continues along the life span, new challenges (e.g., a new Encounter) may bring about the need to "recycle" through some of the stages. Finally, the successful resolution of one's racial identity conflicts makes it possible to shift attention to other identity concerns, such as religion, gender and sexual preferences, career development, social class and poverty, and multiculturalism.

KEY MARKERS OF INTERNALIZATION

If Encounter and Immersion–Emersion usher in cognitive dissonance and an accompanying roller-coaster emotionality, then the Internalization stage marks the point of dissonance resolution and a reconstitution of one's steady-state personality and cognitive style. The person feels calmer, more relaxed, more at ease with self. An inner peace is achieved, as *Weusi* anxiety is transformed into *Weusi* pride (Black pride) and *Weusi* self-acceptance (Black self-acceptance). The shift is away from how your friends see you ("Am I Black enough?") and toward confidence in your personal standards of Blackness; from uncontrolled rage toward white people to controlled anger at oppressive systems and racist institutions; from symbolic, boisterous rhetoric to serious analysis and "quiet" strength; from unrealistic urgency that can lead to dropping out to a sense of destiny that can sustain long-term commitment; from anxious, insecure, rigid, pseudo-Blackness based on the hatred of whites to proactive Black pride, self-love, and a deep sense of connection to, and acceptance by, the Black community.

Habituated and internalized, Blackness becomes a backdrop for life's transactions. It can be taken for granted, freeing someone to concentrate on issues that presuppose a basic identification with Blackness. One *is* Black, thus one is free to ponder matters beyond the parameters of a personal sense of Blackness (e.g., organizational development, community development, problem solving, conflict resolution, institution building).

One of the most important consequences of this inner peace is that a person's conception of Blackness tends to become more open, expansive, and sophisticated. As defensiveness fades, simplistic thinking and simple solutions become transparently inadequate, and the full complexity and inherent texture of the Black condition become the point of departure for serious analysis.

Phenomenologically, at this stage, the person perceives himself or herself to be totally changed, with a new world view and a revitalized personality. Research findings, however, show that nigrescence tends to have more of an effect on the group identity or reference group component of the Black self-concept than it does on the general personality. A person's personality is most certainly put under stress during Immersion–Emersion, and there is a great deal of emotionality associated with conversion, but with internalization and the easing of internal psychological stress, the core of the personality is reestablished. For example, someone who was an effective (or ineffective) leader at Pre-encounter will have the same leadership profile at Internalization. This pattern is likely to be replicated in countless examples: shy at Pre-encounter, shy at Internalization; outgoing and gregarious at Pre-encounter, outgoing and gregarious at Internalization; introverted and mildly uncomfortable around large groups at Pre-encounter, introverted and uncomfortable in large groups at Internalization; calm, rational, and deliberate at Pre-encounter and calm, rational, and deliberate at Internalization; anxious and neurotic at Pre-encounter, anxious and neurotic at Internalization; relatively normal and happy at Pre-encounter, relatively normal and happy at Internalization. In fact, research suggests that during Immersion–Emersion, one's basic personality strengths act as a psychological cushion of stability for the intense struggles taking place at the group identity level of the Black self-concept. (Conversely, personality weaknesses may make nigrescence more stressful to the person, although the point being made here is that a successful completion of nigrescence rides or floats on whatever the person's personality strengths are.) At Internalization, when the dissonance surrounding reference group and world-view change has been resolved, a person is able to fall back on his or her basic personality attributes. Though greatly stressed, perturbed, and excited during the Immersion–Emersion stage, these attributes helped him or her negotiate the group identity change in the first place.

For the fraction of people who were anti-Black at Pre-encounter, nigrescence may enhance the general level of self-esteem, but again the characteristic personality attributes beyond self-esteem are likely to remain the same. As a form of social therapy, nigrescence is extremely effective at changing the salience of race and culture in a person's life. It is *not* a process that lends itself to the needs of personal identity therapy.

What makes one feel completely "new" are the changes experienced at the level of reference group orientation. In moving from Pre-encounter to Internalization, the person has moved from a frame of reference where race and culture had low salience to a perspective that places high salience on Blackness in everyday life. With this change in salience comes membership in new organizations and changes in one's social network, one's manner of dress and personal appearance, one's self-referents, what one reads or views on television, how one socializes children, one's internal image of the capacity and efficacy of Blacks as a group, one's cultural and artistic preferences, one's historical and cultural perspective, the causes and social problems that engage one's activism, and perhaps even changes in one's name. These changes define what is important in adult life, which is why the person feels totally new. Left unnoticed is the fact that his or her basic personality profile is the same as it was during Pre-encounter.

SALIENCE AND IDEOLOGY

While advanced Black identity development results in one's giving high salience to issues of race and culture, not every person in the Internalization stage shares the same degree of salience for Blackness, as this is likely to be determined by the nature of one's ideology. Those who construct a strong nationalist framework from their Immersion–Emersion experiences may continue along this ideological path at Internalization, but others may derive a far less nationalistic stance. The former can lead to total salience on Blackness; for the latter, it is less so. For example, *vulgar* nationalists (people who believe Blacks and whites are biogenetically different, with Blacks of "superior" racial stock and whites an "inferior" mutation of Black stock) and *traditional* nationalists (those who frame their nationalist perspective with other than biogenetic constructs) have saliences about race and culture that in some instances can border on the obsessive. The traditional nationalist presents the more healthy alternative, as his or her high salience and frame of reference are subject to rational analysis and debate. The vulgar nationalist's reactionary racism, which is usually steeped in an odd mixture of pseudoscientific myths, historical distortions, and outright mysticism, offers a salience and orientation beyond the reach of normal discourse. Although vulgar and traditional nationalists are African-Americans by history and culture, both tend to stress a singularity to their cultural emphasis; in some instances, they may even deny that there is anything American or Eurocentric about them. In this sense, their internalized Black nationalist identity, though far more sophisticated than the version espoused during Immersion–Emersion, carries with it, in varying degrees, possibilities of conflict over how to relate to the other half of their cultural–historical makeup.

Other Blacks reaching the Internalization stage derive a *bicultural* reference group orientation from their nigrescence experience. From their vantage point, Internalization is a time for working through and incorporating into the self-concept the realities of one's Blackness as well as the enigmatic, paradoxical, advantageous, and supportive aspects of one's "Americanness." I especially like the way Bailey Jackson addresses this point:

> The individual (in stage four) also has a new sense of the American culture. The person is able to identify and own those aspects of the American culture that are acceptable (e.g., material possessions, financial security, independence, etc.) and stand against those aspects which are toxic (racism, sexism, war, imperialism, and other forms of oppression). The ownership of the acceptable aspects of the American culture does not preclude or override the ownership of Black culture. (Jackson 1976b, 62)

Taking this a step further, still others may embrace a *multicultural* perspective, in which case their concern for Blackness is shared with a multiplicity of cultural interests and saliences. So we see that the cultural identity of the stage 4 person can vary from that of the monocultural orientation of the extreme nationalist to the identity mosaic of the multiculturally oriented Black. Each ideological stance incorporates strengths and weaknesses, and there are times when the holders of one perspective may find themselves at odds with those who share another variant of Blackness. This means that nigrescence may increase the salience of race and culture for everyone who successfully reaches the advanced stages of Black identity development, but Internalization does not result in ideological unity. One can look on this variability as ideological fractionation or as healthy, ideological diversity.

INTERNALIZATION AND THE TOTAL IDENTITY MATRIX

The work of Internalization does not stop with the resolution of conflicts surrounding one's racial–cultural identity. Borrowing again from Bailey Jackson, we note that he believes nigrescence should be viewed as a time when a single dimension of a person's complex, layered identity is first isolated, for purposes of revitalization and transformation. Then, at Internalization, it is reintegrated into a person's total identity matrix:

> For the person who sees him/herself as a Black only or to view his/her Blackness completely separate from the other aspects of the person is seen as a dysfunctional fragmentation of self. While recognizing the necessity for the separation of the person's Blackness from other parts of him/herself in earlier stages as a strategy for making sense of that aspect of self, the person now needs to complete the developmental process by internalizing and synthesizing this new sense of Blackness. (Jackson 1976a, 42)

Jackson sees Internalization as balancing and synthesizing Blackness with other demands of personhood, such as one's sexual identity, occupational identity, spiritual or religious identity, and various role identities, aspects of which may be very race sensitive or, in other instances, race neutral.

THE PSYCHODYNAMICS OF INTERNALIZED BLACKNESS

When discussing difficult social concepts, it is often helpful to vary the approach. With this in mind, a slightly different perspective of the internalized identity is revealed when one seeks an answer to the question "How does the internalized identity function in daily life?" That is, what psychodynamic functions evolve during nigrescence, and how does each functional mode operate in everyday life? In a generic sense, one's identity is a maze or map that functions in a multitude of ways to guide and direct exchanges with one's social and material realities. Of course, Blacks function in two worlds, one Black and one white, and as implied from our earlier commentary, this means that some identity functions and operations in Blacks are no different from those that are evident in most Americans. But the "Blackness" part of Black identity (Cross 1985; Cross, Parham, and Helms, in press) tends to perform three unique functions in everyday Black life: (1) to defend the person from the negative psychological stress that results from having to live in a society that at times can be very racist; (2) to provide a sense of purpose, meaning, and affiliation; and (3) to provide psychological mechanisms that facilitate social intercourse with people, cultures, and human situations outside the boundaries of Blackness. A person may acquire these functions over the course of being socialized from childhood through early adulthood, given that his or her parents or caretakers have strong Black identities. If this is not true, the functions may unfold as part of the *resocialization* that takes place during nigrescence. Let us take a closer look at each functional mode.

Defensive Functions of Black Identity. Recall that people in the Preencounter stage often give low salience to issues of race and Black culture; in addition, they may play down the existence of racism, leaving them psychologically unprepared to deal with racist situations. During nigrescence, one of the first functional modes to evolve is the defensive or protective function of Blackness, which operates to provide a psychological buffer when a person encounters racist circumstances, especially those of a psychological nature (obviously a psychological defense would be inadequate in the face of implied or actual violence). In its most crude manifestation during Immersion–Emersion, a siege mentally may be present. The person sees all white people as racist dogs and all white institutions as inherently racist to the core. He or she is hypersensitive to racism and is "protected" by simply writing off all contact with whites.

At the Internalization stage, the defensive function of Black identity becomes much more sophisticated and flexible. Instead of the iron shield of Immersion–Emersion, it becomes a translucent filter that is often "invisible," undetectable, which allows non–threatening information and experiences to be processed without distortion. The structure of the protective function seems to involve (1) an *awareness* that racism is part of the American experience; (2) an *anticipatory set*—regardless of one's station in American society, one can well be the target of racism; (3) well-developed *ego defenses* that can be employed when confronted with racism; (4) a *system blame* and *personal efficacy orientation* in which one is predisposed to find fault in the circumstances, not the self; and (5) a *religious orientation* that prevents the development of a sense of bitterness or the need to demonize whites.

The first two factors represent the heart of the protective capacity, for it is impossible to defend against something when its existence is denied or even minimized. Of course, if a person sees herself or himself as a special

Negro, beyond the reach of racism, then he or she will hardly be in a position to anticipate being the target of a racist. For a person with Black identity and a well-developed defensive mode, racism is a given; that he or she may well be the target of racism is understood. The third factor refers to the behavioral and attitudinal repertoire that can be employed in negotiating racist situations (e.g., withdrawal, assertion, counteraggression, passivity, avoidance). The stronger, more mature, and more varied the ego defenses, the greater the capacity to handle racist situations. Because Blacks frequently find themselves living in poor and degrading circumstances, the fourth factor helps them maintain a sense of perspective and personal worth in the face of the stress that accompanies racism. They are able to distinguish between what is an extension of self-concept (that which one deserves and should be given credit) and what reflects the racist and oppressive system against which they must endure, survive, and struggle. Finally, the fifth factor, religious orientation, helps people avoid becoming embittered and filled with hatred toward whites. This is important. Time and again, hatred originally directed toward whites spills over and poisons Black-on-Black relationships. The fifth factor keeps the focus on racism as a form of human evil, rather than on the demonization of white people, with its attendant hopelessness (one cannot negotiate with the devil).

The defensive mode helps people deal with the "hassle" of being Black. It operates to minimize the hurt, pain, imposition, and stigma that comes from being treated with disrespect, rudeness, and insensitivity. Instead of being overly hurt or caught "off guard," the defensive mode allows people to maintain control and avoid overreacting. They are also able to pay more attention to "who and what" is instigating the problem.

There are two extremes to this modality (Cross, Parham, and Helms, in press). A person may underestimate the importance of racism; if so, the defensive function will be inadequately developed and his or her identity will offer little protection against racism. (For an excellent example of the consequences of an underdeveloped defensive mode, see the article in the August 20, 1989, issue of the *New York Times* Magazine by Anthony Walton, "Willie Horton and Me.") At the other extreme a person may be overly sensitive or even paranoid, "seeing" racism where it does not exist.

RGO Functions of Black Identity. Human beings need to feel wanted, connected, accepted, and affiliated, but the group from which they derive a sense of well-being need not be the normally ascribed one. (This conclusion is at the heart of the theory and research presented in Part One.)

For example, many Blacks derive their sense of connection and affiliation from groups that have little to do with a nationalist or Black identity. Some Blacks gain personal fulfillment and happiness from being Christians, lawyers, doctors, gamblers, police officers, gays, or believers in obscure cults. Such people cannot be said to have a Black identity because their sense of personal well-being is anchored in something other than their Blackness.

Having a Black identity means that the RGO functions of one's identity *are grounded in one's Blackness*. Being Black has high salience to one's sense of well-being, one's purpose in life, one's sense of connection to other Blacks. Feelings of being wanted, accepted, appreciated, and affiliated are deeply rooted in Black people, Black culture, and the general Black condition. Values, cultural preferences, artistic tastes, leisure activities, cooking styles and food choices, secular and religious musical tastes, church affiliation, organizational memberships, social network or intimate friends— these are all influenced by one's perceived connection to Black people. In brief, some or a great deal of the meaning and hope one has for living a purposeful life is linked to one's perception of the self as an African-American.

This sense of Blackness is either muted or missing at Pre-encounter, becomes an obsession during Immersion–Emersion, and continues as a singular concern (Black nationalism) or shared saliences (biculturalism or multiculturalism) at Internalization. In fact, at Internalization, RGO functions may take on a multidimensional character, as is true for someone whose meaning in life synthesizes his or her gayness, religiosity, and Blackness. Nonetheless, whether of the shared or the single-salience variety, being Black plays an important RGO function in daily life. At its best,

> The reference group functions of Black identity lead to the celebration of Blackness, the press to solve Black problems and a desire to promulgate Black culture and history. At its worst, it provides the basis for inhibiting, if not destructive, social conformity, ethnic chauvinism, reactionary cultural ideologies (biogenetically based ideologies), and a tendency to view as less than human, to one degree or another, those who are "not Black" (such negative and positive potential accompany any and all forms of nationalism, ethnicity or group affiliation, and is thus not unique to the Black experience; one can embrace a cultural perspective without being reactionary, but all biogenetically defined notions of culture are inherently reactionary).
> (Cross, Parham, and Helms, in press)

Bridging or Transcendent Functions of Black Identity.   The defensive and RGO functions combine to form an ethnic identity that is fairly typical of people whose lives revolve around a particular culture, religion, or "race." Such people often show little concern for experiences outside their own. Among Blacks, as long as one operates (works, plays, marries, worships) in an all-Black or predominately Black human environment, then the need to have the functional skills and sensitivities that make Blacks efficacious in interactions with non-Blacks does not exist. Yet it is a paradox of Black life that although Blacks are subject to what recently has been called "hyper-segregation," it is nearly impossible for most Black Americans to escape having to negotiate contracts, transactions, and communications with ethnic whites, Asian-Americans, Jews, Latinos, Cubans, Chicanos, American Indians, and white Protestants. Thus, another identity function that must be performed in the everyday life of many Black people is *bridging*—making connections with other groups, organizations, and individuals who constitute the larger non-Black world within which the Black world is nestled. Keep in mind that because "Black–white" conflict is at the core of nigrescence experience, the initial focus of bridging may be white society, white organizations, and the reestablishment of white friendships.

Bridging is often evident at the Pre-encounter stage, but for the wrong reasons. The focus is not on bridging to share Blackness with whiteness, and vice versa; it is trying to get a handle on the essence of whiteness as a vehicle for becoming the "right kind" of Black person. During Immersion–Emersion, bridging is muted or even destroyed. At Internalization, two trends may be present. Black nationalists may continue to discourage bridging to the white and non-black worlds, stressing instead the need to make connections and build bridges to and from Blacks in the diaspora (i.e., Pan-Africanism). For others, initial concern for Pan-Africanism, Afrocentricity, and Blackness may actually be a prerequisite for bridging to worlds beyond Blackness. Using the lives of Malcolm X and Dr. Martin Luther King, Jr., as examples, Parham, Helms, and I described the evolution of the bridging mode in the following way:

> When Malcolm X returned from Mecca, he was no less com-
> mitted to Black people; however, his "tunnel" vision had been
> expanded, enabling him to see Blackness and Black people as
> but one cultural and historical expression of the *human condi-
> tion*. His new vision did not question the basic integrity of the
> Black experience, rather it made Blackness his point of depar-
> ture for discovering the universe of ideas, cultures, and experi-

ences beyond Blackness, in place of mistaking Blackness for the universe itself. It is often assumed that ethnicity acts as a barrier to humanism, but in its highest expression Black identity functions as a window on the world. The humanism, ever present in the life of Martin Luther King and increasingly apparent in the final period of Malcolm X's life, did not represent a contradiction to their Blackness; on the contrary, it was a product of Blackness. In coming to know Black people, both Malcolm and King had to explain Black diversity. In tracing this diversity to the various cultural, economic, linguistic, social and political *systems* under which Blacks live throughout the diaspora, it was only natural that each would eventually try to make sense of the behavior of non-Black people and nations through a similar analysis. Thus, the more deeply Blacks explore themselves and the lives of those around them, the more likely they are to understand people as reflections of systems and personal experiences, and less so as clusters of ever distinct "racial groups." (Cross, Parham, and Helms, in press)

Transracial, and especially Black–white, bridging activities can lead to conflicts within the Black community. Black nationalists may interpret any bridging other than the Pan-African variety as a waste of limited time and resources; those involved in transracial connections may counter by stating that the Black condition is inherently bicultural, if not multicultural, and that meaningful change cannot take place without bridging. Other Blacks see any debate about "to bridge or not to bridge" as silly because their workplace and community environments are decidedly multiracial and multicultural. Consequently, they see the development of bridging functions of Black identity as a necessity, not an option. Black women are quick to point out that the sexism of white as well as Black men makes it absolutely necessary for them constantly to bridge back and forth from their Black identity to their gender, feminist, or womanist orientation. Finally, bridging adds a crucial element of flexibility to Black identity that allows a person to assimilate rapid culture and technological innovation better (Cross 1985; Cross, Parham, and Helms, in press). Black Americans, and all Americans, must be able to keep abreast of transformations in American society, and a rigid, provincial identity structure cannot handle change. In this sense, bridging may be viewed as a metaphor for future change in Black identity.

Bridging can be problematic in several ways (Cross, Parham, and Helms, in press). First, bridging involves the art of compromise; yet it is possible to make so many compromises that being Black ceases to have meaning. Second, bridging can facilitate the discovery of universals; however, Blacks can become so enchanted with "universal cultural trends" that interest in Blackness may be forsaken. When this happens, Blackness may come to be seen as a contradiction to humanism, rather than its expression, as shaped, voiced, and codified by a particular sociohistorical experience (Cross, Parham, and Helms, in press).

In conclusion, the internalized Black identity functions to fulfill the self-protection, social anchorage, and bridging needs of the individual African-American. African-Americans live in one of the most complex and demanding societies on earth; there should be little surprise in the discovery that the functional structure of Black identity is no less multidimensional.

Stage 5: Internalization–Commitment

It is worth repeating that after developing a Black identity that meets their personal needs, some Blacks fail to sustain a long-term interest in Black affairs. Others devote an extended period, if not a lifetime, to finding ways to translate their personal sense of Blackness into a plan of action or a general sense of commitment. Such people characterize the fifth and final stage of nigrescence: Internalization–Commitment. Current theory suggests that there are few differences between the psychology of Blacks at the fourth and fifth stages of nigrescence other than the important factor of sustained interest and commitment, although, to my knowledge, no empirical studies have focused on the sustained commitment that follows nigrescence. Consequently, other than to repeat what has already been said about Internalization, a more differentiated look at Internalization–Commitment awaits the results of future research.

PARHAM'S CONCEPT OF RECYCLING

A complete nigrescence cycle involves traversing all four or five stages, and as originally conceived, nigrescence was thought to be a "one-time event" in the life of a person. Recently, a young, brilliant nigrescence theorist, Thomas A. Parham, who completed his dissertation under the tutelage of another key figure in the field, Janet E. Helms, has extended the implications of my model across the life span. Parham has noted that having completed their original nigrescence cycle at an earlier point in the life span (say, for example, in adolescence or early adulthood), some people may find that the challenges unique to another life-span phase (middle age or late adulthood) may engender a recycling through some of the stages. For example, a young man may go through nigrescence at age twenty, when he is single and a college student. During this first cycle, he is able to address successfully identity questions that are important to early adult functioning. Subsequently, his marriage may trigger new questions about Blackness; still later, the raising of his progeny may cause him to discover "gaps" in his thinking about Blackness. These new questions and the discovery of "gaps" in thinking, or a powerful racist incident at work or in the community, represent a new Encounter episode, leading to a need to recycle (in all likelihood, recycling does not involve the Pre-encounter stage). In recycling, a person searches for new answers and continued growth in his or her thinking about what it means to be Black. Depending on the nature and intensity of the new encounter, recycling may vary from a mild refocusing experience to passage through full-blown Encounter, Immersion–Emersion, and Internalization stages.

Nigrescence and Afrocentricity

In my 1971 version of nigrescence, I noted that it can revitalize key dimensions of one's reference group orientation, but that for Black scholars in particular, nigrescence was not enough to achieve enlightenment. For their liberation, nigrescence needed to be coupled with the development of a comparative referent (i.e., Western and non-Western insights):

> The significance of non-Western insights is dramatized when considering the problem of liberating Black scholars. The "Negro" (Pre-encounter-oriented) scholar hesitates to become involved in the Black experience because his perspective is distorted by the limitations of the philosophy and epistemology of Western science. In liberating Black scholars, we should add (*the requirement of*) exposure to non-Western thought. (Cross 1971, 25–26; italics added)

As demonstrated in the last chapter, the original version of the Negro-to-Black model was generally well received, although that reception did not make much of my ramblings about the value of developing a non-Western perspective. Nevertheless, my weak exploration of this important theme did reflect a stirring that was taking place among Black graduate students and Black scholars in the 1960s and early 1970s, partly in response to the then widespread circulation of an exciting new work on African philosophy and religions by J. S. Mbiti (1970). Two years after the publication of Mbiti's text, and one year after my nigrescence essay appeared, Wade Nobles (1972) published his seminal essay on the relationship between African philosophy and the psychology of Black America. Unbeknown to Nobles, his essay would mark for many the origin of the Afrocentric movement, although technically the concept of Afrocentricity is usually credited to Molefi Asante (1980).

Essentially, the Afrocentric movement is an attempt to codify and apply a non-Western perspective to the analysis of Black life in the United States. More specifically, it constitutes a *Western* (i.e., Black American) interpretation of what it means to have an African perspective, and in a historical sense, it is an important variant of Black American nationalism. Many of the adherents of Afrocentricity are products of the Black 1960s, and in a sense, their involvement in Afrocentricity is a form of what Parham (1989) would call recycling. That is, to the extent that they experienced Blackness in the 1960s, they now have attempted to take their nationalism to what is thought to be a higher level of analysis in the form of Afrocentricity. Today, for many young Black people, their original nigrescence cycle takes place within the context of the Afrocentric movement; thus, for them, nigrescence and Afrocentricity are perceived as being one and the same.

Intellectually speaking, the two paradigms should remain distinct because one seeks to articulate and explain variability, while the other seeks to delimit what should be called Black. As I have tried to argue in previous sections, nigrescence does not result in a single ideological stance, and it is most certainly true that not all persons in the Internalization stage gravitate toward Black nationalism or Afrocentricism. In making this observation, I am not trying to be contentious, I am simply trying to state a fact: Everyone who has a Black identity may not be Afrocentric, as defined by Afrocentric theorists, and Afrocentricity does not incorporate all legitimate interpretations of Blackness. In fact, the Afrocentric movement itself includes a variety of definitions of what it means to be Black, some of which can hardly be distinguished from a pedestrian, vulgar nationalist identity (Black people as biogenetically superior to whites, and whites as inferior mutations of Blacks). In other instances, Afrocentricity defines an intellectual movement in which scholars and lay people alike explore the significance and applicability of African-derived perspectives on significant aspects of the human condition, including art, history, politics, economics, psychology, and various social problems. Consequently, it remains to be seen whether and which variant of Afrocentricity, if any, becomes popular with scholars, practitioners, and the masses of Black people.

In the meantime, I, along with other nigrescence theorists and researchers, have tried to offer a way of looking at, and talking about, the development of various Black identities—nationalist, bicultural, and multicultural—including Afrocentricity. We have sought to clarify and expand the discourse on Blackness by paying attention to the variability and diversity in Blackness.

｜｜■■■｜｜

APPENDIX

BIBLIOGRAPHY

INDEX

APPENDIX

Summary of Forty-Five Studies of Black Identity That Tested the Relationship between Personal Identity (PI) and Reference Group Orientation (RGO)

Author	Sample	Methodology	Significant Findings
Bennett and Lundgren 1976	42 Black and 42 white 4-year-old boys from three day-care centers that differed in degree of integration (fully integrated, semi-integrated, and segregated).	*PI:* Thomas Self-Concept and Values Inventory. *RGO:* Preschool Racial Attitudes Measure–II (PRAM-II).	No overall correlation but one significant interaction: For children in integrated setting, PI and RGO were negatively correlated.
Brown 1979	929 Black college students (37% males and 63% females).	*PI:* Taylor Self-Esteem Scale. *RGO:* Developmental Inventory of Black Consciousness.	Found high correlation between PI and RGO.
Butts 1963	50 Black children (25 boys and 25 girls), 9–12 years of age.	*PI:* California Test of Personality. *RGO:* Clark Coloring Test; also employed rating scales.	Author erroneously reported significant relationship, but re-analysis by Cross (see text) showed no relationship.
M.L. Clark 1979	210 Black male and female children, grades 3 through 6, attending seven inte-	*PI:* M. Clark Multidimensional Self-Attitude and Self-Esteem Test. *RGO:*	No correlation between PI and RGO.

228 Appendix

Author	Sample	Methodology	Significant Findings
	grated or desegregated elementary schools in two small midwestern cities.	M. Clark measure of racial preference and racial attitude.	
Cole 1979	200 Black and 200 white adults, stratified by SES, age, and sex.	*PI:* Rosenberg Self-Esteem Scale. *RGO:* Morris's 3-item index on racial attitudes; also collected social network data.	No overall correlation but significant interaction. Race esteem found to be more related to self-esteem of Black women than Black men.
Cummings and Carrere 1975	241 Black high school students.	Kuhn-McPartland Sentence Completion Test on "Who Am I?" used to measure PI and RGO.	Racial self-designation on "Who Am I?" (Black, colored, or Negro) test showed no correlation with self-esteem.
Dulan 1975	1,000 third- and fourth-grade Black children, equally divided by gender.	*PI:* 10-item self-esteem scale. *RGO:* 2-item ethnic identity test.	Found no overall relationship between PI and RGO.
Enty 1979	415 undergraduate Black female students from an all-Black college.	*PI:* California Self-Acceptance Scale. *RGO:* Enty Black Identity Scale.	Found significant correlation between PI and RGO ($r = .17, p > .01$).
Fouther-Austin 1978	392 northern and southern Black teenagers from six cities.	*PI:* Tennessee Self-Concept Scale. *RGO:* Banks Black Consciousness Scale.	Overall correlation between PI and RGO $r = .366, p < .01$; however, higher-order interaction accounted for most of the variance. In three test sites, PI and RGO were highly correlated; but in three others there was no relationship.
Garner 1983	24 Black preschool children and their mothers.	*PI:* Children's Self-Social Constructs Test. *RGO:* Porter TV Story Game.	Reported no relationship between esteem of self and racial esteem.
Grossman 1981	21 Black, 98 Chicano, and 320 white eighth- and ninth-grade pupils in Texas high school.	*PI:* Rosenberg Self-Esteem Scale and semantic differential. *RGO:* semantic differential.	No relationship between PI and RGO. Author concluded: "This study provided no basis for

Author	Sample	Methodology	Significant Findings
			assuming a direct relationship from ethnic esteem to self-esteem, or from ethnic identity to behavioral adjustment."
Hall 1980	In-depth study of 30 racially mixed adults (part Japanese and part Black American).	*PI:* self-esteem inferred from structured interview. *RGO:* structured interview data.	No relationship between type of identity respondent stressed (Black or Japanese) and personal self-esteem.
Hendrix 1977	240 Black high school seniors representing a broad range of SES groups in New Orleans.	*PI:* Backman Self-Esteem Test and locus-of-control scale. *RGO:* Noel Group Identification Scale.	Reported highly significant correlation between self-esteem and group identity. Self-esteem also correlated with locus of control. Examination of items in Noel test shows half are locus-of-control items; consequently, overall correlation reported between PI and RGO may be an artifact of the lack of independence between PI and RGO measures.
Hernandez 1984	19 Black and 70 white middle-class children, 6 to 9 years of age.	*PI:* Piers-Harris Self-Concept Scale. *RGO:* Preschool Racial Attitudes Measure-II (PRAM-II); human figure drawing; and matched pair of TAT cards, one set with Black and another with white human figures.	The Black sample attributed more positive characteristics to the Black, relative to white, TAT figures. The white sample attributed neutral characteristics to both Black and white TAT figures. Both groups drew significantly larger white, relative to Black, human figures and perceived the white TAT figures as occupying signifi-

Author	Sample	Methodology	Significant Findings
			cantly higher occupational and social-class positions. No overall relationship was found between PI and RGO; interactions were reported.
Horton 1973	70 Head Start children, 16 from Atlanta and 54 from Baltimore.	*PI:* Thomas Self-Concept and Values Inventory for children. *RGO:* added "color" subscale to Thomas test.	No overall correlation between PI and RGO.
Hughbanks 1977	70 white, 114 Black, and 76 Mexican-American ninth-grade students.	*PI:* Rosenberg Self-Esteem Scale. *RGO:* Social Anchorage and Saliency of Ethnic Identity Test.	No differences were found among the three groups on the saliency of ethnic identification to self-esteem.
Jacques 1976	98 randomly selected Black American couples living in southeastern cities.	*PI:* Kuhn-McPartland Sentence Completion Test; Rosenberg Self-Esteem Scale. *RGO:* spouse's color.	The notion that spouse's self-esteem was related to other spouse's skin color was not substantiated.
Jarrett 1980	48 Black and 48 White children in Atlanta; half from each race were attending either monoracial or biracial kindergartens.	*PI:* Brown IDS Self-Concept Referents Test. *RGO:* doll-play situation.	For Black children, self-concept and measures of racial self-acceptance were not related. Results interpreted with caution because of high scores and low variability on self-concept measure.
J. M. Johnson 1981	60 self-identified Black homosexual men from San Francisco.	*PI:* questionnaire. *RGO:* self-declared primary reference group as "being Black" or "being gay."	Minimal psychological differences recorded in comparison of two primary reference groups.
King 1981	117 fifth- and sixth-grade Black children from three predominantly Black schools in Los Angeles area.	*PI:* Piers-Harris Self-Concept Scale. *RGO:* Black Identity Scale and race-salience measure.	Significant overall correlation between PI and RGO totally accounted for by higher-order interaction. Correlation was practically zero

Author	Sample	Methodology	Significant Findings
			in one school; in two others, it was highly significant. Social desirability was a problem with Black Identity Scale.
Maish 1978	84 college students, 55 professionals, and 31 blue-collar workers from Washington, D.C., area.	*PI:* Tennessee Self-Concept Scale; Behavioral Psychosocial Competence Scale. *RGO:* Black Ideology Scale; Pan-Africanism Scale.	Weak but statistically significant positive correlation between PI and RGO traced to lower-order cells of sample.
Markovics 1974	104 Black children, 7 to 9 years old, from two inner-city schools.	*PI:* Elkins Adjective Checklist; Coopersmith Self-Esteem Inventory; and an egocentrism task. *RGO:* Picture Test of Racial Orientation; Porter TV Story Game.	Several items from Porter test correlated with Elkin's measure of self-esteem; however, no other significant correlations were found between measures of self-esteem and measures of racial orientation. Also found that racial orientation and self-esteem develop independently of social perspective-taking skills.
H. P. McAdoo 1970	78 preschoolers (43 from Mississippi and 35 from Michigan).	*PI:* Thomas Self-Concept and Values Inventory. *RGO:* Williams and Roberson Racial and Sex Role Attitude Test.	No correlation was found between racial attitudes and self-concept.
H. P. McAdoo 1977	133 Black elementary school children from three sections of United States.	*PI:* Thomas Self-Concept and Values Inventory. *RGO:* employed three well-known racial identity measures.	No overall relationship found between PI and RGO, but significant interactions were recorded.
McWhorter 1984	157 Black children in grades 3 through 8 enrolled in public school of Lawndale, N.J.	Personal Attribute Inventory for Children administered in three trials using target stimulus "Yourself" (PI),	No overall correlation between PI and RGO; however, an interaction for one subgroup was noted.

Author	Sample	Methodology	Significant Findings
		"Black People" (RGO), and "White People" (RGO).	
Meyers 1966	23 good and 23 poor achievers, all Black, from grades 4, 5, and 6.	PI: Sentence Completion Test. RGO: Trent Racial Attitude Checklist.	Marginally significant overall positive correlation between PI and RGO.
Mobley 1973	145 male and female Black college students.	PI: Tennessee Self-Concept Scale. RGO: 101-item index of Black identity; 17 bipolar items representative of values in Black ethos.	No overall correlation calculated or reported. Nine of the 101 items from identity index were found to be related to a few of the subscales on PI measure. Such events are accounted for by chance, but author imputes considerable significance to her results.
Paul and Fisher 1980	59 Black 13 and 14 year olds. Girls (N = 32) and boys (N = 27) chosen from 131 students falling into either high or low self-concept groups.	PI: Tennessee Self-Concept Scale. RGO: Black Identity Questionnaire.	Highly significant positive correlation between PI and RGO; however, RGO device was of questionable validity (see text).
Penn 1980	28 Black male and female elementary schoolchildren.	PI: self-concept and motivation inventory. RGO: Cultural Identification Awareness Instrument.	RGO showed no correlation to self-concept, but a slight relationship to achievement.
Porter 1971	58 Black and white 5 year olds.	PI: Draw-a-person. RGO: Porter TV Story Game.	Provided descriptive data that suggested independence of PI and RGO.
Rasheed 1981	66 Black third-graders, equally divided by gender and randomly assigned to various treatment groups.	PI: Piers-Harris Self-Concept Scale; modified Coopersmith Self-Esteem Inventory. RGO: adapted Cheek Black Ethnic Identification Scale for third-graders.	No relationship between Piers-Harris and RGO. The tendency toward significant correlation between Coopersmith and RGO was related to a higher-order interaction in that the relationship approached statis-

Author	Sample	Methodology	Significant Findings
			tical significance for only two of the six subgroups.
J. A. Robinson 1977	125 Black and 87 white community college women from lower-middle-class area of Detroit.	*PI:* Coopersmith Self-Esteem Inventory. *RGO:* Rokeach Value Survey across three administrations for self, Black Americans, and white Americans.	Self-esteem was not found to be a function of racial consciousness nor of difference in perceived value similarity.
Rosenberg 1979a	1,213 Black schoolchildren, grades 3–12, most of whom were teens.	*PI:* Rosenberg Self-Esteem Scale. *RGO:* interview questions.	Concluded that Black child's attitudes toward his/her race and his/her personal self-esteem are virtually unrelated.
Sacks 1973	268 New York City high school boys (grades 9–12), 120 of whom were Black.	*PI:* Self-Attitudes and Self-Regards Test; locus-of-control measure. *RGO:* Draw-a-Person Test.	No relationship was found between racial attitudes and self-attitudes.
Schmults 1975	44 Black and 44 white males, ages 16–21.	*PI:* Personal Orientation Inventory; Embedded Figures Test. *RGO:* semantic differential.	Better-adjusted Blacks were more highly ethnic than maladjusted Blacks. Adjusted Blacks were more highly ethnic than adjusted whites.
Slade 1977	242 urban Black students, 109 from a state college and 133 from a high school in the same community.	*PI:* Rosenberg Self-Esteem Scale. *RGO:* 20-item ethnic-esteem inventory.	No relationship between self- and ethnic esteem.
Spencer 1976	130 children, ages 4–6.	*PI:* Thomas Self-Concept and Values Inventory; SCAMIN. *RGO:* a modified version of PRAM-II and a race-awareness measure.	Using correlational and regression analyses, relationship between global self-esteem and racial attitudes was negative and quadratic.
Spencer 1982	384 lower- and middle-SES Black children of preschool and primary school age.	*PI:* Thomas Self-Concept and Values Inventory. *RGO:* modified version of PRAM-II.	Although the overwhelming majority of the children had average self-esteem, they also recorded

Author	Sample	Methodology	Significant Findings
			an out-group racial orientation, a finding contrary to the notion that PI and RGO are positively related.
Stephen and Rosenfield 1979	51 Black, 192 white, and 103 Mexican-American fourth- and fifth-graders.	*PI:* Rosenberg Self-Esteem Scale. *RGO:* modified semantic differential for image of Black, white, and Mexican-Americans.	PI and RGO highly correlated for Blacks but not for whites or Mexican-Americans. RGO measure was not a true measure of esteem for in-group but a weighted measure that took into account a subject's attitude toward other groups. Correlation between PI and attitudes Blacks hold toward Blacks was not reported.
Storm 1970	72 first-graders, stratified by race, gender, and SES.	*PI:* Pictorial Self-Concept Test. *RGO:* Storm Race Image and Race Preference Test.	No correlation between PI and race image or racial preference for either white or Black children. Also, PI and SES were not related; on some dimensions of self-concept, low-SES children showed more strengths than did middle-income subjects, and vice versa for other PI components.
Vaughan 1977	70 third- and seventh-grade Black pupils.	*PI:* Piers-Harris Self-Concept Scale. *RGO:* Cheek Black Ethnic Identification Scale.	No overall correlation, but the PI and RGO relationship showed a tendency toward significance $(r = 22, p > .065)$. This tendency was clearly related to an interaction because there was no PI and

Author	Sample	Methodology	Significant Findings
			RGO correlation for grade level. While not true for boys at either grade level, girls accounted for most of the association of PI and RGO.
Ward and Braun 1972	60 Black children, 7 and 8 year olds.	*PI:* Piers-Harris Self-Concept Scale. *RGO:* modified Clark and Clark racial-preference task.	Results showed an association between PI and RGO. Although sample size and categorical data should have meant the application of the chi-square statistic, the connection between PI and RGO was based on an analysis employing the Mann-Whitney U Test. Reason for this choice was not clearly discussed by authors.
I. J. Williams 1975	60 Black adults in various stages of Black identity development.	*PI:* Rosenberg Self-Esteem Scale; Tennessee Self-Concept Scale. *RGO:* Cultural Identity Questionnaire plus several identity-related measures.	Subjects in different stages of identity development showed only modest differences in self-esteem, but major differences on RGO measures.
Williams-Burns 1976	115 third-grade Black children of advantaged status.	*PI:* Coopersmith Self-Esteem Inventory. *RGO:* Self-Portrait coloring task.	In subsample of 48 children, no relationship found between PI and RGO.
Wilson 1981	204 Black adults.	*PI:* Multidimensional Psychological Well-Being Scale. *RGO:* 17-item race-awareness scale.	No statistically significant relationship between race awareness and mental health.

‖ ∎ ∎ ‖

BIBLIOGRAPHY

Aboud, F. E. 1980. A test of ethnocentrism with young children. *Canadian Journal of Behavioral Science* 12: 195–209.

Aboud, F. E., and S. Skerry. 1984. The development of ethnic attitudes: A critical review. *Journal of Cross-Cultural Psychology* 15(1):3–34.

Adam, B. D. 1978. Inferiorization and "self-esteem." *Social Psychology* 41: 42–53.

Alejandro-Wright, M. N. 1985. The child's conception of racial classification: A sociocognitive developmental model. In *Beginnings: The social and affective development of Black children*, ed. M. B. Spencer, G. K. Brookins, and W. R. Allen, 185–200. Hillsdale, N.J.: Erlbaum.

Allen, E. G. 1969. An investigation of change in reading achievement, self-concept, and creativity of disadvantaged elementary school children. Doctoral dissertation, University of Southern Mississippi. *Dissertation Abstracts International* 29:3032A.

Allen, J. G. 1972. The effects of an achievement motivation program on the self-concepts of selected ninth-grade students representing three ethnic groups. Doctoral dissertation, North Texas State University. *Dissertation Abstracts International* 33:6048A.

Allen, W. E. 1976. The formation of racial identity in Black children adopted by White parents. Doctoral dissertation, Wright Institute.

Altstein, H., and R. J. Simon. 1977. Transracial adoption: An examination of an American phenomenon. *Journal of Social Welfare* 4(2–3):63–71.

Anderson, J. D. 1988. *The education of Blacks in the South, 1860–1935.* Chapel Hill: University of North Carolina Press.

Asante, Molefi. 1980. *Afrocentricity: The theory of social change.* Buffalo, N.Y.: Amulefi Publishing.

Asher, S., and V. Allen. 1969. Racial preference and social comparison processes. *Journal of Social Issues* 25:157–166.

Atolagbe, E. O. 1975. Correlation of self-concept and values in social classes, races and sexes. Doctoral dissertation, Ohio State University. *Dissertation Abstracts International* 36(3B):1399–1400B.

Bachman, J. G. 1970. *Youth in transition*, vol. 2, *The impact of family background and intelligence on tenth-grade boys.* Ann Arbor: Survey Research Center, Institute for Social Research, University of Michigan.

Baldwin, J. A. 1979. Theory and research concerning the notion of Black self-hatred: A review and reinterpretation. *Journal of Black Psychology* 5(2):51–78.

Banks, H. A. 1970. Black consciousness: Student survey. *Black Scholar* 2(1): 44–51.

Banks, W. C. 1976. White preference in Blacks: A paradigm in search of a phenomenon. *Psychological Bulletin* 83(6):1179–1186.

Banks, W. C., and W. J. Rompf. 1973. Evaluative bias and preference behavior in Black and White children. *Child Development* 44:776–783.

Barbarin, O. 1977. Race and social climate as determinants of effective adaptation in a university setting. *Final report, third conference on empirical research in Black psychology.* NIE–G–76–0059.

Barnes, E. J. 1972. The Black community as a source of positive self-concept for Black children: A theoretical perspective. In *Black psychology*, ed. R. L. Jones, 166–192. New York: Harper & Row.

Bayton, J. A. 1975. Francis Sumner, Max Meenes, and the training of Black psychologists. *American Psychologist* 30(2):185–186.

Beglis, J. F., and A. A. Sheikh 1974. Development of the self-concept in Black and White children. *Journal of Negro Education* 43(1):104–110.

Bennett, L. 1969. Of time, space and revolution. *Ebony* (August): 31–39.

Bennett, P. D., and D. C. Lundgren. 1976. Racial composition of day care centers and racial attitudes and self-concepts of young Black and White children. *Journal of Intergroup Relations* 5(1):3–14.

Bennett-Powell, P. D. 1976. Effects of racially relevant storybooks and learning materials on the racial attitudes and racial identification of young Black children. Doctoral dissertation, University of Cincinnati. *Dissertation Abstracts International* 38(12B):346B.

Bettelheim, B. 1947. The dynamics of anti-semitism in Gentile and Jew. *Journal of Abnormal and Social Psychology* 42:152–168.

———. 1960. *The informed heart*. Glencoe, Ill.: Free Press.

Bottome, P. 1957. *Alfred Adler, apostle of freedom*. London: Faber & Faber.

Bridgeman, B., and V. C. Shipman. 1975. *Disadvantaged children and their first school experiences: Predictive value of measures of self-esteem and achievement motivation in four to nine year old low income children*. Prepared under Grant H-8756, Department of Health, Education, and Welfare. Princeton, N.J.: Educational Testing Service.

Bridgette, R. E. 1970. Self-esteem in Negro and White southern adolescents. Doctoral dissertation, University of North Carolina at Chapel Hill. *Dissertation Abstracts International* 31(5B):2977.

Brody, Eugene B. 1964. Marginality, identity and behavior in the American Negro: A functional analysis. *International Journal of Social Psychiatry* 10:7–12.

Brown, A. 1976. Personality correlates of the developmental inventory of Black consciousness. Master's thesis, University of Pittsburgh.

———. 1979. Black consciousness prototypes: A profile analysis of developmental stages of Black consciousness. Doctoral dissertation, University of Pittsburgh.

Brown, N. W. 1974. Personality characteristics of Negroes attending a predominantly White university and Negroes attending a predominantly Black college. *Personality and Social Psychology Bulletin* 1(1):321–323.

Brown, P. O. J. 1973. A comparison of self-esteem, anxiety, and behavior of Black and non-Black underachieving elementary school students in open and stratified classrooms. Doctoral dissertation, Columbia University. *Dissertation Abstracts International* 34:3011–3012A.

Burbach, H. J., and B. Bridgeman. 1976. Dimensions of self-concept among Black and White fifth grade children. *Journal of Negro Education* 45(4):448–458.

Burke, C. P. 1975. A comparison of pupil self-concepts at the time of enrollment and after a period of attendance in selected continuation high schools in the Los Angeles City Unified School District. Doctoral dissertation, Brigham Young University. *Dissertation Abstracts International* 36(3A): 1383A.

Burnett, M. 1987. The relationship of self and ethnic group esteem to personality in Black Americans. Doctoral dissertation, Duke University.

Butler, R. O. 1976. Black children's racial preference: A selected review of the literature. *Journal of Afro-American Issues* 4(6):168–171.

Butts, H. 1963. Skin color perception and self-esteem. *Journal of Negro Education* 32:122–128.

Cameron, P. 1971. Personality differences between typical urban Negroes and Whites. *Journal of Negro Education* 40(1):66–76.

Caplan, N. 1970. The new ghetto man: A review of recent empirical studies. *Journal of Social Issues* 26:57–73.

Carey, P., and D. Allen. 1977. Black studies: Expectation and impact on self-esteem and academic performance. *Social Science Quarterly* 57(4):811–820.

Carmichael, S., and C. V. Hamilton. 1967. *Black Power: The politics of liberation in America*. New York: Vintage.

Carpenter, T. R., and T. V. Busse. 1969. Development of self-concept in Negro and White children. *Child Development* 40:935–939.

Carter, A. L. 1974. An analysis of the use of contemporary Black literature and music and its effects upon self-concept in group counseling procedures. Doctoral dissertation. Purdue University.

Carter, R. T. and J. E. Helms. 1984. The relationship between radical identity attitudes and socioeconomic status. Paper presented at the American Psychological Association Convention, Toronto, Canada, August.

———. 1987. The relationship of black value-orientations to racial attitudes. *Measurement and Evaluation in Counseling and Development* 17:185–195.

Chang, T. S. 1975. The self-concept of children in ethnic groups: Black American and Korean American. *Elementary School Journal* 76(1):52–58.

Chestang, L. 1972. The dilemma of biracial adoption. *Social Casework* 17:100–115.

Chimenzie, A. 1975. Transracial adoption of Black children. *Social Work* 20:296–301.

Christmas, J. J. 1973. Self-concept and attitudes. In *Comparative studies of Blacks and Whites in the United States*, ed. K. S. Miller and R. M. Dreger, 294–272. New York: Seminar Press.

Cicirelli, V. G. 1977. Relationship of socio-economic status and ethnicity to primary grade children's self-concept. *Psychology in the Schools* 14(2):213–215.

Clark, C. C. 1971. General theory and black studies: Some points of convergence. In *Boys no more*, ed. C. W. Thomas, 28–47. Beverly Hills, Calif.: Glencoe Press.

Clark, E. N. 1971. Analysis of the differences between pre- and post-test scores (change scores) on measures of self-concept, academic aptitude and reading achievement earned by sixth grade students attending segregated and desegregated schools. Doctoral dissertation, Duke University. *Dissertation Abstracts International* 1:2902A.

Clark, K. B. 1955. *Prejudice and your child.* Boston: Beacon Press.

———. 1965. *Dark ghetto.* New York: Harper & Row.

Clark, K. B., and M. P. Clark 1939a. The development of consciousness of self and the emergence of racial identification in Negro pre-school children. *Journal of Social Psychology* 10:591–599.

———. 1939b. Segregation as a factor in the racial identification of Negro pre-school children: A preliminary report. *Journal of Experimental Education* 8(2):161–163.

———. 1940. Skin color as a factor in racial identification of Negro pre-school children. *Journal of Social Psychology* 11:159–169.

———. 1947. Racial identification and preference in Negro children. In *Readings in social psychology*, ed. T. M. Newcomb and E. L. Hartley, 169–178. New York: Holt.

———. 1950. Emotional factors in racial identification and preference in Negro children. *Journal of Negro Education* 19:341–350.

Clark, K. B., and J. Hopkins. 1969. *A relevant war against poverty: A study of community action programs and observable social change.* New York: Harper & Row.

Clark, M. K. P. 1939. An investigation of the development of consciousness of distinctive self in pre-school children. Master's thesis, Howard University. Morland Room, Founder's Library, Howard University.

Clark, M. L. 1979. Race concepts and self-esteem in Black children. Doctoral dissertation, University of Illinois. *Dissertation Abstracts International* 40(10A):5371–5372.

Cole, B. P. 1979. Race and self-esteem: A comparative study of Black and White adults. Doctoral dissertation, University of California at Los Angeles. *Dissertation Abstracts International* 39(10A):6352.

Coleman, J. S., et al. 1966. *Equality of educational opportunity.* Washington D.C.: Office of Education, Department of Health, Education, and Welfare.

Coles, R. 1964. *Children of crisis: A study of courage and fear.* New York: Dell.

Corson, W. R. 1970. *Promise or peril: The Black college student in America.* New York: Norton.

Crain, R. L., and L. S. Weisman. 1972. *Discrimination, personality and achievement.* New York: Seminar Press.

Crawford, T. J. and M. Naditch. 1970. Relative deprivation, powerlessness and militancy. *Journal of Psychiatry* 33(2):208–223.

Crawford, Z. 1979. The effects of Black studies exposure on racial consciousness and Black self-concept. Doctoral dissertation, Stanford University. *Dissertation Abstracts International* 40(7A):4252–4253.

Cross, W. E., Jr. 1970. The Black experience viewed as a process: A crude model for Black self-actualization. Paper presented at the thirty-fourth annual meeting of the Association of Social and Behavioral Scientists, Tallahassee, Florida, April 23–24.

———. 1971. Negro-to-Black conversion experience. *Black World* 20:13–27.

———. 1976. Stereotypic and non-stereotypic images associated with the negro-to-black conversion experience: An empirical analysis. Doctoral dissertation, Princeton University.

———. 1978a. Black families and black identity: A literature review. *Western Journal of Black Studies* 2(2):111–124.

———. 1978b. The Thomas and Cross models on psychological nigrescence: A literature review. *Journal of Black psychology* 4(1):13–31.

———. 1978c. The Mediax Project: The socioemotional domain. Position paper prepared for Mediax Associates, Westport, Conn.

———. 1979. The negro-to-Black conversion experience: An empirical analysis. In *Research direction of Black psychologists*, ed. A. W. Boykin, A. J. Anderson, and J. F. Yates, 107–125. New York: Russell Sage Foundation.

———. 1981. Black families and Black identity development. *Journal of Comparative Family Studies* 12:19–50.

———. 1983. The ecology of human development for Black and White children: Implications for predicting racial preference patterns. *Critical Perspectives of Third World America* 1(1):177–189.

———. 1985. Black identity: Rediscovering the distinction between personal identity and reference group orientation. In *Beginnings: The social and affective development of Black children*, ed. M. B. Spencer, G. K. Brookins, and W. R. Allen, 155–171. Hillsdale, N.J.: Erlbaum.

———. 1987. A two factor theory of Black identity: Implications for the study of identity development in minority children. In *Children's ethnic socialization*, ed. J. S. Phinney and M. J. Rotheram, 117–133. Beverly Hills, Calif.: Sage.

Cross, W. E., Jr., U. Bronfenbrenner, and M. Cochran. 1977. Black families and the socialization of Black children: An ecological approach. Research proposal received and funded by ACYF, 1977–1980.

Cross, W. E., Jr., T. A. Parham, and J. E. Helms. In press. Nigrescence revisited: Theory and research. In *Advances in Black psychology*, ed. R. L. Jones. Los Angeles: Cobb and Henry.

Cummings, C., and R. Carrere. 1975. Black culture, Negroes and colored people: Racial image and self-esteem among Black adolescents. *Phylon* 36(3):238–248.

Cuniff, D. F. 1971. Student perceptions of self-esteem and educational environment. Doctoral dissertation, University of Massachusetts. *Dissertation Abstracts International* 32:4831A.

Curtis, W. M. J. 1975. Enhancing Black self-concept through Black studies. Doctoral dissertation, University of Arizona. *Dissertation Abstracts International* 36(10B):5252.

Dale, J. D., and J. F. Keller. 1972. Self-concept scores among Black and White culturally deprived adolescent males. *Journal of Negro Education* 41(1): 31–34.

Daly, W. T. *The revolutionary: A review and synthesis.* Sage Comparative Politics Paper, vol. 3, series 01–025. Beverly Hills, Calif.: Sage.

Davids, A. 1973. Self-concept and mother-concept in Black and White preschool children. *Child Psychiatry and Human Development* 4(1):30–43.

Davidson, J. P. 1974. Empirical development of a measure of black student identity. Doctoral dissertation, University of Maryland.

Davis, C. 1974. The analysis of self-concept and self-actualization manifestations by incarcerated and free Black youth. Doctoral dissertation, University of Pittsburgh. *Dissertation Abstracts International* 35(11B):5636–5637B.

Davis, W. A. 1980. The effects of Black consciousness and Black identity on the self-concept of Black elementary school children. Doctoral dissertation, Atlanta University. *Dissertation Abstracts International* 41(5A):1995.

Dennis, W. 1968. Racial change in Negro drawings. *Journal of Psychology* 69:129–130.

Denton, S. E. 1985. A methodological refinement and validation analysis of the develomental inventory of black consciousness. Doctoral dissertation, University of Pittsburgh.

Deutsch, G. 1923. Conformity in human behavior with a test for its measurement. Master's essay, Columbia University Library.

Dickerson, D. C. 1986. *Out of the crucible: Black steelworkers in western Pennsylvania, 1875–1980.* Albany: State University of New York Press.

Dixon, V., and B. Foster. 1971. *Beyond Black or White.* Boston: Little, Brown.

Dizard, J. E. 1970. Black identity, social class, and Black power. *Journal of Psychiatry* 33(2): 195–207.

Douglas, L. 1969. A comparative analysis of the relationship between self-esteem and certain selected variables among youth from diverse racial groups. Doctoral dissertation, University of Michigan. *Dissertation Abstracts International* 31:641–642.

244   Bibliography

Dover, C. 1960. *American Negro art*. London: Studio Books.

Downton, J. V. 1973. *Rebel leadership: Commitment and charisma in the revolutionary process*. New York: Free Press.

Du Bois, W. E. B. 1903. *Souls of Black folk*. Chicago: A. C. McClurg.

Dulan, C. G. 1975. Ethnic identification and stereotyping by Black children in desegregated elementary schools. Doctoral dissertation, University of California at Riverside. *Dissertation Abstracts International* 38(10A):6352A.

Durley, G. L. 1973. A variance analysis of the self-esteem among Black elementary school children: Sex and grade level the determining variables. Doctoral dissertation, University of Massachusetts. *Dissertation Abstracts International* 34:6514.

Edwards, H. E. 1970. *Black students*. New York: Free Press.

Ellison, R. 1964. *Shadow and act*. New York: Random House.

Enty, J. E. 1979. Clothing symbolism: A study of Afro fashions and their relation to Black identity and university students. Doctoral dissertation, Pennsylvania State Unversity. *Dissertation Abstracts International* 40(1B):186–187.

Erikson, E. 1968. *Identity, youth and crisis*. New York: Norton.

Evans, D., and S. Alexander 1970. Some psychological correlates of civil rights activity. *Psychological Reports* 26:899–906.

Evarts, A. B. 1913. Dementia praecox in the Negro. *Psychoanalytic Review* 1(1):388–403.

Fanon, F. 1963. *The wretched of the earth*. New York: Grove Press.

———. 1967a. *Black skins, white masks*. New York: Grove Press.

———. 1967b. *A dying colonialism*. New York: Grove Press.

Feigelman, W., and A. R. Silverman. 1984. The long-term effects of transracial adoption. *Social Service Review* 58(4):588–602.

Finnegan, D. G., and E. B. McNally. 1987. *Dual identities: Counseling chemically dependent gay men and lesbians*. Center City, Minn.: Halzelton.

Foster, B. G. 1971. Toward a definition of Black referents. In *Beyond Black or White: An alternate America*, ed. V. Dixon and B. G. Foster, 7–22. Boston: Little, Brown.

Foster, M., and L. R. Perry. 1982. Self-valuation among Blacks. *Social Work* 27(1):60–66.

Fouther-Austin, A. 1978. Education, personality development and mental hygiene. Doctoral dissertation, Syracuse University. *Dissertation Abstracts International* 38(3A):4650A.

Fox, D., and V. B. Jordan. 1973. Racial preference and identification of Black, American Chinese, and White children. *Genetic Psychology Monographs* 88(2):229–286.

Fox, D. J., C. Stewart, and V. Pitts. 1968. *Services to children in open enrollment receiving schools, evaluation of ESEA title 1 projects in New York City, 1967–68.* New York: Center for Urban Education, November. Mimeographed.

French, J. T. 1972. Educational desegregation and selected self-concept of lower-class Black children. Doctoral dissertation, Florida State University. *Dissertation Abstracts International* 33:2167A.

Frenkel-Brunswik, E. 1948. A study of prejudice in children. *Human Relations* 13:295–306.

Frisch, G. R., and L. Handler. 1967. Differences in Negro and White drawings: A cultural interpretation. *Perceptual and Motor Skills* 24:667–670.

Gaier, E. L., and H. S. Wambach. 1960. Self-evaluation of personality assets and liabilities of southern White and Negro students. *Journal of Social Psychology* 51:135–143.

Garner, M. E. M. 1983. The esteem of the Black urban preschooler's developing self-concept of worth and race. Doctoral dissertation, City University of New York. *Dissertation Abstracts International* 44(1B):307B.

Gates, H. L. 1988. *The signifying monkey: A theory of African-American literary criticism.* New York: Oxford University Press.

Gayle, A. 1971. *The Black aesthetic.* Garden City, N.Y.: Doubleday.

Gerlach, L. P., and V. H. Hine. 1970. *People power and change: Movements of social transformation.* Indianapolis: Bobbs-Merrill.

Getsinger, M., et al. 1972. Self-esteem measures and cultural disadvantagement. *Journal of Consulting and Clinical Psychology* 38(1):149.

Gibby, R. G., and R. Gabler. 1967. The self-concept of Negro and White children. *Journal of Clinical Psychology* 23:144–148.

Gilman, S. L. 1986. *Jewish self-hatred.* Baltimore: Johns Hopkins University Press.

Glasgow, D. G. 1981. *The Black underclass.* New York: Vintage.

Goodman, M. E. 1946. Evidence concerning the genesis of interracial attitudes. *American Anthropologist*, new series 48:624–630.

———. 1952. *Race awareness in young children.* Cambridge, Mass.: Addison-Wesley.

Gopaul-McNicol, S. 1986. The effects of modeling, reinforcement, and color meaning word association of Black pre-school children and White pre-school children in New York and Trinidad. Doctoral dissertation, Hofstra University.

———. 1988. Racial identification and racial preference of Black preschool children in New York and Trinidad. *Journal of Black Psychology* 14(2):65–68.

Gordon, C. 1963. Self-conception and social achievement. Doctoral dissertation, University of California at Los Angeles.

———. 1972. *Looking ahead: Self-conceptions, race and family factors as determinants of adolescent achievement orientations*. Arnold and Caroline Rose Monograph Series. Washington, D.C.: American Sociological Association.

Gordon, D. 1971. *Self-determination and history in the Third World*. Princeton: Princeton University Press.

Gordon, V. V. 1976. Methodologies of Black self-concept research: A critique. *Journal of Afro-American Issues* 4(3 and 4):373–381.

———. 1980. *The self-concept of Black Americans*. Washington, D.C.: University Press of America.

Greenwald, H. J., and D. P. Oppenheim. 1968. Reported magnitude of self-misidentification among Negro children—artifact? *Journal of Personality and Social Psychology* 8:49–52.

Gregor, A. J., and D. A. McPherson. 1966. Racial attitudes among White and Negro children in a Deep South standard metropolitan area. *Journal of Social Psychology* 68:95–106.

Gregory, R. D. 1977. Self-concept across sex, color, and teacher estimated annual family income level for students in grades seven thru twelve. Doctoral dissertation, Duke University. *Dissertation Abstracts International* 38 (4B):1859B.

Griffin, J. D. 1975. The design, implementation, and evaluation of a group experience for increasing the Black consciousness of Afro-Americans. Doctoral dissertation, University of Pittsburgh.

Gross, E. 1976. A highly structured academic program and self-concept of urban Black lower socio-economic status kindergarten children. Doctoral dissertation, Fordham University. *Dissertation Abstracts International* 37(2A):881A.

Grossack, M. M. 1957. Group belongingness and authoritarianism in southern Negroes—a research note. *Phylon* 18(2):261–266.

Grossman, B. 1981. Ethnic identity and self-esteem: A study of Anglo, Chicano, and Black adolescents in Texas. Doctoral dissertation, New School for Social Research. *Dissertation Abstracts International* 42(8B):3423B.

Grow, L., and D. Shapiro. 1974. *Black children—White parents*. New York: Child Welfare League of America.

Guggenheim, F. 1969. Self-esteem and achievement for White and Negro children. *Journal of Projective Techniques and Personality Assessment* 33:63–71.

Gurin, P., and E. Epps. 1975. *Black consciousness, identity and achievement.* New York: Wiley.

Gutman, H. G. 1976. *The Black family in slavery and freedom, 1750–1925.* New York: Pantheon Books.

Haggerstrom, W. C. 1963. Self-esteem and other characteristics of residentially desegregated Negroes. Doctoral dissertation, University of Michigan. *Dissertation Abstracts International* 23(8):3007–3008.

Hahn, H. 1970. Black separatists: Attitudes and objectives in a riot-torn ghetto. *Journal of Black Studies* 1(7):35–43.

Hall, C. C. 1980. The ethnic identity of racially mixed people: A study of Black-Japanese. Doctoral dissertation, University of California at Los Angeles. *Dissertation Abstracts International* 41(4B):1565B.

Hall, W. S., W. E. Cross, Jr., and R. Freedle. 1972. Stages in the development of black awareness: An exploratory investigation. In *Black psychology*, ed. R. Jones. New York: Harper & Row.

Hall, W. S., R. Freedle, and W. E. Cross, Jr. 1972. *Stages in the development of a black identity.* ACT research report 50. Iowa City: Research and Development Division, American Testing Program.

Hansberry, L. 1958. *A raisin in the sun.* New York: Signet.

Hardiman, R. 1982. White identity development: A process oriented model for describing the racial consciousness of White Americans. Doctoral dissertation, University of Massachusetts–Amherst.

Hare, B. R., and L. A. Castenell, Jr. 1985. No place to run, no place to hide: Comparative status and future prospects of Black boys. In *Beginnings: The social and affective development of Black children*, ed. M. B. Spencer, G. K. Brookins, and W. R. Allen, 201–214. Hillsdale, N.J.: Erlbaum.

Harms, N. C. 1977. Relationships among learner self-concept, internality and ethnic group. Doctoral dissertation, University of Colorado. *Dissertation Abstracts International* 38(5A):2724A.

Harren, V. A. 1979. A model of career decision-making for college students. *Journal of Vocational Behavior* 14:113–119.

Harris, S., and J. Braun. 1971. Self-esteem and racial preference in Black children. *Proceedings of the seventy-ninth annual convention of the American Psychological Association* 6:259.

Harrison, A. O. 1985. The Black family's socializing environment: Self-esteem and ethnic attitude among Black children. In *Black children: Social, educational and parental environments*, ed. H. P. McAdoo and J. L. McAdoo, 174–193. Beverly Hills, Calif.: Sage.

Hartley, E. L., and R. E. Hartley. 1952. *Fundamentals of social psychology.* New York: Knopf.

Hartnagel, T. F. 1970. Father absence and self conception among lower class White and Negro boys. *Social Problems* 18(2):152–163.

HARYOU 1964. *Youth in the ghetto.* New York: Harlem Youth Opportunities Unlimited.

Hauser, S. T. 1972. Black and White identity development: Aspects and perspectives. *Journal of Youth and Adolescence* 2(2):113–130.

Hawkin, P. L. 1971. The interaction of achievement related motives in children. Doctoral dissertation, Case Western Reserve University. *Dissertation Abstracts International* 32:239A.

Hayes-Bautista, D. E. 1974. Becoming Chicano: A "dis-assimilation" theory of transformation of ethnic identity. Doctoral dissertation, University of California–San Francisco.

Heacock, D., and C. Cunningham. 1977. Self-esteem in the Black child placed in a white family: An introductory study. Manuscript.

Healy, G. W., and R. R. DeBlassie. 1974. A comparison of Negro, Anglo, and Spanish-American adolescents' self concepts. *Adolescence* 9(33):15–24.

Hedgebeth, J. E. 1970. The relationship of self and academic attitudes and academic achievement of Negro and White students to school racial composition: An exploratory study. Doctoral dissertation, Michigan State University. *Dissertation Abstracts International* 31:5846A.

Helegerson, E. 1943. The relative significance of race, sex, and facial expression in choice of playmate by the preschool child. *Journal of Negro Education* 12:612–622.

Helms, J. E., and T. A. Parham. In press. The relationship between black racial identity attitudes and cognitive styles. In *Black and White racial identity: Theory, research, and practice*, ed. J. E. Helms. Westport, Conn.: Greenwood Press.

Hendrix, B. L. 1977. Internal versus external control and group identification influences on self-esteem. Doctoral dissertation, State University of New York at Buffalo. *Dissertation Abstracts International* 38(9A):5742.

Hentoff, N. 1982. Profiles: The integrationist—Kenneth B. Clark. *New Yorker* 58(27):37–73.

Herman, M., et al. 1967. *Study of the meaning, experience, and effects of the neighborhood Youth Corps on Negro youth who are seeking work.* New York: Center for the Study of Unemployed Youth, New York University Graduate School of Social Work.

Hernandez, M. 1984. A study of children's racial attitudes and self-esteem. Doctoral dissertation, New York University. *Dissertation Abstracts International* 45(6B):1914B.

Herskovits, M. J. 1941. *The myth of the Negro past*. Boston: Beacon Press.

Hine, D. C. 1989. *Black women in white: Racial conflict and cooperation in the nursing profession, 1890–1950*. Bloomington and Indianapolis: Indiana University Press.

Hines, P. Y. 1978. Differential components of self-esteem. Doctoral dissertation, University of Delaware. *Dissertation Abstracts International* 39(12B): 6120.

Holtzman, J. 1973. Color caste changes among Black college students. *Journal of Black Studies* 4(1):92–101.

Horowitz, E. L. 1936. The development of attitude toward the Negro. *Archives of Psychology*, no. 104. Columbia University.

———. 1944. "Race" attitudes. In *Characteristics of the American Negro*, ed. O. Klineberg, 139–247. Evanston, Ill.: Harper & Row.

Horowitz, E. L., and R. E. Horowitz. 1938. Development of social attitudes in children. *Sociometry* 1:301–338.

Horowitz, R. 1939. Racial aspects of self-identification in nursery school children. *Journal of Psychology* 7:91–99.

Horowitz, R., and L. B. Murphy. 1938. Projective methods in the psychological study of children. *Journal of Experimental Education* 7:133–140.

Horton, R. G. 1973. Black parent–child participation in preventive–intervention programs: Implications for self-concept values and racial identification. Doctoral dissertation, University of Michigan. *Dissertation Abstracts International* 34(4A):1733.

Hraba, J., and J. Grant. 1970. Black is beautiful: A reexamination of racial preference and identification. *Journal of Personality and Social Psychology* 16:398–402.

Hughbanks, J. O. 1977. Self-esteem and social anchorage of adolescent White, Black, and Mexican American students. Doctoral dissertation, Georgia State University. *Dissertation Abstracts International* 38(11A):6411A.

Hughes, R. E., and E. Works. 1974. The self-concepts of Black students in a predominantly White and in a predominantly Black high school. *Sociology and Social Research* 59(1):38–43.

Hunt, D. E., and R. H. Hardt. 1969. The effects of upward bound programs on the attitudes, motivation and academic achievement of Negro students. *Journal of Social Issues* 25:122–124.

Hunt, J. G. 1973. Race and identity: A study of Black and White urban school boys. Doctoral dissertation, Indiana University. *Dissertation Abstracts International* 34:4452A.

Hunt, J. G., and L. L. Hunt. 1977. Racial inequality and self-image: Identity maintenance and diffusion. *Sociology and Social Research* 61(4):539–559.

Hyman, J. J., and E. Singer. 1968. *Readings in reference group theory and research*. New York: McGraw-Hill.

Jackson, B. W. 1976a. The functions of black identity development theory in achieving relevance in education. Doctoral dissertation, University of Massachusetts.

———. 1976b. Black identity development. In *Urban social and educational issues*, ed. L. Golubschick and B. Persky, 158–164. Dubuque, Iowa.: Kendall/Hunt.

Jackson, G. G., and S. A. Kirschner. 1973. Racial self-designation and preference for a counselor. *Journal of Counseling Psychology* 20(6):560–564.

Jacques, J. M. 1976. Self-esteem among southeastern Black-American couples. *Journal of Black Studies* 7(1):11–28.

Jamerson, R. F. 1973. A study of self-concept of art and academic ability of secondary students with emphasis on the Black perspective. Doctoral dissertation, University of Massachusetts. *Dissertation Abstracts International* 34: 6261–6262A.

James, D. H. 1970. The effects of desegregation of the self-concept of Negro high school students. Doctoral dissertation, University of Southern Mississippi. *Dissertation Abstracts International* 31(9A):4464.

Jarrett, O. S. 1980. Assessment of racial preferences and racial identification of Black and White kindergarten children in mono-racial and bi-racial settings. Doctoral dissertation, Georgia State University. *Dissertation Abstracts International* 41(6A):2489.

Jefferson, F. C. 1981. A learning procedure that increases self-esteem and Black identity development in Black college students. Doctoral dissertation, University of Massachusetts, Amherst.

Johnson, D. J. 1983. Racial attitudes and biculturality in interracial preschoolers. Master's thesis, Department of Human Development and Family Studies, Cornell University.

Johnson, H. 1970. The relationship of the self-concepts of Negro and White college freshmen to the nature of their written work. Doctoral dissertation, North Texas State University. *Dissertation Abstracts International* 31:1623A.

Johnson, J. B. 1970. A comparison of physical fitness and self-concept between junior high Negro and White male students. Doctoral dissertation, University of Alabama. *Dissertation Abstracts International* 31:5180A.

Johnson, J. M. 1981. Influence of assimilation on the psychosocial adjustment of Black homosexual men. Doctoral dissertation, California School of Professional Psychology at Berkeley. *Dissertation Abstracts International* 42(11B): 4620.

Johnson, L. P. 1972. The correlates of the Black identity complex. Doctoral dissertation, University of Minnesota.

Johnson, P. R., J. F. Shireman, and K. W. Watson. 1987. Transracial adoption and the development of Black identity at age eight. *Child Welfare* 66(1):45–55.

Jones, C. H. 1973. The relationship of self-esteem, general anxiety and test anxiety in Black and White elementary school students in grades four through six. Doctoral dissertation, Northern Illinois University. *Dissertation Abstracts International* 34:1131A.

Jones, E. D. 1972. On transracial adoption of Black children. *Child Welfare* 52(3):156–164.

Jordan, T. J. 1981. Self-concepts, motivation, and academic achievement of Black adolescents. *Journal of Educational Psychology* 73(4):509–517.

Kardiner, A., and L. Ovesey. 1951. *The mark of oppression.* New York: Norton.

Katz, P. A. 1974. Doll preferences: An index of racial attitudes. *Journal of Educational Psychology* 66(5):663–668.

Kelley, A. 1976. Self-concept and career selection of Black community college students. Doctoral dissertation, California School of Professional Psychology at Berkeley. *Dissertation Abstracts International* 38(6B):294B.

Kelman, H. C., and D. P. Warwick. 1973. Bridging micro and macro approaches to social change: A social-psychological perspective. In *Processes and phenomena of social change*, ed. G. Zaltman et al., 13–59. New York: Wiley.

Kiesler, S. 1971. Racial choice among children in realistic situations. Manuscript, University of Kansas.

Kilson, M. 1973. The Black experience at Harvard. *New York Times Magazine*, September 2.

Kim, J. 1981. Processes of Asian-American identity development: A study of Japanese American women's perceptions of their struggle to achieve positive identities as Americans of Asian ancestry. Doctoral dissertation, University of Massachusetts, Amherst.

King, E. L. 1981. Ethnicity as a relevant dimension of the self-concepts of Black children. Doctoral dissertation, University of California at Los Angeles. *Dissertation Abstracts International* 42(12B):4917.

King, R. E. G. 1974. A workshop method for improving self-concept of Black youth. Doctoral dissertation, Temple University. *Dissertation Abstracts International* 34:4876A.

Kircher, M., and L. Furby. 1971. Racial preference in young children. *Child Development* 42:2076.

Klein, B. L. 1974. Development, validation and experimental application of an instrument to assess self-concept. Doctoral dissertation, University of Texas at Austin. *Dissertation Abstracts International* 35:4864A.

Kline, J. 1971. *An exploration of racism in ego ideal formation*. Smith College Studies in Social Work. Northampton: Smith College.

Klineberg, O. 1944. *Characteristics of the American Negro*. Evanston, Ill.: Harper.

Kluger, R. 1975. *Simple justice*, vol. 1. New York: Knopf.

Knight, O. B. 1969. The self concept of Negro and White educable mentally retarded boys. *Journal of Negro Education* 38(2):143–146.

Kohn, M. L. 1969. *Class and conformity: A study in values*. Chicago: Dorsey Press.

Koslin, S. C., B. L. Koslin, and J. Caldwell. 1969. Quasi distinguished and structured measure of school children's racial preferences. *Proceedings of the seventy-seventh annual convention of the American Psychological Association* 4(pt. 1):661–662.

Krate, R., G. Leventhal, and B. Silverstein. 1974. Self-perceived transformation of negro-to-black identity. *Psychological Reports* 35:1071–1075.

Kuhlman, T. L., and V. J. Bieliauskas. 1976. A comparison of Black and White adolescents on the HTP. *Journal of Clinical Psychology* 32(3):728–731.

Landreth, C., and B. C. Johnson. 1953. Young children's responses to a picture and inset test designed to reveal reactions to person of different skin color. *Child Development* 24:63–80.

Lanza, E. R. 1969. An investigation of various antecedents of self-esteem as related to race and sex. Doctoral dissertation, Ball State University. *Dissertation Abstracts International* 31:1077A.

Laryea, E. B. 1972. Race, self-concept and achievement. Doctoral dissertation, Columbia University. *Dissertation Abstracts International* 33(5A):2172–2173.

Lassiter, C. S. 1976. The relationship of self-concept as learners to Black students compared to selected variables. Doctoral dissertation, United States International University. *Dissertation Abstracts International* 38(3B):1385B.

Lefebvre, A. 1973. Self-concept of American Negro and White children. *Acta Psychologica Taiwanica* 15:19–23, 25–30.

Lewin, K. 1935. Psycho-sociological problems of a minority group. *Character and Personality* 3:175–187.

———. 1936. *Principles of topological psychology*. New York: McGraw-Hill.

———. 1941. Jewish self-hatred. *Contemporary Jewish Record* 4:219–232.

———. 1948. Self-hatred among Jews. In *Resolving social conflicts*, ed. G. W. Lewin. New York: Harper & Row.

Lewis, H. E. 1966. A descriptive study of self-concept and general creativity of southern and northern undergraduate students. Doctoral dissertation, Pennsylvania State University. *Dissertation Abstracts International* 27:3625–3626A.

Likert, R. 1947. Foreword. In *Readings in social psychology*, ed. T. M. Newcomb and E. L. Hartley, v–vi. New York: Holt.

Lind, J. E. 1913a. The color complex in the Negro. *Psychoanalytic Review* 1(1):404–414.

——. 1913b. The dream as simple wish-fulfillment in the Negro. *Psychoanalytic Review* 1:295–300.

Little, F. W. 1971. The effects of a personal growth experience upon measured self-concept of a selected group of Black college freshman. Doctoral dissertation, Purdue University. *Dissertation Abstracts International* 32: 4957A.

Little, J. A. 1981. Research summary of studies measuring both personal identity and reference group orientation. Manuscript, Cornell University.

——. 1983. An exploration of the relationships among reference group orientation, self-esteem, and reference group dilemmas. Doctoral dissertation, Cornell University.

Livingston, L. B. 1971. Self-concept change of Black college males as a result of a weekend Black experience encounter workshop. Doctoral dissertation, Arizona State University.

Locke, A. 1925. *The new Negro*. New York: A. C. Boni.

Logan, S. L. 1981. Race, identity, and Black children: A developmental perspective. *Social Casework* 62(1):47–56.

Long, G. H., and E. H. Henderson. 1968. Self-social concepts of disadvantaged school beginners. *Journal of Genetic Psychology* 113:41–51.

——. 1970. Social schemata of school beginners: Some demographic correlates. *Merrill-Palmer Quarterly of Behavior and Development* 16:305–324.

Lunceford, R. D. 1973. Self-concept change of Black college females as a result of a weekend Black experience encounter workshop. Doctoral dissertation, United States International University.

McAdoo, H. P. 1970. Racial attitudes and self-concepts of Black preschool children. Doctoral dissertation, University of Michigan. *Dissertation Abstracts International* 22(11):4114.

——. 1977. The development of self-concept and race attitudes in Black children: A longitudinal study. In *Third conference on empirical research in black psychology*, ed. W. Cross, 47–64. Washington, D. C.: National Institute of Education, Department of Health, Education, and Welfare.

——. 1985. Racial attitude and self-concept of young Black children over time. In *Black children: Social, educational and parental environments*, ed. H. P. McAdoo and J. L. McAdoo, 213–242. Beverly Hills, Calif.: Sage.

McAdoo, J. 1970. An exploratory study of racial attitude change in Black preschool children using differential treatments. Doctoral dissertation, University of Michigan. *Dissertation Abstracts International* 22(11):4114–4115.

McCarthy, J., and W. L. Yancey. 1971. Uncle Tom and Mr. Charlie: Metaphysical pathos in the study of racism and personal disorganization. *American Journal of Sociology* 76:648–672.

McDill, E. L., et al. 1966. *Sources of educational climate in high school.* Final Report, Project 1999, Contract #OE–3–10–080. Department of Social Relations, Johns Hopkins University. Washington, D.C.: Office of Education, Department of Health, Education, and Welfare.

McDonald, R. L., and M. D. Gunther. 1965. Relationship of self and ideal-self descriptions with sex, race and class in southern adolescents. *Journal of Personality and Social Psychology* 1:85–88.

McElroy, J. L. 1971. A study of the relationship among stability of social class position, race and self-esteem. Doctoral dissertation, University of Akron. *Dissertation Abstracts International* 32:1859–1960A.

McKinney, A. W. 1977. Black or White socio-economically disadvantaged pupils—they aren't necessarily inferior. *Journal of Negro Education* 46(4): 443–449.

McRoy, R. G. 1981. A comparative study of the self-concept of transracially and inracially adopted Black children. Doctoral dissertation, University of Texas at Austin.

McRoy, R. G., L. A. Zurcher, M. L. Lauderdale, and R. E. Anderson. 1982. Self-esteem and racial identity in transracial and inracial adoptees. *Social Work* 27(6):522–526.

———. 1984. The identity of transracial adoptees. *Social Casework* 65(1): 34–39.

McWhorter, S. G. 1984. Self-concept and racial preference in Black children. Doctoral dissertation, Temple University. *Dissertation Abstracts International* 45(1A):114A.

Maish, K. A. 1978. Black political orientation, political activism, and positive mental health. Doctoral dissertation, University of Maryland. *Dissertation Abstracts International* 39(4B):1962–1963.

Maliver, B. L. 1965. Anti-Negro bias among Negro college students. *Journal of Personality and Social Psychology* 2:770–775.

Markovics, C. B. 1974. Racial identity formation and personal self-esteem: Cognitive influences in Black children. Doctoral dissertation, University of Rochester. *Dissertation Abstracts International* 35(4B):1893.

Marx, G. T. 1967. *Protest and prejudice: A study of beliefs on the Black community.* New York: Harper & Row.

Mbiti, J. S. 1970. *African religions and philosophy.* Garden City, N.Y.: Doubleday.

Mead, G. H. 1934. *Mind, self and society*. Chicago: University of Chicago Press.

Mediax. 1980. *Accept my profile: Perspectives for headstart profiles of program effects on children*, vol. 1. Contract #HEW-105-77-1006. Washington, D.C.: Department of Health, Education, and Welfare.

Meenes, M., and J. A. Bayton. 1936. Personality traits of Negro college students. *Psychological Bulletin* 33(9):775.

Melancon, D. 1976. The evaluation of the impact of multi-ethnic curriculum materials upon elementary students. Doctoral dissertation, University of Illinois at Urbana–Champaign. *Dissertation Abstracts International* 37(5A): 2641.

Meltzer, H. 1939. Differences in nationality and race preferences of children. *Sociometry* 2:86–105.

Memmi, A. 1967. *The colonizer and the colonized*. Boston: Beacon Press.

Meyers, E. O. 1966. Self-concept, family structure and school achievement: A study of disadvantaged Negro boys. Doctoral dissertation, Columbia University–Teacher's College. *Dissertation Abstracts International* 27:3960A.

Miller, T. W. 1975. Effects of maternal age, education and employment status on the self-esteem of the child. *Journal of Social Psychology* 95:141–142.

Milliones, J. 1973. Construction of the developmental inventory of black consciousness. Doctoral dissertation, University of Pittsburgh.

———. 1980. Construction of a Black consciousness measure: Psychotherapeutic implications. *Psychotherapy: Theory and Practice* 17(2):175–182.

Milner, D. 1983. *Children and race*. 2nd ed. Harmondsworth, England: Penguin.

Mobley, B. D. 1973. Self-concept and conceptualization of ethnic identity: The Black experience. Doctoral dissertation, Purdue University. *Dissertation Abstracts International* 34(9B):4638.

Moore, C. L. 1976. The racial preference and attitude of preschool Black children. *Journal of Genetic Psychology* 129(1):37–44.

Morland, J. K. 1958. Racial recognition by nursery school children in Lynchburg, Va. *Social Forces* 37:132–137.

———. 1962. Racial acceptance and preference of nursery school children. *Merrill-Palmer Quarterly of Behavior and Development* 8:217–280.

———. 1963. Racial self-identification: A study of nursery school children. *American Catholic Sociological Review* 24:231–242.

———. 1966. A comparison of race awareness in northern and southern children. *American Journal of Orthopsychiatry* 36:23–31.

256 Bibliography

Morten, G., and D. R. Atkinson. 1983. Minority identity development and preference for counselor race. *Journal of Negro Education* 52(2):156–161.

Moses, E. G., P. A. Zirkel, and J. F. Greene. 1973. Measuring the self-concept of minority group pupils. *Journal of Negro Education*, 93–98.

Munro, R. W., and H. J. Oles. 1975. Self-perception, socio-economic status and related variables in Black, Mexican-American and White youths. Paper presented at the annual meeting of the American Educational Research Association, Washington, D.C., March 30–April 3.

Murphy, G., and L. B. Murphy. 1931. *Experimental social psychology*. New York: Harper.

Murphy, G., L. Murphy, and T. Newcomb. 1937. *Experimental social psychology*. New York: Harper.

Napper, G. 1973. *Blacker than thou*. Grand Rapids, Mich.: W. B. Eerdmans.

Newcomb, T. M., and E. L. Hartley. 1947. *Readings in social psychology*. New York: Holt.

Nobles, W. 1972. African philosophy: Foundations for Black psychology. In *Black psychology*, ed. R. L. Jones, 18–32. New York: Harper & Row.

Ogbu, J. U. 1985. A cultural ecology of competence among inner-city Blacks. In *Beginnings: The social and affective development of Black children*, ed. M. B. Spencer, G. K. Brookins and W. R. Allen, 45–66. Hillsdale, N.J.: Erlbaum.

Ogletree, E. 1969. Skin color preference of the Negro child. *Journal of Social Psychology* 79:143.

Olsen, H. D. 1972. Effects of changes in academic roles of self-concept of academic ability of Black and White compensatory educational students. *Journal of Negro Education* 41(2):365–369.

Onwuachi, P. C. 1967. Identity and black power: An African viewpoint. *Negro Digest* (March): 31–37.

Parham, T. A. 1989. Cycles of psychological nigrescence. *Counseling Psychologist* 17(2):187–226.

Parham, T. A., and J. E. Helms. 1981. The influence of black students' racial identity attitudes on preferences for counselor's race. *Journal of Counseling Psychology* 28(3):250–257.

———. 1985. Relation of racial identity attitudes to self-actualization and affective states of black students. *Journal of Counseling Psychology* 32(2): 431–440.

Paul, M. J., and J. L. Fisher. 1980. Correlates of self-concept among Black early adolescents. *Journal of Youth and Adolescence* 9(2):163–173.

Payne, R. B. 1977. Racial attitude formation in children of mixed Black and White heritage: Skin color and racial identity. Doctoral dissertation, California School of Professional Psychology–San Francisco.

Penn, M. C. 1980. An investigation of the educational impact of cultural group identification and self-esteem. Doctoral dissertation, University of San Francisco. *Dissertation Abstracts International* 41(4A):1458.

Perry, J. 1977. Some effects of selected Black literature on the self-concept and reading achievement of Black male eighth grade students. Doctoral dissertation, University of California–Berkeley. *Dissertation Abstracts International* 38(9A):5318.

Peterson, B., and M. Ramirez. 1971. Real ideal self-disparity in Negro and Mexican-American children. *Psychology* 8(3):22–26.

Pettigrew, T. F. 1964. *A profile of the American Negro.* New York: Van Nostrand Reinhold.

———. 1978. Placing Adam's argument in a broader perspective: Comments on the Adam paper. *Social Psychology Quarterly* 41(1):58–61.

———. 1983. Group identity and social comparisons. In *Minorities: Community and identity,* ed. C. Fried, 51–60. New York: Springer-Verlag.

Picou, J. S., A. G. Cosby, E. W. Curry, and H. Wells. 1977. Race and the formation of academic self-concept: A causal analysis. *Southern Journal of Educational Research* 11(2):57–70.

Pinderhughes, C. A. 1968. The psychodynamics of dissent. In *The dynamics of dissent,* ed. J. H. Masserman, 56–79. New York: Grune and Stratton.

Pleasants, D. J. 1973. An exploratory study of the relationship of socio-cultural variables to the self-concepts of selected Black and White teachers. Doctoral dissertation, University of North Carolina. *Dissertation Abstracts International* 33:3710A.

Porter, J. D. R. 1967. Racial attitude formation in pre-school age children. Doctoral dissertation, Harvard University.

———. 1971. *Black child, white child: The development of racial attitudes.* Cambridge: Harvard University Press.

Porter, J. D. R., and R. E. Washington. 1979. Black identity and self-esteem: A review of studies of Black self-concept, 1968–1978. *Annual Review of Sociology* 5:53–74.

Posner, C. A. 1969. Some effects of genetic and cultural variables on self-evaluations of children. Doctoral dissertation, Illinois Institute of Technology. *Dissertation Abstracts International* 29:4833–4834A.

Powell, G. J., and M. Fuller. 1970. School desegregation and self-concept. Paper presented at the forty-seventh annual meeting of the American Orthopsychiatric Association, San Francisco, March 23–26.

Powell-Hopson, D. L. 1985. The effects of modeling, reinforcement and color meaning word associations on doll color preferences of Black preschool children and White preschool children. Doctoral dissertation, Hofstra University. *Dissertation Abstracts International* 47(01B):387.

Powell-Hopson, D., and D. S. Hopson. 1988. Implications of doll color preferences among Black preschool children and White preschool children. *Journal of Black Psychology* 14(2):57–63.

Powers, J. M., et al. 1971. A research note on the self-perception of youth. *American Educational Research Journal* 8(4):665–670.

Prendergast, P., S. M. Zdep, and P. Sepulveda. 1974. Self-image among a national probability sample of girls. *Child Study Journal* 4(3):103–114.

Proshansky, H., and P. Newton. 1968. The nature and meaning of Negro self-identity. In *Social class, race, and psychological development*, ed. M. Deutsch, I. Katz and A. R. Jensen, 178–218. New York: Holt, Rinehart and Winston.

Radke, M. J., M. J. Sutherland, and P. Rosenberg. 1950. Racial attitudes of children. *Sociometry* 13:154–171.

Radke, M. J., and H. G. Trager. 1950. Children's perception of the social roles of Negroes and Whites. *Journal of Psychology* 29:3–33.

Radke, M. J., H. G. Trager, and H. Davis. 1949. Social perception and attitudes of children. *Genetic Psychology Monographs* 10:327–447.

Ramseur, H. P. 1989. Psychologically healthy Black adults: A review of theory and research. In *Black adult development and aging*, ed. R. Jones, 215–241. Berkeley: Cobb and Henry.

Rasheed, S. Y. 1981. Self-esteem and ethnic identity in African American third grade children. Doctoral dissertation, University of Michigan. *Dissertation Abstracts International* 42(6B):2604.

Reeder, E. N. 1978. Clothing preferences of male athletes in relation to self-concept, athletic ability, race, socio-economic status, and peer perception. Doctoral dissertation, University of Tennessee. *Dissertation Abstracts International* 28(9B):4179B.

Richardson, S. A., and J. Royce. 1968. Race and physical handicap in children's preference for other children. *Child Development* 39:467–480.

Rio, A. T. 1980. Defensiveness, self criticism and self-concept in a sample of Black, Mexican, and White American adolescents. Doctoral dissertation, Michigan State University. *Dissertation Abstracts International* 40(9A):4971.

Roberts, A., L. K. Mosley, and M. W. Chamberlain. 1975. Age differences in racial self-identity of young Black girls. *Psychological Reports* 37(3, pt. 2):1263–1266.

Robinson, C. C. 1976. The modification of racial attitudes in Black and White pre-school children. Doctoral dissertation, Emory University. *Dissertation Abstracts International* 37(8B):4221.

Robinson, J. A. 1977. Self-esteem, racial consciousness, and perception of difference between the values of Black and white Americans. Doctoral dissertation, University of Detroit. *Dissertation Abstracts International* 40(5B):2386.

Rodriguez, A. 1972. The relationship of self-concept and motor ability in certain selected Negro and Caucasian tenth grade girls. Doctoral dissertation, University of Alabama. *Dissertation Abstracts International* 33:4923A.

Rohrer, J. H., and M. S. Edmonson. 1960. *The eighth generation: Cultures and personalities of New Orleans Negroes*. New York: Harper & Row.

Rosenberg, M. 1965. *Society and the adolescent self-image*. Princeton: Princeton University Press.

———. 1979a. Group rejection and self-rejection. *Research in Community Mental Health* 1:3–20.

———. 1979b. *Conceiving the self*. New York: Basic Books.

Rosenberg, M., and R. G. Simmons. 1971. *Black and White self-esteem: The urban school child*. Arnold and Caroline Rose Monograph Series. Washington, D.C.: American Sociological Association.

Ross, S., and J. A. Bayton. 1979. Contributions of the history of psychology: Max Meenes, 1902–1974. *Psychological Reports* 44:774.

Roth, R. W. 1969. The effects of Black studies on Negro fifth grade students. *Journal of Negro Education* 38:435–439.

Rubin, R. H. 1974. Adult male absence and the self-attitudes of Black children. *Child Study Journal* 4(1):33–46.

Sacks, S. R. 1973. Self-identity and academic achievement of Black adolescent males: A study of racial identification, locus of control, self-attitudes and academic performance. Doctoral dissertation, Columbia University. *Dissertation Abstracts International* 34(6B):2911.

St. John, N. H. 1975. *School desegregation: Outcomes for children*. New York: Wiley.

Samuels, S. C. 1973. An investigation into the self-concepts of lower- and middle-class Black and White kindergarten children. *Journal of Negro Education* 42(4):467–472.

Schmults, T. C. 1975. The relationship between black ethnicity to field dependence and adjustment. Doctoral dissertation, University of Rhode Island. *Dissertation Abstracts International* 36(11B):5816.

Schofield, J. W. 1977. Racial identity and intergroup attitudes of children in segregated and desegregated schools. ERIC #ED 11863. Manuscript, Department of Psychology, University of Pittsburgh.

Seeman, M. 1946. Skin color values in three all-Negro school classes. *American Sociological Review*, 315–321.

Semaj, L. 1979. Reconceptualizing the development of racial preference in children: The role of cognition. In *The fourth conference on empirical research in Black psychology*, ed. W. E. Cross, Jr., and H. Harrison, 180–198. Ithaca: Africana Studies Center and National Institute of Education, Department of Health, Education and Welfare.

———. 1980. The development of racial evaluation and preference: A cognitive approach. *Journal of Black Psychology* 6(2):59–79.

Sherif, M., and C. Sherif. 1970. Black unrest as a social movement toward an emerging self-identity. *Journal of Social and Behavioral Sciences* 15(3):41–52.

Shireman, J. F., and P. R. Johnson. 1981. *Adoption: Three alternatives*. Chicago: Chicago Child Care Society.

———. 1986. A longitudinal study of Black adoptions: Single parent, transracial and traditional. *Social Work* 31(3):173–176.

Silverman, A. R. 1980. The assimilation and adjustment of transracially adopted children in the United States. Doctoral dissertation, University of Wisconsin–Madison.

Silverman, A. R., and W. Feigelman. 1981. The adjustment of Black children adopted by White families. *Social Casework* 62(9):529–536.

Simmons, R. G. 1978. Blacks and high self-esteem: A puzzle. *Social Psychology* 41:54–59.

Simon, R. J., and H. Altstein. 1977. *Transracial adoption*. New York: Wiley.

———. 1981. *Transracial adoption*: A follow-up. Lexington, Mass.: Lexington Books.

Sisenwein, M. 1970. A comparison of the self-concept of Negro and White children in an integrated school. Doctoral dissertation, Columbia University. *Dissertation Abstracts International* 31:1633A.

Slade, P. J. 1977. An examination of the relationship between ethnic-esteem and personal self-esteem among urban Black senior high school and college students. Doctoral dissertation, Columbia University–Teacher's College. *Dissertation Abstracts International* 38(4B):1961–1962.

Smith, A. N. 1974. Self-concept: Analysis of participants and non-participants in Black studies. Doctoral dissertation, North Carolina State University at Raleigh. *Dissertation Abstracts International* 35(10A):6442.

Smith, L. M. 1980. Contributions to understanding self-image in Black Americans: Do Black Americans feel that Black is beautiful? Doctoral dissertation, Wright Institute. University of Michigan Microfilm 8104797.

Soares, A. J., and L. M. Soares. 1969. A comparative study of culturally disadvantaged children. *American Educational Research Journal* 9:31–45.

Southern, E. 1971. *The music of Black Americans*. New York: Norton.

Sowell, T. 1973. *Black education: Myths and tragedies*. New York: McKay.

Spencer, M. B. 1976. The socio-cognitive and personality development of Black preschool children: An exploratory study of developmental process. Doctoral dissertation, University of Chicago. *Dissertation Abstracts International* 38(2B):970B.

———. 1982. Personal and group identity of Black children: An alternative synthesis. *Genetic Psychology Monographs*, 106:59–84.

———. In press. Transitions and continuities in cultural values: Kenneth Clark revisited. In *Advances in Black psychology*, vol. 1, ed. R. L. Jones. Berkeley: Cobb and Henry.

Spencer, M. B., and F. D. Horowitz. 1973. Effects of systematic social and token reinforcement on the modification of racial and color-concept attitudes in Black and White pre-school children. *Developmental Psychology* 9: 246–254.

Sperber, M. 1974. *Masks of loneliness: Alfred Adler in perspective*. Translated by Krishna Winston. New York: Macmillan.

Spivey, W. L. 1976. A study of the self-concept and achievement motivation of Black versus White high school male achievers. Doctoral dissertation, California School of Professional Psychology at San Franciso. *Dissertation Abstracts International* 36(9B):4711B.

Stanfield, J. H. 1985. *Philanthropy and Jim Crow in American social science*. Westport, Conn.: Greenwood Press.

Stephen, W. G., and D. Rosenfield. 1979. Black self-rejection: Another look. *Journal of Educational Psychology* 71(5):708–716.

Stevenson, W. W., and E. C. Stewart. 1958. A developmental study of racial awareness in young children. *Child Development* 29:399–409.

Stewart, C. M. 1975. Research literature on self-image and disadvantaged children. Doctoral dissertation, Columbia University Teacher's College.

Stone, C. 1968. *Black political power in America*. New York: Dell.

Storm, P. A. 1970. An investigation of self-concept, race image and race preference in racial minority and majority children. Doctoral dissertation, University of Maryland. *Dissertation Abstracts International* 31(B):6246B.

Strang, W. J. 1972. The self-concepts of children in elementary schools with differing proportions of Negro and White students. Doctoral dissertation, University of Alabama. *Dissertation Abstracts International* 33:5567A.

Suggs, R. H. 1979. The effects of an identity group experience on Black college students. Doctoral dissertation, State University of New York at Albany.

Sumner, F. C. 1931. Mental health statistics of Negro college freshmen. *School and Society* 33(852):574–576.

Taylor, J. 1986. Cultural conversion experiences: Implications for mental health research and treatment. Paper presented at the Menninger Foundation for the Fortieth Anniversary of the Menninger School of Psychiatry, June 20.

Taylor, R. 1976. Psychosocial development among Black children and youth: A reexamination. *American Journal of Orthopsychiatry* 46:4–19.

Teeland, L. A. 1971. The relevance of the concept of reference groups to the sociology of knowledge. Report 12. Department of Sociology, University of Grothenburg. Read at Olin Library, Cornell University.

Teplin, L. A. 1977. Racial preference as artifact? A multitrait-multimethod analysis. *Social Science Quarterly* 57:834–848.

Terrell, F., J. Taylor, and S. Terrell. 1980. Self-concept of juveniles who commit Black-on-Black crimes. *Journal of Corrective and Social Psychiatry* 26: 107–109.

Thomas, C. W. 1971. *Boys no more.* Beverly Hills, Calif.: Glencoe Press.

Thorsell, B. A. 1976. Inter-generational factors in ethnic differences in self-esteem. Paper presented at the annual meeting of the Western Psychological Association, Los Angeles, April 8–11.

Toldson, I., and A. Pasteur. 1975. Developmental stages of black self-discovery: Implications for using black art forms in group interaction. *Journal of Negro Education* 44:130–138.

Tomlinson, T. M. 1970. Determinants of Black politics: Riots and the growth of militancy. *Journal of Psychiatry* 33:242–264.

Trager, H. G., and M. Yarrow. 1952. *They live what they learn.* New York: Harper & Row.

Trent, R. D. 1957. The relation between expressed self-acceptance and expressed attitudes toward Negroes and Whites among Negro children. *Journal of Genetic Psychology* 91:25–31.

Trotter, J. W. Jr. 1985. *Black Milwaukee: The making of an industrial proletariat, 1915–1945*. Urbana: University of Illinois Press.

Trowbridge, N., L. Trowbridge, and L. Trowbridge. 1972. Self-concept and socio-economic status. *Child Study Journal* 2(3):123–143.

Tucker, B. S. 1977. The development of directionality of self-concept of low socioeconomic young children as it relates to grade, sex and race. Doctoral dissertation, Florida State University. *Dissertation Abstracts International* 38(4A):2016A.

Urry, J. 1973. *Reference groups and the theory of revolution*. London: Routledge & Kegan Paul.

Valentine, C. A. 1971. Deficit, difference and bicultural models of Afro-American behavior. *Harvard Educational Review* 41(2):137–157.

Vaughan, P. B. 1977. A developmental study of race esteem and self-esteem of Black boys and girls in third and seventh grade. Doctoral dissertation, University of Michigan. *Dissertation Abstracts International* 38(6A):3735A.

Vershure, B. 1976. Black is beautiful: A re-examination of racial self-identification. *Perceptual and Motor Skills* 43(3, pt. 1):842.

Walton, A. 1989. Willie Horton and me. *New York Times Magazine* (August 20): 52–53, 77.

Ward, S. H., and J. Braun. 1972. Self-esteem and racial preference in Black children. *American Journal of Orthopsychiatry* 42(4):644–647.

Watson, J. G. 1974. An analysis of the self-concept, personal values and levels of achievement motivation of Black and White managers. Doctoral dissertation, St. Louis University. *Dissertation Abstracts International* 35:2480–2481A.

Wax. D. E. 1972. Self-concept in Negro and White preadolescent delinquent boys. *Child Study Journal* 2(4):175–184.

Wendland, M. M. 1968. Self-concept in southern Negro and White adolescents as related to rural–urban residence. Doctoral dissertation, University of North Carolina at Chapel Hill. *Dissertation Abstracts International* 29:2642B.

Weston, R. 1975. Commitment and awareness. Master's thesis, Rutgers University.

————. 1977. Level of black awareness, race of experimenter, race of model, and modeling tasks as factors in vicarious learning. Doctoral dissertation, Rutgers University.

Wheatley, L. A., and F. C. Sumner. 1946. Measurement of neurotic tendency in Negro students of music. *Journal of Psychology* 22:247–252.

White, D. E. 1975. The effect of hearing and viewing realistic picture story books on self-concept of first grade students. Doctoral dissertation, University of Virginia. *Dissertation Abstracts International* 36(5A):251A.

White, M. L. 1973. A comparative analysis of the self-concepts and philosophic orientations of a selected group of White and Black public school teachers. Doctoral dissertation, East Texas State University. *Dissertation Abstracts International* 34:2452A.

White, M. O. 1968. Alienation and self-esteem as they relate to race, sex, socio-economic and school variables in urban high school age youth. Doctoral dissertation, Wayne State University. *Dissertation Abstracts International* 32:803–804A.

Williams, I. J. 1975. An investigation of the developmental stages of Black consciousness. Doctoral dissertation, University of Cincinnati. *Dissertation Abstracts International* 36(5B):2488–2489.

Williams, J., and J. Morland. 1976. *Race, color and the young child*. Chapel Hill: University of North Carolina Press.

Williams, R. L. 1981. Special issue: Culture-specific testing, pt. 1. *Journal of Non-White Concerns* 10(1).

Williams, R. L., and H. Byars. 1970. The effect of academic integration on self-esteem of southern Negro students. *Journal of Social Psychology* 80:183–188.

Williams-Burns, W. 1976. An investigation into the self-esteem level and skin color perceptions of self-portraits of advantaged Afro-American children in New Orleans, Louisiana. Doctoral dissertation, Southern Illinois University. *Dissertation Abstracts International* 38(2A):686A.

Wilson, M. J. 1981. Evaluating the mental health status of Black adults. In *The fifth conference of empirical research in Black psychology*, ed. J. McAdoo, H. McAdoo, and W. Cross, 200–218. Washington, D.C.: National Institute of Mental Health.

Winnick, R. J., and J. A. Taylor. 1977. Racial preference: Thirty-six years later. *Journal of Social Psychology* 102(1):157–158.

Wise, J. H. 1969. Self-reports by Negro and White adolescents to the Draw-a-Person. *Perceptual and Motor Skills* 28(1):193–194.

Woodson, C. G. 1919. *The education of the Negro prior to 1861*. Washington, D.C.: Associated Press.

———. 1933. *Mis-education of the Negro*. Washington, D.C.: Associated Press.

Wortham, A. 1981. *The other side of racism: A philosophical study of black race consciousness*. Columbus: Ohio State University Press.

Wright, R. N. 1953. *The outsider*. New York: Harper.

Wylie, R. C., and B. Hutchins. 1967. Schoolwork ability estimates and aspirations as a function of socio-economic level, race and sex. *Psychological Reports* 21:781–808.

Yancey, W., et al. 1972. Social position and self-evaluation: The relative importance of race. *American Journal of Sociology* 78:338–359.

Yeatts, P. P. 1968. An analysis of developmental changes in the self-report of Negro and White children, grades three through twelve. Doctoral dissertation, University of Florida. *Dissertation Abstracts International* 29(3A):823.

Young, R. A. 1977. Results of values clarification training on the self-concept of Black female upperclassmen residence hall students at Mississippi State University. Doctoral dissertation. Mississippi State University. *Dissertation Abstracts International* 38(7A):3967.

INDEX